The Common Thread

PRAISE

"Somehow, Jerry Gladstone has gotten dozens of famous people to candidly discuss their successes and failures. It is the cautionary tales that separate *The Common Thread* from other books of its kind. You will learn a lot, you will not be bored!"

BILL O'REILLY, ANCHOR, FOX NEWSCHANNEL

"I am thrilled to be part of *The Common Thread!* Both Garfield and I have had the privilege to work with Jerry Gladstone over the years. With his winning attitude and the many stories Jerry has shared in his book, there is no doubt we can all benefit and be empowered to reach our fullest potential."

JIM DAVIS, EMMY AWARD WINNER AND "GARFIELD" CREATOR

"If you're looking to get real strategies to make real productive and positive changes in your life, then *The Common Thread* is a must-read!"

DAN CALDWELL, A.K.A. "PUNK ASS," FOUNDER AND PRESIDENT, TAPOUT

"After spending 12 years in the NFL dealing with a variety of personalities and characters while being named to 3 Pro Bowls, all NFL twice and 2 Super Bowl Championships, you learn how to play judge and jury. You learn in order to win championships one must dive into teamwork with both feet and lead with every ounce of energy. This is what author Jerry Gladstone's book *The Common Thread* speaks off. I am quite certain after reading and absorbing this book you are destined for success!"

LEONARD MARSHALL, AUTHOR,
WHEN THE CHEERING STOPS (2010: TRIUMPH BOOKS)
EXECUTIVE DIRECTOR, *THE GAME PLAN FOUNDATION*

"*The Common Thread* book is awesome! Jerry Gladstone shows how we all are meant for success."

GLORIA GAYNOR, "THE QUEEN OF DISCO"

"People search for ways to succeed and achieve; they will find the answers they seek in *The Common Thread*. Through well-known celebrities they admire and respect, the reader will see a little of themselves in this book, motivating and guiding them to pursue their dreams."

MIKE ERUZIONE, CAPTAIN OF THE 1980 "MIRACLE ON ICE"
USA GOLD MEDAL HOCKEY TEAM

"I very much enjoyed the interview with Jerry and his book '*The Common Thread* ... I have no doubt you will be inspired!"

EVANDER HOLYFIELD, CRUISERWEIGHT AND HEAVYWEIGHT WORLD
BOXING CHAMPION, OLYMPIAN

"If you're looking for a book that not only motivates you but teaches the life lessons of super achievers then look no further than Jerry Gladstone's *The Common Thread of Overcoming Adversity and Living your Dreams!*"

RANDY "THE NATURAL" COUTURE, UFC THREE-TIME HEAVYWEIGHT
CHAMPION, TWO-TIME LIGHT HEAVYWEIGHT CHAMPION

"*The Common Thread* is a perfect read for those who want to hit great heights of success!"

MOTI HORENSTEIN, MARTIAL ARTS GRAND MASTER
EIGHTH DEGREE BLACK BELT; WORLD TITLES IN 5 DIFFERENT STYLES

"Jerry Gladstone gets the 'Common Thread' of GREATNESS. He knows it's not a gift, it's not an accident, it's not a natural ability, and Jerry knows it's not good luck. *The Common Thread of Over Coming Adversity and Living Your Dreams* provides the seamless commonality of greatness. Jerry helps us all recognize that greatness is all about redefining and forging the human will and the willingness to be great; the willingness to outwork talent!! It is an honor for me to know Jerry."

JUAN CARLOS SANTANA
WORLD CLASS PERFORMANCE AND FITNESS TRAINER
FOUNDER INSTITUTE FOR HUMAN PERFORMANCE
PH.D. IN EXERCISE PHYSIOLOGY

"There is a life plan for all of us. Too many people try to live a life that is not theirs. I think it is masterful what Jerry Gladstone does in his book *The Common Thread,* to take the thoughts that we all have in our heads and then to place them into the context of our own individual game plan, our own action plan for success.

"In Jerry Gladstone's book *The Common Thread Of Over Coming Adversity and Living Your Dreams,* he has masterfully captured the insight of the most successful people on how they overcame obstacles and how they have persevered to attain their success. Share in their secrets and how they overcome their individual hurdles to achieve their dreams. This book is an insightful guide on what to do when you hit obstacles, how to overcome others negativity and stay focused on your goals the way the most successful people have done. This book will inspire you to take action and forge a path toward your personal and professional success and has made me realize we all have what it takes within us, sometimes we just need the tools to start the work, that is what Jerry's book is, your tool. It is now your time to find your "common thread", to get past the fear and limitations that hold you back from achieving your greatness."

DUANE PERKINS, DIRECTOR
WHEEL PASSION YOUTH SCHOLARSHIP ORGANIZATION,
DANBURY, CONNECTICUT

"*The Common Thread* book is a great project...the interview with Jerry was insightful and I believe it can really make an impact on people looking for more out of life."

DAVE DIEHL, ALL PRO, 2 X SUPER BOWL CHAMPION

"*The Common Thread* book is like a three point shot for anybody looking to win at the game of success!"

KEITH ASKINS, MIAMI HEAT 3X NBA CHAMPION

The
Common
Thread

Of Overcoming Adversity
& Living Your Dreams

NEW YORK

The Common Thread
Of Overcoming Adversity and Living Your Dreams

© 2016 Morgan James.

Published in New York, New York, by Morgan James Publishing. Morgan James and The Entrepreneurial Publisher are trademarks of Morgan James, LLC.
www.MorganJamesPublishing.com

The Morgan James Speakers Group can bring authors to your live event. For more information or to book an event visit The Morgan James Speakers Group at
www.TheMorganJamesSpeakersGroup.com.

Morgan James Publishing
The Entrepreneurial Publisher
5 Penn Plaza, 23rd Floor, New York City, New York 10001
(212) 655-5470 office • (516) 908-4496 fax
www.MorganJamesPublishing.com

9781630475277   paperback
9781630475284   eBook
9781630475291   hardcover

Library of Congress Control Number:
2014959306

A **free** eBook edition is available
with the purchase of this print book.

CLEARLY PRINT YOUR NAME ABOVE IN UPPER CASE

Instructions to claim your free eBook edition:
1. Download the BitLit app for Android or iOS
2. Write your name in **UPPER CASE** on the line
3. Use the BitLit app to submit a photo
4. Download your eBook to any device

Cover Design by:
George Foster, www.fostercovers.com;
www.3DogDesign.net

Images ©Getty Images

Interior Design by:
Brittany Bondar
www.SageDigitalDesign.com

In an effort to support local communities, raise awareness and funds, Morgan James Publishing donates a percentage of all book sales for the life of each book to Habitat for Humanity Peninsula and Greater Williamsburg.

Get involved today, visit
www.MorganJamesBuilds.com

Habitat
for Humanity®
Peninsula and
Greater Williamsburg
Building Partner

TABLE OF CONTENTS

Personal Stories and Lessons as Told By...

SYLVESTER "SLY" STALLONE
ACTOR, WRITER, ACADEMY AWARD WINNER

BILL O'REILLY
FOX NEWS, BEST SELLING AUTHOR

SMOKEY ROBINSON
"KING OF MOTOWN"

JOE BARBERA
HANNA-BARBERA CARTOON STUDIO FOUNDER

BROOKS ROBINSON
BASEBALL HALL OF FAME

MARK CUBAN
ENTREPRENEUR

PREFACE

I was just 16 years old when Sylvester Stallone's *Rocky* hit the theatres. Watching Rocky Balboa beat impossible odds to rise from underdog to bona fide champion opened my eyes to new possibilities, while simultaneously igniting a fire deep within my heart. For me, the transformation wasn't immediate, but a seed was planted. It was then that I began to understand that just because I was not the biggest, strongest, smartest or most talented guy in the world, it really did not matter. With heart, drive and determination, I could accomplish just about anything that I set my mind to.

Who would have ever thought that years later I would be fortunate enough to personally sit down with Sly Stallone and listen to his insights and wisdom on what it takes to be a winner—a real-life version of Rocky, the iconic role he brought to life on the big screen.

As a youngster I had very low self-esteem; I was overweight and never did very well in school. As I entered my teens, I was always in trouble for one thing or another. It seemed that the odds of making something out of my life were a long shot at best. Down deep, I felt there was something special within me—some type of inner strength. But the negative self-image I carried, almost as an outcast, acted as a constant roadblock to any potential path of success I envisioned.

Like many, my beginnings were humble. When my mom was only a child, she was put out on the street and raised in an orphanage. As a youngster, my dad endured a life of abuse. At the age of 16, he escaped that abuse by misstating his age and joining the U.S. Marine Corps. Years later, my parents would tell me that no one ever taught them how to raise children, but they did understand how to love. So my two sisters and I grew up in a home where there was never a lack of love, kindness and understanding.

Supported by family, by athletic coaches and by other role models, I managed to become somewhat of an overachiever in sports and in my business career.

I was able to embrace and sustain a very strong mindset that I have since used throughout my life. Crazy as it sounds, I was the kid who was laughed at in gym class because I couldn't do any sit-ups—but as an adult, driven by that *Rocky* attitude, I placed first in a sit-up contest by doing 5,002 consecutive sit-ups. I was awarded a football scholarship and earned a college degree. I've run numerous 26-mile marathons, earned a black belt and became an instructor in martial arts. My achievements had little to do with my abilities—and much to do with my understanding of perseverance and dedication.

I believe that my interest in, and my understanding of, the inner workings of success and self-improvement have played an integral part in my life-long journey.

At the age of 26, with an investment of $2,000 and with a dedicated and loyal staff, I started a small art publishing and distribution company and then grew it into an organization that has represented some of the most important and best-known celebrities, business leaders, movie studios, and athletes of the 20th century. Years later, I sold my business to Getty Images, a multi-national organization.

Throughout my career, I have been very fortunate and humbled to have interacted with Academy and Grammy Award Winners, Super Bowl and World Series Champions, Rock and Roll Hall of Fame Legends, Talented Artists, Best-selling Authors, Olympians, Boxing Legends, Ultimate Fighting Championship (UFC) Fighters, and even Billionaires.

When interacting with many of these cultural icons from all different walks of life, I observed that there was a common theme, a common way, and a common thread to their success. Thus, the idea to write *The Common Thread of Overcoming Adversity and Living Your Dreams* was born. I had a simple goal and a deep desire to share with others the same thrill and empowerment I felt while getting to know many of these highly successful individuals. No matter who you are or where you come from, all things are truly possible when the proper mindset is in place.

I felt it was very important to feature a varied group of people in this book. As we are all unique, I strived to find a diverse selection of individuals to interview. My hope is that you, the reader, will find at least one story that speaks directly to your inner fabric and then inspires you toward a personal breakthrough, coming to the conclusion that "if they can do it, then I can do it, too!"

Many of these interviews and experiences came from my personal relationships—while others were arranged by friends.

I challenged each person with whom I spoke to reflect on his or her life and career and give thoughtful insight and inspiration to pass along to others. These superstars are often interviewed about their next movie, next award or next big event. But this book is different. My quest was to find out *why* and *how* these people had reached such a high level of achievement.

I wanted to find the answers to questions like:

- What did they do in the face of extreme adversity?
- How did they handle competition?
- How did they stay passionate?
- How did they rebound from defeat?
- What strategies did they use when they didn't have the support of others?
- What would they recommend regarding daily disciplines, habits and "must-do" things?
- And most importantly, what did they believe held other people back from reaching their potential, along with their advice on what could be done about it?

Many commented that they really enjoyed being interviewed for *The Common Thread* because it offered them the opportunity to help others by sharing their personal life lessons about how they overcame their own adversity.

As you read through these interviews, you will be amazed to discover that the same celebrities we place on pedestals have a lot of the same kinds of struggles and difficulties as each of us. They lose jobs, face fears, and experience rejection and setbacks. In addition, most of the people featured in this book deal with ups and downs, and roller coaster like careers as business executives, athletes or entertainers. But for many of the interviewees in this book, those same challenges and obstacles turned out to be the gateway that brought out their inner strength and ultimately propelled them to greatness.

The Common Thread of Overcoming Adversity and Living Your Dreams is a comprehensive, easily read "Instant Motivator." But it can also bring about long-term benefits as you focus on highlighted insights, wisdom, motivation, empowering thoughts and "do it daily" tips included at the end of each story to help you build your own roadmap for success.

My wish is that you will find this book to be of great benefit because it is not based on a theory of what may or may not work. Rather, it describes *real* people and their *real* success.

The reality is that at one time or another, we will all experience challenges and circumstances that test our resolve. So, I invite you to discover, explore and use this treasure trove of proven strategies, methodologies, and perspectives from people in the public eye who have proven to be more than "one-hit wonders." These are lifelong learners, creators and achievers who have turned what could have been ordinary lives into extraordinary adventures.

The Common Thread of Overcoming Adversity and Living Your Dreams will become a valuable tool and guide to help you master new skills and habits by understanding and incorporating into your life the same qualities and characteristics that make successful people tick. Analyzing these personal success stories will help you discover how to defeat obstacles and over-come challenges to live your personal dreams of achievement. And you will better understand that *you* have the ability to develop your own suc-cess code and the power to influence your own destiny.

Make self-discovery and growth your primary focus. Then take these principles, lifestyles and routines and apply them daily to truly reach your fullest potential. After meeting the achievers in this book, I hope you walk away with a renewed vision and a new "I Can Do It" attitude. I want you to see a bigger picture and a brighter future for yourself—far greater than you had previously imagined.

You will no longer allow your circumstances, your lack of resources, or your past to define who you are or what you can become.

Enjoy,
Jerry

A SPECIAL ACKNOWLEDGEMENT

To Brooke:

This book is centered on the common threads or themes that tie amazing and successful people together. Although they all come from different walks of life, various upbringings, and an enormous array of life experiences, an additional thread they all share is they didn't do it alone. Throughout each of these amazing men and women's lives, they looked to their left, and then to their right, and found a mentor, support system, loved one, or friend that elevated their ability to achieve their massive goals.

In fact, most of these famous folks can literally point to that one person who acted as the guiding light through thick and thin. And, as your narrator for this journey, I am no different. I would like to introduce to you the most important person in my life. She is my rock, my foundation, and my everything. Her name is Brooke. She is intelligent, special, unique, and my wonderful bride. Just like many of the people featured in this book needed a lift from time to time, so did I. This guardian angel picked me up during a very dark time in my life and was able to help me persevere and endure.

Brooke is a wonderful caring person and the mother of our three awesome kids: Austin, Allie and Emma. On the outside she is a beauty, on the inside you can endlessly multiple it. Most people who know Brooke would tell you she is a "spiritual guide" and a kindred spirit. Her warmth, love, and compassion for everyone resonate at an extremely high level.

She has a gift for making others feel good about themselves, and during difficult times few can convey the message of hope better than Brooke.

She has been by my side faithfully not only in my personal life, but in my business life as well.

My professional career started at the age of 26 with a couple of thousand dollars. For more than 25 years I entered into licensing agreements with some of the most well known companies including Disney, Fox, Warner Bros, DreamWorks and many more. I did business with the likes of Sylvester Stallone, Seth MacFarlane and Howard Stern. I came into contact with Academy Award Winners, Super Bowl and World Series Champions, Rock & Roll Hall of Fame Legends, Best-selling Authors, Olympians and UFC World Champions. Most of these relationships were developed from past success and referrals.

Together, Brooke and I began learning more about these people and discussing the common threads that tied them together. This was the beginning of the journey in writing *The Common Thread*, and the journey was pretty smooth. That is, until life intervened.

My business concentrated mostly on the production and distribution of licensed entertainment fine art. However as the business grew, we sometimes offered signed memorabilia to our clients. Some of what we bought were signed guitars from a vendor who was in business for over 30 years. The guitars were autographed by different celebrities. The vendor supplied me with photos of each celebrity signing the guitars, as well as the date and location of the signings. In the collectibles industry, this is called provenance.

To take the authentication process even further, after we purchased the autographed guitars from the vendor we sent them to an accredited Forensic Examiner who provided me with credentials and training certification he had received from the United States Secret Service as a handwriting expert. He examined each one of the guitars and authenticated the signatures as genuine.

I was confident I did all I could do to be a responsible businessman to ensure these items for our clients were indeed genuine.

Unfortunately, the vendor who sold me the guitars, actually used Photoshop to insert images of the guitars he sold to me into the photographs without my knowledge, making it appear the celebrity was signing it. In other words, the guitars may or may not have been signed by the celebrity. Regardless, the provenance was seriously flawed. Not knowing this at the time, I featured the guitars and the photos in our national advertising campaign.

A group of people in the industry who discovered the photos did their best to ruin me and my business. Instead of contacting me directly with this news so I could rectify the situation, they used the photos as ammunition to discredit me in a public forum.

A tidal wave came my way. They exploited me and took every opportunity they could to get out in the world and tell all who would listen that I was a fraud. I experienced the ugly side of human nature. Many relationships that I spent years building were compromised. Even when I produced the documents, emails and original photos I received from the vendor to show I had nothing to do with the doctored photos, these individuals could care less. They had an agenda and a mission to do as much harm to me as they could; holding back the facts to hurt me, and others, was just a means to an end.

For several years I did my best to get out the truth, but deceitful people will stop at nothing to make sure their lies are heard. I was in the firing line and it brought me to the most difficult time in my life. And that is when my wonderful wife lifted me up. You see, Brooke has a gift: She has the ability to completely change one's mindset with a sincere belief that all will pass and the best days are ahead. More times than I care to remember,

Brooke picked me up during those dark days. She simply would not let me give up.

With each passing day, Brooke stood by me and uplifted my spirits even more. I began to visualize a finish line out there with my name on it. I did not know where it was, or when I would pass it, but I knew I would get there if I had my wife in my corner encouraging me every step of the way. Eventually, we made it through this difficult time. And the silver lining was truly remarkable. Brooke was strong when I wasn't. She was steadfast and dedicated when I couldn't be. And she shined her light when mine was extinguished.

My children and I are very fortunate to have such a strong advocate and loving mother who would go to the ends of the world for her family. And we are all lucky to have a person like Brooke in our world.

ACKNOWLEDGEMENTS

Mom and Dad—I will forever love you.

Austin, Allie and Emma—You are our heart and soul. Never forget how special you are and how much you are loved.

My beautiful sisters Bonnie and Marla—You've always been there to support me. Our memories will live on forever.

Jerry and Ellen Levine, my extended family and my old time friends— I love you all.

Agnes Palmer—Thank you for your loyalty, your friendship and going beyond the call of duty over so many years.

The many co-workers over the years—Thank you for your efforts, devotion and love.

Justin Spizman and Tim Boden—Thank you for bringing this book to life.

Morgan James Publishing and George Foster—Thank you for all your efforts with this project.

The individuals featured within this book—Thank you for sharing your heart, knowledge and wisdom in the pursuit of empowering others.

Sylvester "Sly" Stallone

Sly's Journey:

COMPLICATIONS AT BIRTH → BULLIED → #1 FILMS ACROSS FIVE DECADES

It is easy to be a spectator and root for the underdog. But it is much more difficult to be the one in the ring, fighting for your life and trying to overcome the competition. In my opinion, that is when true heroes are born. With your back against the wall, sometimes you just have to dig deep to fight your way out. We celebrate these underdogs, and are unbelievably excited to witness the unexpected victories. The heart and soul of the underdog is one paved with hard-work, dedication, and an endless amount of determination to overcome the obstacles and get it done.

One of the greatest underdogs of our time, Sylvester Stallone, reminds us, *"We're all underdogs in our own way, but there's a little Rocky in all of us."* A common thread trait observed with Sly is his quality of pushing through despite being an underdog.

When it was released in 1976, the iconic film *Rocky* and its message of overcoming the odds deeply resonated with me. I was a typical sixteen-year-old struggling with school and low self-esteem. It seemed like all my peers outperformed me at almost everything. I readily identified with the film's title character, Rocky, who was a million-to-one shot.

The music, the training scenes, and Rocky's struggles captivated me—I even started eating raw eggs before working out! I figured if it was good enough for Rocky, it was good enough for me.

Common wisdom says you should never meet your idols, because they can't help but disappoint you. But when I scored the opportunity to meet Sly Stallone, I found that he not only lived up to my personal hopes, he exceeded them. Of course, just about anyone would enjoy meeting a Hollywood luminary like Sylvester Stallone, but beyond that I enjoyed hearing Sly's well-thought-out answers to my interview questions. I deeply appreciate the wisdom he shared with me, and I feel honored to pass it along to others.

The "Italian Stallion" was born Michael Sylvester Gardenzio Stallone in 1946 in New York's gritty Hell's Kitchen neighborhood. His extraordinary career as an actor, filmmaker, screenwriter, and film director is the stuff legends are made of.

Sly's two best-known action heroes—boxer Rocky Balboa (*Rocky*, 1976) and Vietnam Green Beret veteran John Rambo (*First Blood*, 1982)—were his own creations. He was the writer or screenwriter for those incredibly triumphant films. The *Rocky* and *Rambo* franchises are among the most successful in Hollywood history. Along with several other films, they've earned close to $3 billion in box office sales.

From the beginning, Sly faced challenges. Complications and the misuse of forceps during his birth accidentally severed a nerve that caused paralysis in his face. As a result, part of the lower left side of his face is paralyzed—including parts of his lip, tongue, and chin.

Like others who have tried to break into the entertainment industry, Sly soon found out there are overwhelming odds against making it in Hollywood. He held down plenty of odd jobs—from being a hairdresser in his family's business, to cleaning out lion cages at Central Park Zoo, and working on the Philadelphia waterfront. He said his first apartment was a mere eight feet by nine feet.

He was bullied as a youngster, but those negative experiences motivated him to take up bodybuilding. As the legend goes, he couldn't afford proper weightlifting equipment, so he attached cinderblocks to a pole as substitute barbells. As underdog from the start, he wasn't going to let anything stop him!

Sly certainly paid his dues. While living in New York with barely fifty dollars to his name, he sold an original movie script, *Paradise Alley*, for a hundred bucks. Years later after *Rocky's* success, he was able to direct and star in the film, which went on to gross over seven million dollars at the box office.

But long before his Hollywood career, Sly had his first starring role in a soft-core porn film. He was paid two hundred dollars for two days' work. He said he did the film out of sheer desperation—he was homeless after being evicted from his apartment. When he saw the casting notice for the film, he had been sleeping in the New York City Port Authority bus station for three weeks. In Sly's own words: "It was either do that movie or rob someone, because I was at the end—the very end—of my rope."

Over the next five years, Sly landed several minor movie and TV roles. Then, one day in 1975, inspiration struck. On March 24th, Stallone watched the bloody fifteen-round fight between Muhammad Ali and Chuck Wepner. The epic battle inspired him, and the idea of *Rocky* was born that night. Sly went home directly, and within three days he completed the story's first draft.

The script looked promising, but the movie studios wanted a well-established actor for the title role. They wanted a star like Burt Reynolds, James Caan, or Ryan O'Neal—they all were in their heyday, and any of them would be a big draw at the box office. Sly, on the other hand, was relatively unknown. But he had a dream that he simply wouldn't give up on.

He was offered $25K for the script—then $50K, $150K, and finally over $300K! But Sly would have nothing to do with it. He wanted to play the part, and he wasn't about to give up on himself. He stood his ground despite the fact that he had less than $100 to his name, a pregnant wife, and a dog named Butkus. (Yes, that was Sly's real dog in the movie.)

Later, he told an interviewer, *"I never would have sold it. I told my wife that I'd rather bury it in the backyard and let the caterpillars play Rocky. I would have hated myself for selling out."*

In the end Sly accepted less money—but *he* would play the role of Rocky Balboa, and he played it like no one else could.

Fast forward thirty years after Rocky was first shown on the silver screen: MGM Studios contacted my company to commission one of our artists to create artwork for the thirtieth-anniversary release of the film. We had done business with MGM executives before, so we had a good track record. I was ecstatic to be involved with the *Rocky* brand in any way.

The first thing I did was to call Joe Petruccio, an accomplished artist who understands how to capture the essence and inspiration of a legend like *Rocky*. Over the years we have published Joe's art under license agreements with Elvis Presley Enterprises, Muhammad Ali Enterprises, and many others.

Joe really knocked it out of the ballpark with this assignment. He not only captured *all* the key scenes, but his work truly embodied the persona and emotion, true to the spirit of *Rocky*. Once we developed a comprehensive marketing program, we were off to the races.

From the beginning MGM cautioned us that Sly had final approval of the artwork, but that our company would have limited direct contact with him. I convinced the studio that the more we could involve Sly, the better our chances for success. They arranged for me to meet with him and discuss the program. Our first meeting took place in a very unassuming office. Sly was editing the then soon-to-be-released film *Rocky Balboa*. We hit it off right away—he was gracious and generous, even letting me hold the original *Rocky* championship belt.

He loved our artwork and the marketing plan, and was very impressed with what we had in mind for its release to the public. We sat down, and I asked him his thoughts on dealing with life's challenges and obstacles.

It soon became obvious that at this point in his incredibly successful career Sly has little interest in working for the money. He's had more fame than most of us would ever *dream* of having. He simply loves what he does. I inquired, "What motivates you? What do you do when adversity strikes? How do you stay so focused?" He took his time to respond and was thoroughly generous with his insights.

"Most people don't understand how powerful they can be. The human body is an amazing thing. If people can learn to push themselves, there's no limit to how far they can go to become the best. We all need to be competitors. I love to compete; I always have and I always will."

His humility and honesty struck me as he contemplated the future:

"One day somebody is going to try and take my spot, and I guess that may happen. But until then, I plan on doing all I need to do to be the best I can."

The next time I saw Sly was during the press junket for *Rocky Balboa*. He signed all the artwork we created. It was fantastic. He even wanted a couple of pieces for his home, and I gladly gave them to him. My wife Brooke and I were invited to the red carpet for the film's premier. Not only did we hang out with Sly, but with Burt Young—good old "Paulie"—as well. Sly gave a very uplifting speech, helping the crowd see the film as more than a story about a fighter. Rather, **it was about a man who still had something left—who still had something in his tank. A lot of people reach**

a certain age and think it's over, he explained. But it's not over until *you* **say it's over.**

If you have not already seen *Rocky Balboa*, please do. It will inspire you with faith in the fact that "it ain't over till it's over" for any of us. In the film, Rocky sums it up this way: *"Let me tell you something you already know. The world ain't all sunshine and rainbows. It's a very mean and nasty place, and I don't care how tough you are. It will beat you to your knees and keep you there permanently if you let it. You, me, or nobody is gonna hit as hard as life. But it ain't about how hard ya hit. It's about how hard you can get hit and keep moving forward—how much you can take and keep moving forward. That's how winning is done!"*

Soon after the premier festivities, Sly invited me to his office to sign more art. He was busy editing the 2008 version of *Rambo*, and we continued our conversation about competing: *"Way back when, I knew I wanted to get to a better place, so I was never afraid of rejection. I figured that's just the way it was—that it's part of life."*

Sly's many quotes over the years keep on inspiring the masses: *"Once in one's life, for one mortal moment, one must make a grab for immortality; if not, one has not lived. I believe there's an inner power that makes winners or losers. The winners are the ones who really listen to the truth of their hearts. When you're scared, when you're hanging on, when life is hurting you, then you're going to see what you're really made of. For every guy, there is an opportunity to be a lot better than he thought he could be. We can't all be the star of the team, but we can be a star in our life."*

My wife Brooke and I were invited to a party at Prince's house, and Sly was there. When he spoke to me about the possibility of the next *Rocky*, it almost felt like he was pitching me the idea. Maybe he was. He described Rocky seeing a street light out in the old neighborhood and being inspired to run for political office and get things fixed. It was great to see how his mind was working and the enthusiasm he had for his beloved character.

Sly went out of his way to thank me for putting together the art program for the thirtieth anniversary of *Rocky*. "You guys really did a great job," he said. From my perspective, it was pretty impressive to meet such an iconic, yet humble person. He loves movies, art, and certainly boxing. Although never a professional boxer, Stallone was inducted into the International Boxing Hall of Fame in June 2011.

Stallone and his iconic Rocky character will be hitting the big screen again late in 2015 with Creed, a movie produced by Sly that tells the story of the son of Apollo Creed, Adonis Johnson Creed, traveling to Philadelphia, where he meets Rocky Balboa and requests that the elder boxer train him. Plans are also underway for a fifth Rambo movie to be released – Rambo: Final Blood.

Early in his career, Sylvester Stallone bet on himself and won. He has created a legacy of inspiration for future generations to come. But maybe most important, he has shown us all that if you believe in yourself, being the underdog is not always the worst thing in the world.

SLY'S EMPOWERING THOUGHT: *"Until you start believing in yourself, you ain't gonna have a life."*

DO IT DAILY:

▶ *Embrace Life's Obstacles.* Life will throw punches at you and sometimes knock you down. Learn to take the hit, but more importantly, learn to get back up and keep punching every single day!

▶ *Believe in the Underdog.* There will be times when each of us is the underdog. The odds may not be in your favor, and the onlookers will expect you to fall short. But it's your choice and your attitude that will be the difference between winning and losing in the ring of life.

Bill O'Reilly

FOX NEWS, BEST SELLING AUTHOR

Bill's Journey:

SCHOOLTEACHER → THE O'REILLY FACTOR → EMMY AWARD WINNER

The world thirsts for straightforward people. You know, the type of folks with great character and morals that will stand up and stay true, unwilling and even unable to do anything but tell it like it is. Having the ability to be straightforward is one of the most coveted and necessary traits for each of us to possess. So much is forgiven and forgotten with just a little bit of sincerity. It is the lies and cover-ups that are deal breakers. For Bill O'Reilly, being viewed as straightforward has been a defining quality on both a personal and professional level. And that quality has launched a career that has spanned decades.

Whichever way you lean politically, it's not difficult to recognize Bill O'Reilly's success as a talk show host, journalist, five-time bestselling author, and two-time Emmy Award winner. Bill O'Reilly, a registered independent and self-described "traditionalist," hosts *The O'Reilly Factor*, the most-watched cable news show for more than fourteen years. It is broadcast in more than thirty countries worldwide and has amassed an audience of loyal viewers numbering in the millions. It really doesn't matter which side of the issue you fall on, many Americans respect Bill's straightforward approach.

While Bill has gained amazing notoriety and respect, he still does have his share of critics and naysayers. His fiery, argumentative style and his outspoken, opinionated conclusions draw a lot of heat from those who oppose his views. In this day and age, the Internet provides plenty of forums (blogs, social media, and so on) through which his detractors can express their counter-arguments. But all too often these "keyboard warriors" cross the line from expressing different views and go on the attack with venom and hatred. In his bestselling book, *Culture Warrior*, Bill writes: *"I am routinely threatened with physical harm and loathed by many. Early in my career it was tough, but now we are established. We have a brand, and criticism does not bother me anymore—I have a job to do."*

Bill's advice should come in handy for all of us during our own trying situations. *"At times you have to fight, no way around it. At some point every one of us is confronted with danger or injustice. How we choose to combat that challenge is often life-defining."* But for Bill, the approach has always been head on and with integrity, valuing his honest assessment and opinion.

Bill has shown over the years that he has tremendous resilience, and his relentless stamina offers invaluable insights we all can learn from. During our interview, I quickly saw his very straightforward and focused style.

I learned that Bill grew up just a few minutes from my old neighborhood on Long Island, New York. On his rise to the top—from high school history teacher to local news broadcaster and anchor for the popular TV show *Inside Edition*—he has always been willing to put in the necessary work. That drive and dedication led him at age forty-six to earn his second master's degree from Harvard's Kennedy School of Government.

While attending Harvard, Bill worked on his game plan for *The O'Reilly Factor*, which was eventually picked up by the Fox News Channel. Bill's hard-driving interview style is "an attempt to bring honest information about complicated and important matters." Bill has interviewed hundreds of well-known people from a variety of fields—even U.S. Presidents George Bush and Bill Clinton. And, just before the 2014 Super Bowl, President Barack Obama.

No matter what side of the aisle you are on, Bill asks the challenging and tough questions we all want to ask. A true innovator, he is not afraid to question the establishment. Unlike many authors, Bill does not use a ghostwriter. He puts in the time to do the research and certainly does his homework before any interview.

To succeed Bill suggests: *"Try and be a realist: Acknowledge the fact that you will have negative thoughts. I practice a style of Eastern philosophy and meditation called "Tantra." This helps me accept any negative thoughts I have and replace them with positive thoughts—almost like exercise. The positive needs to overwhelm the negative thoughts. I myself have a plan in place. I always follow through with what I say I will do for myself and others. There is no safety valve—no escape. I have to do it. I accept all the responsibility and obstacles that go along with my journey. Do not let what people say matter to you. Don't let them determine your success. Outlast them. Out-fight them! If you want to be a competitor, then you need to mentally handle all the critics. Life has a way of letting the chips fall where they may. If you're a good person and you give the necessary effort for something you desire, you have a good chance of having a happy life."*

Bill says he has requested that his headstone be inscribed: "He'll Never Spin in His Grave." The author of more than sixteen books, Bill's growing list runs the gamut from fiction to nonfiction to children's stories. His *NY Times* bestselling book *Killing Lincoln,* released in 2011, was adapted into a movie by the National Geographic Channel in 2013 and featured Tom Hanks as the narrator.

Killing Lincoln met with such great success that the same was done for Bill's 2012 book *Killing Kennedy.* Released in 2013 to coincide with the fiftieth anniversary of JFK's assassination, the docudrama starred Rob Lowe as President John F. Kennedy.

In September 2014, Bill released *Killing Patton*, and it quickly became a New York Times best seller. *Killing Patton* takes readers inside the final year of World War II and recounts the events surrounding Patton's tragic demise, naming names of the many powerful individuals who wanted him silenced.

Bill also writes a weekly self-titled syndicated newspaper column that appears in numerous papers, including the *New York Post* and the *Chicago Sun-Times*. He is a fan of The Beatles, The Rolling Stones, Luther Vandross, Elvis, and "Ol' Blue Eyes" Frank Sinatra. In addition, he's a fan of two of my favorite movies, *Rocky* and *Young Frankenstein*.

Another one of Bill's passions is collecting historical documents. Whether he realizes it or not, the tremendous amount of worthy material he has produced will become historical in nature for future generations to enjoy and learn from. He is certainly creating a legacy.

Bill is committed to giving back. He regularly contributes to dozens of charities and organizations including Wounded Warriors, Doctors without Borders, New York Coalition for the Homeless, Autism Speaks, and the Crohn's and Colitis Foundation of America.

Bill is a lot of things to a lot of different people, but remaining straightforward is one consistency you'll see in everything he touches. And for that simple reason, Bill will always be one of the most straightforward people around.

BILL'S EMPOWERING THOUGHT: *"When you get knocked down, get back up. Outlast them. Out-fight them!"*

DO IT DAILY:

- ▸ ***Be Honest***. Obvious, right? But the truth is that we all should strive to be honest with ourselves. Survey how often you lie or even exaggerate the situation to appease your conscious. The more transparent you are in addressing the present situation, the better the result will be.

- ▸ ***Don't Cut Corners.*** No shortcuts, no compromise, and no letup. You either carry yourself in a straightforward manner, or you don't. When you take the time to put integrity first, you will attract people who respond with the same level of that amazingly important quality.

Smokey Robinson

Smokey's Journey:

DRUG ADDICTION → SINGER-SONGWRITER → GRAMMY WINNER

I t is not always easy to turn the mirror inward and take a deep and thoughtful look at yourself and your life. In fact, most people simply refuse to do it. They would rather maintain the status quo, and remain content with exactly the way things appear. But for Smokey Robinson, reflection has become a personal calling card.

He said, *"Those of us lucky enough to live our dreams can find ways to turn them into nightmares if we're not too careful. I know this first-hand because I nearly threw all my blessings away."*

For Smokey, reflection became almost a daily ritual. It would have been easy to maintain his current status, but it would have eventually killed him. It took unbelievable self-reflection for Smokey to acknowledge his status quo was simply not cutting it. In reality, it was killing him. So when he turned the mirror back onto himself, it was easy to see the immediacy and necessity for change.

"The truth is that I'm probably one of the most blessed people on the face of the earth," says the legendary Smokey Robinson, one of the leading singer-songwriters of all time. Smokey is unquestionably one of the cornerstone artists who made Motown Records into "The Sound of Young America," as it was once known.

"I thank God all the time for all those blessings. See, my life truly has been filled with miracles, and I'm talking about more than my great group—The Miracles. There have been so many times along the way when I was in the right place at the right time. First and foremost, we were in Detroit more than a half-century ago, and fortunate enough to run right into Berry Gordy just as his dream was beginning to take shape. We were all so lucky to be part of something historic—something never done before and never to be again—the whole Motown story."

Smokey Robinson's key part in the Motown Story went beyond his success as a best-selling artist with hits such as "Shop Around," which became Motown's first million-selling hit record, "You've Really Got a Hold on Me," and "I Second That Emotion." He also served as an executive producer and songwriter behind countless classics and soulful hits including "My Guy" for Mary Wells, and "The Way You Do the Things You Do" and "My Girl" for The Temptations, as well as numerous others.

Today he remains very proud—and thankful—for the Motown experience:

"People talk about Motown like it was just this big music factory, but I'm here to tell you that Motown was an amazing family. And in our family we were blessed to have some of the greatest artists of all time: Stevie Wonder, Marvin Gaye, The Temptations, The Four Tops, Diana Ross and the Supremes—all of whom people around the world are still listening to today, and will be listening to for many years to come. Our family was very special, and we were blessed to have one another and share so much together. Then there was my "baby brother" Michael Jackson and the Jackson 5. They came to Motown a little later, and they took things to a whole other level. Michael was probably the greatest

entertainer of all times and a total natural. I know because I saw it for myself."

A remarkable tribute from a man who, during the course of his fifty-year music career, released more than four thousand songs featuring his signature tenor voice, impeccable timing, and profound sense of lyric. He has received numerous awards including the Grammy Living Legend Award, NARAS Lifetime Achievement Award, Honorary Doctorate (Howard University), the National Medal of Arts Award from the President of the United States, and the 2006 Kennedy Center Honors.

But Smokey came close to throwing away his towering success: *"As I said before, I've been very blessed in my life, but it turned out that the biggest obstacle in my life was drugs. I had two and a half years doing weed and cocaine—when I was old enough to know better. I never did the pipe, but I mixed the weed with cocaine, and for me that was a recipe for disaster."*

"Now I'm a national drugs spokesperson for the government, and I speak to judges and at drug rehab facilities around the country. As smooth as people might think I am, drugs destroyed me for a time. It was my toughest obstacle—and the way I overcame it was spiritual, through God. I went and got prayed for, and that made all the difference in my life.

That was back in May of 1986. I had lost two and a half years of my life to drugs. At the end of it, I was virtually dead—and this was all pre-crack, thankfully! When I speak at rehab centers and talk to people who've been doing drugs for twenty years (and some of them are only thirty years old), I'm amazed, because two and a half years of drugs just about finished me off."

"Thankfully, a friend came and got me to a prayer service. I realized that I didn't have all the answers in the world. It was the turning point in my life."

That was in 1986. Sometimes you face your biggest obstacle in the midst of your biggest success, but you can always turn it around. In 1987, Smokey made a comeback with the album *One Heartbeat* and the singles "Just to See Her" and "One Heartbeat," which became Top 10 hits on *Billboard's* Pop, Soul, and Adult Contemporary charts. "Just to See Her" won Smokey his first Grammy Award in 1988. In 1989, Smokey opened up about his drug abuse when he wrote and published his memoirs, titled *Inside My Life.*

"Success will tell you that you are a god—that you can do whatever you want. Drugs will tell you the same thing, and that's a very big lie. Drugs were killing the best part of me. I had always been a spiritual person, but I let that slip away for cocaine and weed, and my life went to hell, literally. I had to look to God for strength, and since then I've never touched the stuff again or even been tempted. My advice is: We must each find our own God and truth system—something bigger than ourselves that we can rely on to tell us the truth about ourselves...even when we don't want to hear it."

SMOKEY'S EMPOWERING THOUGHT: *"I'm at war against drugs because young people—and not so young people—need to know that drugs will kill your dreams and they will kill you. So follow your dreams, and don't block your blessings with the drugs that will kill you."*

DO IT DAILY:

▸ *Survey Your Life.* Practice honest self-reflection to better yourself. Always work to be sincere with your life so you can provide an accurate assessment of your successes and the areas in which you can improve.

▸ *Don't Settle.* The truth is that no one should hold you to a higher standard than yourself. When it comes to self-reflection, don't ever be willing to go easy on your heart and soul. They need care and tenderness, but tough love will also do the trick.

Joe Barbera

HANNA-BARBERA CARTOON STUDIO FOUNDER

Joe's Journey:

DELIVERY BOY → NUMEROUS REJECTIONS → SEVEN OSCARS, EIGHT EMMYS

For most us, we know persistence to be that "never give up" attitude. You know, the type of character trait that constantly forges you forward, blasting through those obstacles that lie in your path. It is the willingness to act like a rubber-ball, and have considerable bounce-back. For Joe Barbera, his persistency and unwillingness to give up has been a staple and behavioral norm.

He said, *"Making cartoons means very hard work. At every step of the way it's a lot like the task Dr. Frankenstein set for himself: nothing less than the creation of life—or at least a reasonable facsimile thereof."* Even though it often lives in the imagination of movies and television, creating life takes a great deal of persistence.

"Yabba dabba doo!" was Fred Flintstone's signature cry whenever he was overwhelmingly happy. That's *exactly* how I felt about the times I spent with legendary animator, director, producer, storyboard artist, and entrepreneur Joe Barbera. He was about eighty-two years "young" when I first had the opportunity to meet him. What a privilege to spend time with someone who had had so many life experiences.

Joe and his business partner of more than sixty years, Bill Hanna, were better known on our TV screens as Hanna-Barbera. To audiences around the world this legendary duo brought some of the most loveable cartoon characters—including many I used to run home from school to watch: *The Flintstones, The Jetsons, Tom and Jerry, Yogi Bear and Boo-Boo, Huckleberry Hound, Quick Draw McGraw, Top Cat*, and my favorite, *Magilla Gorilla*. Together they produced over three thousand animated half-hour shows featuring more than two thousand characters.

Joseph Roland Barbera was born in 1911 in Little Italy, New York, and raised in Flatbush, Brooklyn. His mom married at sixteen. His dad was a barber who seemed more committed to his gambling habits than to providing for his family. In his book, *My Life in Toons: From Flatbush to Bedrock in Less Than a Century*, Joe talks about his early love of drawing: **"Drawing was just something to do on a rainy day, but it was the first inkling I had that I could do something nobody else could do."**

As a young man, Joe worked as a delivery boy for a tailor, filled out tax forms for a bank, and dabbled as a boxer. He found humor in his first adult job: *"The problem I had working in the accounting field was that I couldn't add, subtract, divide, or multiply. Even so, I worked in the bank for more than six years—and dreaded every day!"*

Joe grew up during the Great Depression and graduated high school in 1928, but there were few jobs to be had: *"I loved to draw and began submitting my drawings to different magazines. For two years I received reject letter after reject letter. Why did I persist? It was survival—it was staying alive. It was having something to look forward to."*

Joe managed to get a number of his cartoons published in *Redbook, Saturday Evening Post*, and *Collier's*. He even went so far as to write to Walt Disney for his advice on getting started in the animation industry. After paying his dues doing ink and storyboard work for Van Beuren Studios and Terrytoons, he eventually landed a job with MGM's cartoon unit in

California in 1937. There he met Bill Hanna, and quickly they both recognized that they would make a good team.

At MGM Studios, Joe and Bill created *Tom and Jerry*, the animated cat-and-mouse duo famous for their hard-hitting rivalry. Over the next seventeen years, *Tom and Jerry* cartoons collected fourteen Oscar nominations, winning seven—the most awards ever garnered by a theatrical-based animated series.

The silver lining, however, had some dark clouds. After creating the award-winning series, developing the characters, writing the scripts, and producing and directing each cartoon, Joe and Bill's boss took full credit for their work.

Joe remembers that he "begged to be out on stage" on Oscar night, but year after year neither Joe nor Bill were allowed to receive the awards. Their boss not only snubbed them at the award ceremonies, but he went so far as to imprint his own name on the cartoon credits as sole producer. He completely left these two creative geniuses out of the limelight.

Joe and Bill were placed in charge of MGM's cartoon division when their boss finally retired in the mid-1950s, but television was beginning to siphon off much of their revenue. After almost two decades of success with *Tom and Jerry*, their business manager received a phone call from the front office: "Close the studio and lay everybody off."

As Joe tells it, ***"With a single call—conveyed to us secondhand—a whole career disappeared...but in reality, it was merely the end of one career and the beginning of another."*** Talk about a persistent attitude.

They founded their own company in 1957 and pursued both theatrical and television productions. Hanna-Barbera Productions went on to produce some of the most successful animated features in history. Joe and Bill invented a new technique to bring their onscreen characters to life. They developed *limited animation,* which reduced the number of individual drawings necessary for a thirty-minute cartoon from the standard thirty-eight thousand to fewer than six thousand. The time and cost savings were dramatic.

After learning that half the viewers of their popular *Huckleberry Hound* and *Yogi Bear* shows were adults, the studio decided to take a huge risk and produce a prime time, half-hour animated series aimed at the whole family.

Joe thought it sounded crazy, but about this seemingly impossible project he said: ***"With our families to feed, we learned to say 'yes' to anything that had the remote possibility of working and making a living for us. It was either figure out a new way to do business…or find another career."***

Joe and Bill's *limited animation* technique made the impossible possible. And their success with America's first prime time animation series, *The Flintstones*, vaulted the new company to the top.

The stone-age couple Fred and Wilma Flintstone, along with their neighbors Barney and Betty Rubble, and their respective children, Pebbles and Bamm-Bamm—not to mention their lovable pet dinosaur Dino—became part of the very fabric of 1960s America. This "impossible" half-hour cartoon ended up being the most financially successful animated franchise for three decades, until *The Simpsons* debuted in 1989.

Even after Turner Broadcasting System bought the cartoon-making factory of Hanna-Barbera for an estimated $320 million in 1991, Joe continued to be active as an advisor and executive producer. Despite several more mergers and ownership changes, Joe worked on projects right up to his death in 2006, at the age of ninety-five, thus ending his seventy-year career in animation.

Joe was one of the humblest people I've ever met. When my company opened a new gallery in Boston, he not only agreed to come be our celebrity guest for the grand opening, but he also willingly shot a commercial while at our gallery and signed every piece of art our clients bought.

As we made our plans to open the Boston gallery, Joe, a fellow New Yorker, asked me why we would want to operate a business so far from our main operation. I guess like Joe, I had a little bit of persistence in my blood as well.

I was already several years into a successful business and had become one of the country's leading animation art dealers with many licenses and distribution agreements in place with the likes of Warner Bros. and Hanna-Barbera. We also had landed deals to work with legendary cartoon directors Chuck Jones and Friz Freleng. The missing piece for us was the Walt Disney Company.

For more than three years I did my best to secure an agreement with Disney. Every letter and every call was ignored. A competing dealer did all he could to keep us off the Disney art program. He had friends in high places, and he used any and all tactics to discourage Disney from working with us.

I will never forget running into one of Disney's executives at a trade show and asking what it would take for us to get on the Disney art program. She bared her teeth just like a Disney villain and snarled, "You will *never* get on the Disney program!" I politely walked away, but that didn't mean I would give up. A Disney license would mean millions of dollars to our organization.

Finally, I tracked down somebody who could potentially help us. He said if I wanted the Disney art then I should consider opening up a gallery in Boston because they had no dealers there. I operated my business out of New York. I had no interest in opening up in Boston. But, the day after he hinted that I could get on their program if I did, I hopped on a plane and flew to Boston to find the best location on Newbury Street. From a

Boston pay phone I dialed the Disney executive and told him where I was—I had called his bluff.

With a big laugh he said, "If you have that type of passion, then we need you on the Disney art program!" And just like that, my three years of effort finally paid off. Within six months we became the largest dealer of Disney animation art in the United States. We maintained that achievement for more than fifteen years, and I was asked to serve on the Disney animation art advisory board.

Passion and persistence really do pay off. They can be the difference between endless success and complete failure. We can all agree that Joe could have given up on countless occasions. But there was no give up inside of him. And that attitude certainly made him "smarter than the average bear."

JOE'S EMPOWERING THOUGHT: *"I persisted to survive. It was staying alive. It was having something to look forward to."*

DO IT DAILY:

▸ *Be Inspired.* Use each setback as a motivating reason to continue, not as a reason to stop. At the end of the day, your success will be defined by your attitude towards those times you fell short.

▸ *Evaluate Failure.* Most people use failures or obstacles as a reason to quit. But they should simply be learning experiences. Take the time to assess where you fell short, brush yourself off, and continue to forge ahead.

Brooks Robinson

BASEBALL HALL OF FAME

Brooks' Journey:

NEWSPAPER BOY → BAT BOY → BASEBALL LEGEND

Humble beginnings make for humble and powerful legacies. So is true for Brooks Robinson, known to most as "The Human Vacuum Cleaner," and considered to be the greatest defensive third-baseman in MLB history. When speaking with Brooks, you'd probably never know of the amazing accomplishments on his resume; mostly because he is extremely humble, and doesn't take himself all that seriously. But that is what makes him so truly unique. Humility is one of those traits you can't always identify. Humility is a pleasant surprise; it catches people off-guard, and only adds to the aura of success an individual achieves. Remain humble through your life and people will respect you not for what you say about yourself, but for what you don't say.

"I am in the Hall of Fame not because of my ability—it was my love of the game that overrode everything else." This humble statement comes from one of the greatest baseball Hall-of-Famers of all time, Brooks Calbert Robinson Jr. He grew up in Little Rock, Arkansas, where his dad worked for a bakery until joining the Little Rock Fire Department, eventually rising to the rank of captain. His mom worked for Sears, Roebuck & Company.

He continues, *"When I was signed in 1955, I was not a great player. I had average speed and was average all around. No one saw me as a great prospect. But I loved the game of baseball and always believed that I could make it."*

And make it he did. Brooks played his entire twenty-three-year major league career for the Baltimore Orioles—from 1955 to 1977. He won sixteen consecutive Gold Glove Awards, played in four World Series (winning against the LA Dodgers in 1966), and was selected for the All-Star Team fifteen consecutive years (1960-74). In 1964, Brooks was named the American League MVP—beating out Mickey Mantle.

Over his baseball career, Brooks accumulated 2,848 hits, 268 home runs, and 1,357 runs batted in. The Baltimore Orioles retired his number 5 in 1977, and he was elected to the Major League Baseball All-Century Team.

Even as a New York sports fan, I was thrilled and honored to speak with Brooks Robinson. His sense of history and optimism was a constant: *"My dad was my hero. He gave me my love for the game. As a young kid, I delivered the* **Arkansas Gazette** *newspaper on my bike. I also operated the scoreboard, served as a batboy, and sold soft drinks at the ball field. I never wanted to do anything else but play in the big leagues."*

Even when he made it to the majors, he still remained humble and always focused on his work ethic and performance. He explained to me, *"My mindset was always to perform at a high level each and every day. Motivated by baseball history, I constantly needed to prove myself not only to others, but to myself as well. People have challenges—and I had my fair share. I remember what I had thought could be the worst thing that happened to me turned out to be the best: Early in my career I hurt my knee; it was devastating. I was sent down to Triple-A ball. But being sent down turned out to be a blessing: I came back a completely different player. I had time to refine my skills in the minors, and in turn I became a stronger and faster player."*

"Ball players, and anybody who wants to have success, should keep in mind that the love of the game should be your most important thing. Professional athletes and successful people have a lot in common—they both started with an early drive for success and a love for what they do. That's what it takes: love and drive. The way I see it, it's important to do the things you don't want to do—whatever is hard for you to do—for the love and the joy success can bring. In the big leagues, I went to bat more than eleven thousand times. During the playoffs and the World Series, I was a pretty good clutch hitter. My sense of concentration was enhanced because of all my experience. **The problem I see these days is that people want to start at the top. They need to understand that you must pay your dues, learn the business, and put in the time to learn the ropes."**

"Tell your readers: You will not just somehow get better; nobody will give you anything. You need to work overtime to get better and better, no matter what you do in life."

Brooks has always been a man of deep faith and has always been committed to giving back. He has long been a supporter of the Boy Scouts of America, has served as an executive board member for the Baltimore Area Council, and has received its Silver Beaver Award. In 1972, he won the Roberto Clemente Award, honoring the player who best exemplifies the game of baseball both on and off the field.

Brooks has served as president of the Major League Baseball Players Alumni Association. After retiring from baseball, he worked as a color commentator for the Orioles in the 1980s. In 2012, the Orioles unveiled a bronze sculpture of him in Oriole Park at Camden Yards. Brooks' humility and character are truly part of what has made him such a tremendous athlete and person. When speaking with him, it is impressive and surprising that the last thing he tells you about is his on-the-field successes. His humble beginnings and humility are not just refreshing, but also a great lesson to us all.

BROOKS' EMPOWERING THOUGHT: *"If you're not practicing, somebody else is—somewhere, and he'll be ready to take your job."*

DO IT DAILY:

- *Appreciate What You Do.* Put forth your full effort into whatever you may do. You are only given one life-so make the most of it and constantly respect all that surrounds you.

- *Remember Your Origins.* Don't ever forget that there was a time when you were not where you are today. There were times when you needed the guidance and support of others. Never forget those times, so you remain humble and can pass along that same generosity to those in need.

Mark Cuban

ENTREPRENEUR

Mark's Journey:

BARTENDER → BILLIONAIRE → NBA TEAM OWNER

Author and speaker John Ortberg said, "Over time, grit is what separates fruitful lives from aimlessness." For me, grit is (and always has been) the ability to dig in, bear down, and work harder than the next guy. Grit begins when you want to give up, feel as if you cannot succeed, and simply run out of gas. It is easy to get to that point without grit, but to overcome the hump, you simply have to have it. The grittiest people are often those that refuse to stop until they reached their goals.

For most of us, we feel drawn to people with substantial amounts of grit. It is a term often used to describe athletes and coaches, but it is totally relevant to the business world. It is an attitude, a way of thinking, and a resiliency that uplifts and helps people to hit higher goals.

When I think of grit, Mark Cuban comes to mind. You probably know him as the billionaire Entrepreneur, Shark Tank phenom, and owner of the National Basketball League's Dallas Mavericks. Mark's successes brought notoriety in financial circles and among the hi-tech savvy. But his purchase of the Dallas Mavericks in 2000, and his success at turning a flailing NBA franchise into a world championship team in just 11 short years (by NBA standards) made Mark a household name for the rest of us. He is gritty, passionate, and started from humble beginnings, hustling his way to his current social status. Throughout his life, he has worked to buck the common wisdom, and has realized that success is a definition all your own; it is never dependent on outside factors like good luck, connections, and other people.

Talk about a gritty attitude. Mark simply has no give-up and losing is not within his vocabulary. He says, "*I want to kick the ass of the people I am competing with and that always motivates me to push myself to know as much as I can about my business and puts me in a position to create new ideas.*"

This son of working-class parents from Pittsburgh became a multi-billionaire overnight. But it was the gritty journey leading up to that moment that truly defines Mark and his perspective on success. He quotes his dad, an automotive upholsterer, when he says, "*Nothing will come easy…hard work is something everyone talks about, but rarely does… if you do something you love, then working hard is easy. If you can work hard enough to be really, really good at something—anything— you can usually find a way to reach your goals.*"

More than 10 years later, I found this insanely busy mega-mogul hasn't forgotten his roots, and he remains generous and willing to tell his story with others who need motivation as they follow their own paths. I was actually surprised by how open and excited he was to be a part of this project.

Don't think that Mark's success began and ended with the historic sale of Broadcast.com to Yahoo. He was definitely not a "one-hit wonder." He went on to finance television shows and movies. He invested in a multitude of tech companies and bought a string of art-house theaters. Today his net worth exceeds some $3 billion.

And the best part is that one of his personal *common threads* was making money through turning losers into winners. He has an amazing ability in identifying the opportunity where others simply cannot. He has done it through the course of his career and constantly looks to those occasions where it takes grit and hard work to turn it around.

But how did this common guy from a Pittsburgh suburb come to land on the Forbes richest people list?

No one handed success to Mark—he didn't inherit it. At the age of 12, he made his inauspicious entrée into the business world selling garbage bags to purchase a pair of expensive basketball shoes. He learned early to do whatever it takes to get what you want. To grit up. Later he tended bar, collected and sold stamps to pay for college, taught disco dancing and worked as a party promoter.

There lies within Mark an innate drive that has catapulted him to the top of his game and has turned him into a master self-motivator. He is pretty good at getting inside his own head and remaining there. He is his own best friend, never allowing the naysayers or the doubters take control. If that were the case, he may still be selling garbage bags.

Mark Cuban has an intense need for competition. He thrives on it. He tells his Mavericks players, ***"Business is the ultimate sport: 365 days a year, seven days a week and 24 hours a day, somebody is trying to take you down."*** And when he identifies a "win" within his reach, he sets his sights on it with a laser focus and drives toward his endgame, never stopping until he gets where he is going. That ambition and competitive mentality generates his vivacious confidence to win.

Staying on top of his game is one way to live out another of his father's lessons—in fact, it's one of his favorite quotes: ***"Today is the youngest you will ever be, so live life to the fullest."*** Playing to win helps Mark live life to the utmost.

His confidence comes out in an optimistic, "glass-half-full" attitude. When it comes to business planning, he disagrees with strategic approaches that include specific contingency plans for overcoming projected adversity. *"That's a loser's game,"* he says, *"You have to have strategies to achieve success"*—not to project failure! Difficult challenges can be a positive force. Setting smaller goals helps you build a roadmap to success. And always retaining a large amount of grit can help to overcome those obstacles as they present themselves.

You can view your challenges as walls that hinder or stop your progress, or like Mark did, you can *grit up* and use those apparent obstacles as learning experiences that help propel you to greater heights. Seeing your "walls" as merely obstacles to overcome will increase your chances for huge success.

Grit is a term we use to describe people that are willing to go just a little farther than the competition. They are the type of people that don't just roll with the punches; they take the punches, and brush them off, recovering quickly so they can continue the journey. Grit can be a game-changer, a differentiator of sorts. For Mark Cuban, it has made all the difference.

MARK'S EMPOWERING THOUGHT: *The power to achieve success lies within you: "Sweat equity is the best equity—and everyone has a bank full of it. They just have to choose to use it."*

DO IT DAILY:

▸ *Forget Contingency Plans.* Instead, create strategies to achieve success and view your challenges as lessons to help you reach your goals.

▸ *Grit Up.* Remain dedicated, determined and strong in the face of adversity. Grit is the simple notion of doing just a little bit more than the next guy. It is about realizing that today's failures are tomorrow's successes and not forgetting that in the process.

Montel Williams

TALK SHOW ICON

Montel's Journey:

MULTIPLE SCLEROSIS → NAVAL ACADEMY → EMMY AWARD WINNER

There are few words in the English language that have such important meaning as the word *determination*. Determination is smashing through the obstacles and the brick walls that often stand in your path. Determination is what separates the winners from the losers, and those that sit on the sideline from those that win the game.

At the time of our interview, Montel Williams shared that he was "in pain twenty-four hours a day." You'd never know it—not even when you see this American media icon in person. He has been a public personality for over twenty years, best known for the long-running *Montel Williams Show*, for which he received a Daytime Emmy Award for Outstanding Talk Show Host in 1996.

The show received three more Emmy nominations before it was finally canceled in 2008. Montel went on to host a national radio program and serve as an infomercial spokesman for several products.

Montel's constant pain comes from multiple sclerosis (MS). He was diagnosed with the degenerative disease in 1999, near the peak of his career.

He explained how he lives with MS: *"Years ago, the doctor told me I would be in a wheelchair—and I am in pain 24 hours a day, 365 days a year, but I am determined to walk around this planet with positive thoughts. And I have no doubt that that attitude helps me deal with my MS.*

I learned to become my own advocate—to take charge of my diet and exercise. I accept responsibility for my own overall health and wellness."

Montel Williams proved to be one of the most inspiring, determined, and insightful people I have ever interviewed. Montel's success journey started long before he achieved celebrity status—a fact that became more and more evident as I learned about his background and achievements.

Born in Baltimore, Montel showed himself to be a good student, athlete, and musician. His firefighter father became Baltimore's first African-American fire chief in 1992.

Montel enlisted in the U.S. Marine Corps directly out of high school in 1974. He distinguished himself almost immediately and got promoted to platoon guide while in basic training at boot camp on Parris Island, South Carolina.

He continued to impress his superiors and was eventually recommended for a career track in the U.S. Naval Academy. He entered the academy in 1976, where he studied Mandarin Chinese, engineering, and international security affairs. Montel is justifiably proud of his record: *"I became the first black, enlisted Marine to complete and graduate from both the Naval Academy Prep School and the U.S. Naval Academy."*

A freak medical accident during his last year ruined Montel's plans to return to the Marines after graduation. He was one of one hundred seniors who received the wrong dose of an immunization. His severe reaction landed him in the hospital for two and a half weeks and cost him the vision in his left eye.

He made a partial recovery and served as a naval intelligence officer, further specializing in foreign languages—eventually working with the National Security Agency. After three years aboard submarines, Montel, then a full lieutenant, was made supervising cryptologic officer with the Naval Security Fleet Support Division at Ft. Meade, Maryland.

While counseling the servicemen in his command, as well as their wives and families, he discovered his gift for public speaking. Soon he was invited to speak to different groups about the importance of leadership and how to overcome obstacles on the road to success. Montel enjoyed this new role, and it would pave his way to a career in motivational speaking.

He left the Navy with the rank of lieutenant after receiving the Navy Achievement Medal, the Meritorious Service Medal, and the Navy Commendation Medal. Montel continued to excel at public speaking, and it eventually led to the *Montel Williams Show,* which first aired in 1991.

A 22-year military veteran, Montel remains a staunch advocate for veterans. In October 2014, he played a major role in bringing home Marine Sgt. Andrew Tahmooressi who spent 214 days in a Mexican prison. Tahmooressi served two tours of duty in Afghanistan and suffers from Post-Traumatic Stress Disorder.

When asked to reflect on his upbringing and identify what made him what he is today, Montel responded: *"There were two very powerful forces in my life—my parents and their insistence that education was the most important part of growing up. They made me read at the dinner table—and it paid off! I had a super vocabulary, and I could read and write by the time I was in the first grade. I was a product of 'bussing' every day from the ghetto where I lived to a school in an all-white neighborhood. Even some of the teachers were openly racist. One teacher actually said to me, 'That is why you people will never get any-where!' I took the sting of that remark and made a promise to myself, that I will be the only person who defines me. Tell your readers: As far as I'm concerned, you need to be your own advocate. You alone have to own the definition of who you are!"*

He continued: *"You need knowledge. Knowledge is king—get it so you can help yourself. Learn everything you need to know, including what-ever is stopping you from reaching your goals. Evaluate yourself con-stantly, but don't stop believing in yourself. Every day, ask yourself: 'What did I do today that's worth talking about tomorrow?' At the end of the day I write down three good things that happened that day. When I wake up in the morning, I read those three things again. It starts my day with positive thoughts and helps me better understand who I am. Surround yourself with good people, not people who tell you why you can't do something. When someone points out your limita-tions, you must counter with an attitude that says, 'How dare they try and define who I am!' Recognize the fact that they are only describing themselves. People are held back by their own thoughts—that they can't be successful. Don't look back with critical regret. Look at the things you've done right, and learn from your mistakes."*

Montel sums up his message of self-determination: **"Stop worrying about being 'in the right place at the right time.'"** Instead, *always transform the place you're in* so that it becomes the right place and the right time. You need to realize that genes and environment influence 60 percent of who you are—the other 40 percent is in *your* control.

As I listened to Montel, it was easy to understand why so many companies seek him out as a spokesperson. Montel's mission is clear: "I want to encour-age as many people as I can. With the right attitude, anything is possible."

Determination. Simple as that. Montel has no give-up. He is dedicated to his goals and determined to overcome all that stands in his way. It is easy to give-in. It is unbelievably effortless and undemanding to simply throw in the towel. But to reach insurmountable levels of success, you have to be determined and dedicated to the mission, whatever it may be.

For Montel, he remains dedicated to his trade and his life's goals even in the face of an overbearing medical diagnosis and constant barriers in his path. It was not easy. It remains difficult. But Montel's attitude positions him to implement a dedicated force that drives him to overcome any and all obstacles along the way.

MONTEL'S EMPOWERING THOUGHT: *"You need knowledge. Knowledge is king—get it so you can help yourself. Learn everything you need to know, including whatever is stopping you from reaching your goals."*

DO IT DAILY:

- ▶ *Manifest Your Life.* At the end of the day, write down three good things that happened that day. Wake up in the morning and reread those three things to start your day with a mindset of positive thoughts to build momentum and set the tone for the rest of your day.

- ▶ **Don't Give Up.** Easy to say, hard to do. But if you subscribe to this integral mantra, you'll always remain ahead of the game. Implementing a no give-up attitude will position you for success. Sure, it takes more than just determination, but that's at least half of the battle.

Howard Stern

Howard's Journey:

FINED $3.2 MILLION → RADIO LEGEND → AMERICA'S GOT TALENT

"*Hey now!*" You may like him; you may not like him. Say what you want about Howard Stern, but the outspoken and sometimes controversial icon is truly a cultural phenomenon that many consider a creative genius and visionary. Visionaries are those people amongst us that see things in just a little brighter and more unique light. They inspire us, motivate us, and improve our lives through their commitment to becoming difference-makers, game-changers, and elevating the status quo to something far more exciting than what it once was.

For Howard Stern, being ahead of the curve has been the norm. While some may not consider him to be a visionary, the truth is that there are few people that have left a larger footprint on popular culture than Howard Stern. He's easily one of the most successful broadcasters of all time, and he grew up not too far from my hometown.

Howard freely admits that as a child he was awkward, and as a teenager he was ridiculed and picked on. When he started out as a radio DJ, he says, "I was just plain awful." He speaks often of the mishaps in the early days, but he emphasizes that he had a dream from childhood to become a radio personality, and it drove him to keep moving forward.

Through the years, he has been quoted as saying, ***"Some kids wanted to be a fireman, others a policeman—I always wanted to be a disc jockey."***

"The King of All Media" is more than his self-proclaimed boast; it is a well-deserved description of his thirty-five-plus-year career. Howard Stern has become a successful radio entertainer, a bestselling author, a movie star, and a judge on TV's *America's Got Talent*. He has hosted numerous late-night television shows, pay-per-view events, home video releases, and, in 1993, he starred in a hit movie about his life: *Private Parts*. Not bad for a guy who's first job paid him ninety-six dollars a week!

I did not interview Howard specifically for this book, but during the time I spent with him I came to understand the type of person he is and how he deals with challenges and adversity. I have been a fan since the WNNNBC days. My company advertised on Howard's radio show. Our marketing plan to promote heavyweight-boxing champ "Smokin'" Joe Frazier included an interview with Howard. During our advertising campaigns, not only was I lucky enough to have great meetings with Howard to discuss our promotions, but I also had the good fortune of being invited to a couple of his birthday parties.

You might think that with the level of success Howard has achieved he wouldn't make time for one-on-one meetings with advertisers. But I found just the opposite to be true. Howard could not have been nicer to me. He walked into the meeting and said, "Let's get to it. What do you need from me to make your campaign successful?" As an advertiser, that was like music to my ears. Howard sincerely desired to put together spots for us that would work. He shared many creative ideas that worked very well on air. Every time I spoke to Howard or one of his staff members it was all about **"tell us what you need and we'll make it happen."**

He understands that for him to be successful and win against his competitors, he needs to help sponsors like me beat *my* competitors. "You can't just take their money," he says. Rather, he wants to make sure he delivers—and from my standpoint, Howard *more* than delivered!

When we advertised on his radio show, the results were amazing. Back then, in the mid-1990s, Howard had many "closet" listeners—people who listened but would not admit it. I knew I had a hit when my lawyer, accountant, and business associates from around the country called me and said they'd heard our spot.

As a businessman and media personality, few have come close to Howard's vision and creativity over the last few decades. His unique way of broadcasting made him a pioneer of his format. He knows his medium like no other. He went from one market to another, conquering each one and building up his audience the old-fashioned way—through hard work and creativity.

Howard is a prime example of someone who works extremely hard to make it look easy. Even with more success under his belt than most people could ever achieve, Howard publicly admits, *"I still feel like I gotta prove something. There are a lot of people hoping I'll fail. But I like that; I need to be hated."*

Howard remained true to himself, despite being fired numerous times and enduring attacks from countless groups demanding he be taken off the air. From 1990 to 2004, the Federal Communications Commission (FCC) fined owners of radio stations carrying the *Howard Stern Show* a total of $3.2 million for indecent programming. Nevertheless, Howard stayed strong and continued to add new sponsors, building his career and his audience. He describes it like this: *"I'm in a war, a cultural war."*

Looking back at Howard's decision to move to Sirius satellite radio, it would be easy to conclude that was a slam-dunk. But in 2004, Sirius was very much an unproven business, operating in the shadow of its much larger competitor, XM Radio. Howard was at the top of his game—even after dealing with the FCC. He had built an enormous fan base, was making plenty of money, and was enjoying more success than any other radio personality.

But now, on Sirius, Howard's fans that always listened to his show for free would be asked to pay. Without any guarantee of success, Howard still believed in himself and his abilities. He had the vision. He clearly knew that achieving his goals required him to be driven—to embrace competition and to remain focused when others may lose sight. There are no two ways about it: Howard Stern embraces competition.

Howard has no interest in discussing how much money he makes, and I won't speculate. The lesson he shares is about gratefulness and giving back. He and his wife Beth have made a huge impact through their support of the North Shore Animal League, the world's largest no-kill animal rescue and adoption organization. As a child, I was very familiar with North Shore Animal League as we adopted most of our family pets from this shelter.

Many of Howard's loyal listeners will tell you that he has significantly impacted their lives by providing plenty of laughs and pick-me-ups when they were going through difficult down times. I am one of those fans, and I still treasure a handwritten letter Howard sent me after our meeting. The note ends with this sentence: "Let's eliminate the competition!"

HOWARD'S EMPOWERING THOUGHT: *"If you are passionate and competitive about seeing your vision come true, you will defy the odds and achieve what others (or even you) might think is impossible."*

DO IT DAILY:

▸ *Maintain Your Work Ethic.* The value of having a vision backed up by a strong work ethic should not be underestimated.

▸ ***Remain Focused.*** Visionaries are hyper-focused on their dreams. They often know they are ahead of the curve and have a purpose slightly different than the accepted norm. Be willing to follow your vision no matter how dark the journey may seem.

Quentin Tarantino

Quentin's Journey:

HIGH SCHOOL DROPOUT → VIDEO STORE CLERK → $3 BILLION AT THE BOX OFFICE

There are times in life when we will benefit from the knowledge of others; however, sometimes we have to just teach ourselves if we want to succeed. Acclaimed director Quentin Tarantino is an excellent example of someone who did not have anyone to show him the ropes, and as a result had to provide his own entrée into the world of filmmaking. It is exactly this independent and unorthodox approach to the film industry that makes Tarantino the ultimate maverick. Being a maverick requires that you think outside of the box, and use extreme adaptability and wit to move towards your goals. According to the legend himself,

"You have to break down your own doors—because a lot of times in life, there's no one else to do that for you...I really had to mentor myself by trial and error. And it made me tougher in a very tough business."

Tarantino's life is a testament to those words. One of the world's most acclaimed and influential filmmakers, Quentin Tarantino was born March 27, 1963, in Knoxville, Tennessee. He grew up in some less than glitzy stretches of Torrance, California, and in the Harbor City neighborhood of Los Angeles.

From childhood on, Quentin was driven by an almost singular passion for movies. Despite dropping out of high school at age fifteen, he studied acting while working at Video Archives, a now-defunct video rental store in Manhattan Beach, California. Not only did he pick up a much-needed paycheck there, but he also received a good deal of informal film education. Clearly, Quentin learned his lessons well.

In true maverick style, Tarantino went on to become an Oscar-winning screenwriter and critically acclaimed filmmaker who brought us the genuinely groundbreaking movies:

Reservoir Dogs (1992)
Pulp Fiction (1994)
Jackie Brown (1997)
Kill Bill, Volumes 1 & 2 (2003, 2004)
Inglorious Basterds (2009)
Django Unchained (2012)

Quentin's movies have garnered international critical acclaim; won dozens of prestigious nominations, awards, and honors; *and* have grossed over $3 billion at the box office. He has won two Oscars for screenwriting (*Pulp Fiction* and *Django Unchained*).

His new movie, *Hateful Eight*, is already generating 2016 Oscar buzz. The distribution of this post-Civil War western will be a major event as it is being billed as the widest 70mm film release in more than twenty years.

When asked about the biggest obstacle he overcame on his path to success, Quentin didn't hesitate to talk about his experiences:

"Even though I grew up around Los Angeles, I didn't know anybody who was part of that world I dreamed of getting into—nobody. I didn't even know anybody who knew anybody! That's how out of it I was."

"It's true that [Hollywood] can be a very "clubby" place, and I was definitely not part of that club—not by a long shot. I didn't even have any sense of where that club was or if anyone would ever let me in. But my passion for the movies—watching them, thinking about them, and actually making them myself—overcame my sense that I couldn't possibly do it."

Tarantino refused to be dismayed by his lack of resources or connections. Instead, he let his drive and passion chart his course towards success.

"Ultimately I was lucky not to have any sense of just how long the odds against me were. Ignorance really can be bliss! If all you really want to do is one thing, then you have to follow that dream wherever it leads you. That's definitely what I did."

When asked about his greatest mentor along the way, Quentin Tarantino's answer is unusual but not surprising given the unique path his career has followed. With a laugh he responded:

"I'm sorry—and proud—to say that I ended up having to be my own mentor! Truthfully, I didn't have one—as much as I wanted one. And, trust me, there were many times I dreamed of having a mentor."

"Harvey Keitel gave me my first and biggest break when he agreed to be in Reservoir Dogs. *He made that whole experience possible, thus making a very big difference in my life. But honestly, by that point, I was already not taking no for an answer."*

"I was already bound and determined to make movies. I believed in myself—and eventually other people started to believe in me too. But I had to believe in myself first. You hear people talk about how a mentor made all the difference for them—and that's great. But I think kids

need to learn that sometimes you have to be your own mentor. And you have to break down doors for yourself."

Quentin's maverick approach to filmmaking and life is no doubt what has made him incredibly successful. He is known for having his own unique style both in writing and directing, which gives him an edge in a competitive industry. Even though the odds were against him from the beginning, he never gave up on his passion, and he followed his dream.

QUENTIN'S EMPOWERING THOUGHT: *"If all you really want to do is one thing, then you have to follow that dream wherever it leads you. That's definitely what I did."*

DO IT DAILY:

▸ **Don't wait for someone else to open doors for you.** If you want to get somewhere, you are going to have to take charge and forge your own path.

▸ **Believe in yourself, have faith in your abilities, and stay the course!** There will be times when the odds are against you, but you must stay focused and continue to visualize yourself achieving your dreams.

Jimmy Kimmel

LATE NIGHT TALK SHOW HOST

Jimmy's Journey:

FIRED AS RADIO DJ → GAME SHOW HOST → JIMMY KIMMEL LIVE!

It is not always easy to truly believe in yourself. Often times, life creates plenty of noise that can overpower the inner-voice that tells you to keep going and reassures you that you absolutely will succeed. But there should never be a louder and more impactful voice than the one in your heart and soul. It should keep you moving, determined, and dedicated to your dreams.

Jimmy Kimmel has always been strong in his ability to believe in his goals and aspirations. He says, *"I do not like anybody else telling me what I am capable or not capable of doing. That can be very inspirational, because you run into a lot of people who will tell you what you can't do in life. And it's fun to prove those people wrong!"*

Jimmy Kimmel's teenage hero was David Letterman, but the would-be television talk show host and comedian actually began his show business career in the radio industry as a college DJ. He turned pro at twenty-one, working his way into bigger and bigger radio markets before arriving at LA's legendary station KROQ, where he was "Jimmy the Sports Guy" on *The Kevin and Bean Show.*

In 1997, he made the leap from radio to TV as host of the game show *Win Ben Stein's Money*. He eventually became a member of the elite club of late-night talk show hosts when ABC's *Jimmy Kimmel Live!* hit the air in 2003. Jimmy's show was not an instant success but he fought on, earning the respect of A-list stars and getting top 10 ratings. In 2012, ABC moved *Jimmy Kimmel Live!* to an earlier time slot to compete against NBC's *The Tonight Show with Jay Leno*.

Jimmy was eager to share his experiences on his journey to the top:

"The biggest obstacle I've overcome in my life is probably that it's very hard for people to take someone as handsome as I am seriously in the world of comedy."

One night on his show, Jimmy included himself in the "Handsome Men's Club," along with such famously good-looking members as Patrick Dempsey, Sting, Taye Diggs, Matthew McConaughey, and Rob Lowe. "Clearly being so damn handsome has been very difficult for me," said this Brooklyn boy.

"Now, if you want a serious answer—which is not my specialty—the biggest obstacle I have had to overcome in my career is being pigeonholed. And that's not just true in television. It's been true going back to my days when I was on the radio. I remember when I was starting out in radio there would be certain program directors and general managers who felt that I should just be a behind-the-scenes guy or maybe a writer. They felt that I shouldn't be "on-the-air talent." They felt that I would be more suited toward a support role to other people who were—in their minds—more talented. I was even let go from a couple of radio jobs."

"It's weird that the way I was able to overcome that sort of stuff was by just moving from one radio station to another. It's sort of like going to a different high school and being able to "reinvent yourself," for lack of a better phrase.

But in a way, it enabled me to sort of start over each time, and to try and be seen the way that I wanted to be seen."

Self-belief is a crucial trait to possess, especially when you are trying to accomplish tasks and goals that others might not support. There will always be naysayers and non-supporters, along with people that simply cannot see what you see. But if you have a strong inner-voice, and actually take the time to listen to it, you'll be amazed by how far that will get you on your journey through your personal and professional life.

JIMMY'S EMPOWERING THOUGHT: *"Try to help and advise other people the way that you were once helped. But only do that if they want your advice and help, and if they actually listen to you."*

DO IT DAILY:

▸ *Listen Hard.* Every failure is an opportunity to reinvent yourself and move forward. But you have to listen hard to the voice in your heart and soul that forges you ahead and overcomes the noise.

▸ *Share Your Beliefs.* Broadcast your inner-voice and self-beliefs to the world. When you share those mantras with others, you'll find that the world and those around you will support your vision and goals.

Gloria Gaynor

Gloria's Journey:

ABSENTEE FATHER → 63-YEAR-OLD COLLEGE GRADUATE → GRAMMY
AWARD WINNER

F aith is a little word with a pretty big meaning. Martin Luther King, Jr. said, "Faith is taking the first step even when you don't see the whole staircase." Faith isn't blind reliance, but it does require you to put one step in front of the other without knowing what lies ahead. We are all intrinsically wired to have faith. But as we experience life, we often forget to believe and lose this important trait. But for some, faith becomes second nature; a breath of fresh air that blows through when needed the most. Gloria Gaynor told me, *"One of the benefits of having little in life is that it makes it easier to be grateful for all you have."* And an attitude like that is what helps to build great faith. Faith in the ability to succeed, overcome, and achieve even when life seems utterly impossible.

Fresh out of high school in 1978, I worked as a bouncer in a wide range of establishments—from local dives to upscale clubs. I was a classic rock fan, with no use for the new dance music that was invading my world. Then I heard the *disco* song "I Will Survive" by Gloria Gaynor. As it did with so many others, the song struck an emotional chord deep down inside of me. That song became somewhat of an internal anthem that I played in my head when facing my own challenges and obstacles.

At our most desperate moments those three words, *I will survive*, can get us through situations that may feel like the end of the world. Now—more than thirty years later—I had the opportunity to interview Gloria about the meaning behind the song and her insights on life. What an inspiration!

Born in Newark, New Jersey, Gloria came from a relatively poor family, but she describes life at home as a "house filled with laughter and happiness." She said, ***"My dad was an absentee father; my mom dropped out of school by the seventh grade. Growing up we had limited means, but being poor made me appreciate all we did get that much more."***

Gloria loved music from an early age, and music was in her family. Her father played the nightclub circuit and her brothers sang Gospel music. Although she participated in school choirs, Gloria wasn't noticed for musical ability. But still, her real dream was to have a singing career.

To appease her mom, who insisted she have something "to fall back on," Gloria studied hard, graduated with honors, attended Beauty College, and took business courses. She worked a number of nonmusical jobs as she developed her singing. Early on, she wanted to be a teacher, but there was no money for a real college education. Yet she never stopped dreaming about becoming a college graduate: ***"After all these years I am so grateful and proud that I went back and fulfilled my dream when I received my college degree in 2012."***

Gloria sang with a jazz/pop group, the Soul Satisfiers, in the 1960s and recorded a few solo singles for a small Chicago label. Working four to five sets a night in the New York nightclub The Wagon Wheel, Gloria certainly paid her dues. You never knew who might be in the audience, and one night a producer caught her show. That producer arranged a meeting for Gloria with the president of Columbia Records, Clive Davis.

Davis signed her to Columbia, where she recorded the 1975 album *Never Can Say Good-Bye*. The album featured a nineteen-minute dance marathon that included three songs: "Honey Bee," sometimes referred to as the "Disco National Anthem," "Never Can Say Good-Bye," and "Reach Out, I'll Be There." She was on her way to being recognized as the Queen of Disco. She said, ***"I never considered myself a disco artist. I considered myself a singer who had gotten her success by using disco music as a medium. It was the popular genre at the time."***

Gloria's success was moderate as she released two more albums, but in 1978 her career skyrocketed when the album *Love Tracks* came out—and its "I Will Survive" climbed to the top of the charts. Success seldom runs in a straight line. Record company executives didn't consider "I Will Survive" to be radio-friendly, so Polydor released it as the "B-side" behind her cover of a Righteous Brothers' tune, "Substitute." The Righteous Brothers cover did well in the charts, but club DJs started playing the B-side, and it developed a life of its own. Radio stations picked it up, and Polydor finally released it as an A-side. In March 1979, "I Will Survive" topped the charts. In 1980, the song won the Grammy Award for Best Disco Recording.

History continued to prove those original recording executives wrong: "I Will Survive" has been further recognized as one of *Billboard* magazine's "All-Time Hot 100" songs and *Rolling Stone* magazine included it in its list of "500 Greatest Songs of All Time."

Gloria recognizes a deeper truth behind her greatest hit, however. A woman of deep faith and conviction, she says, ***"Without faith, inspiration, and encouragement, 'I Will Survive' is little more than an empty catchphrase."***

She has had her share of naysayers and negative people who have criticized her. Some sounded almost jubilant as they pronounced the demise of disco and cruelly proclaimed of her, "The Queen is dead!" But she responds: ***"I have learned that when people criticize you, they are really*** *talking about themselves. They have limited belief in what they can do. Filled with self-doubt, they want to feel important. If they can't do it in a productive and positive way, they will do it in a negative and harmful way—and they don't care if they hurt others. But I've learned that even if I get hurt for a minute, it does not change who I am. My value comes from God and what He placed in me. We all have God-given talents, abilities, and gifts. Each and every one of us should use them: Nobody is destined to fail! God has made me unique—he has made each of us unique. I will do some things better than others, and others will do some things better than I can. This means that if you use these gifts, it will make you like nobody else. I will not let anybody but myself define who I am."*

When asked for her advice on getting ahead in life, Gloria emphasized facing the truth as it is, not as you would like it to be. To up-and-coming singers, she offers three important principles:

Make sure others believe you have talent besides yourself and your mom.

Surround yourself with people who love you when you are a "nobody" who has nothing. Once you make it, these people will protect you.

Follow your passion. Do the type of music you are driven to, not what others say you should do.

Gloria continued with some timeless advice for us all ... *"Discipline is the only bridge between thought and accomplishment, because consistency is key to accomplishing your goals. Procrastination is a thief, because it steals your choices, opportunities, and time. Overall, surrender to the truth. Don't try to go around it or over it—just deal with it. The truth is what it is. Don't try to change it and you will thrive."*

Gloria Gaynor has certainly thrived, but she doesn't believe it takes worldwide fame and fortune to be happy: *"I see and speak with people from all over the world, and I've found that money or talent does not make happiness. I know plenty of street sweepers who are happy. Inner peace and joy come in many different forms. Society tries to tell us what we should be and what should make us happy, but I believe we should each have our own definition of happiness."*

Faith has always remained a supporting pillar for Gloria. No doubt about it, she is completely dedicated to her strong belief and faith in that which has yet to come. Even when she was told, time and time again, that she wasn't good enough or her music wasn't catchy enough, faith always prevailed. It acted as a guiding light, moving her through the torrential waters and toward safe shores. Remember, a little bit of faith can go a long way.

GLORIA'S EMPOWERING THOUGHT: *"My value comes from God and what he placed in me. I will not let anybody but myself define me."*

DO IT DAILY:

▸ *Support your faith and support your truth.* Distance yourself from people who do not move you in the right direction. Your faith should be tended to like a garden. Overall, surrender to the truth. Don't try to go around it or over it—just deal with it. The truth is what it is. Don't try to change it and you will thrive.

▸ *Remain disciplined.* Discipline is the only bridge between thought and accomplishment, because consistency is key to accomplishing your goals. Procrastination is a thief, because it steals your choices, opportunities, and time.

Stevie Nicks

Stevie's Journey:

DESTRUCTIVE EGO → DRUG ABUSE → ROCK AND ROLL HALL OF FAME

As most of us know, being grounded isn't easy. It takes concentration, effort, and a sense of overall balance—in addition, it also takes time. Stevie Nicks wasn't always grounded—she has faced much self-imposed adversity in her life and career. In fact, she advises, "***people, especially young people, should know that ego can be just as dangerous as any drug.***" It is our ego that often throws us off balance, as Nicks learned the hard way. However, we can learn a lot about how to find that grounding in our own lives, by hearing Nicks speak about her own.

Stevie Nicks, one of the most successful and beloved singer-songwriters ever, has long been open about her personal struggles and heartbreak. Her music, both as a solo artist and as part of Fleetwood Mac, has chronicled her pain throughout her long career. Stevie remembers recording her first song, "I Loved and I've Lost," on a cassette player on her fifteenth birthday. That song (sadly lost long ago) foreshadowed the tone of her turbulent life and songwriting career.

The raw honesty that marks her deeply personal lyrics shows in her willingness to share some of the wisdom she's gained along the way. No one can describe her journey better than Stevie Nicks herself. So here, in her own words, is Stevie's story:

"A lot of people would expect me to say that drugs have been the biggest obstacle in my life. And in a way, it's true. That's because, like way too many people of my generation, I paid a very high price in my life for the drugs that I took."

"Cocaine was one of the great lies my generation fell for—and we fell hard. They told us that cocaine was a drug without consequence, but that turned out to be a very big and wildly destructive lie. I know because that particular lie cost me at least a million dollars and put a hole in my nose that could have killed me. Now if that wasn't bad enough, cocaine use inflated our egos beyond reason—making it even more destructive."

"In the eighties, I fell for the lies regarding the drug Klonopin (clonazepam, a medication used to treat convulsive disorders and anxiety). That drug nearly brought me down when it was completely overprescribed to me. This tranquilizer not only caused me to lose weight, it actually resulted in me losing interest in my work. And that was a total disaster because it essentially stopped me from being me. After years of sacrifice to focus on creating the best music I could, I was suddenly tranquilized right out of being true to myself and my music."

"But ultimately, the truth about drugs is how they are usually a symptom of an even bigger problem—in my case, an ego out of control. Sometimes the biggest and most dangerous lies are the ones we tell ourselves. With fame comes the danger of thinking that you are bigger and better than anyone else, and that you can live 'above it all.' Letting your ego get out of control can often bring you crashing back down to earth. Like a drug, your ego can stop you from listening to your true self."

"My true self is someone who writes and sings songs. Then I get to perform those songs—bringing them alive for other people! It's such an honor to be able to do that: to go around the world and see how your songs—your children in

a way—are so deeply loved, understood, and appreciated by others who only know you through your words and music. Sometimes it feels like a lot of work, but ultimately it's a privilege. Too many of us who have succeeded in the popular arts have somehow forgotten that."

"So my best advice goes well beyond just staying away from drugs. Check your ego too! If you're lucky enough to figure out what you are meant to do with your life, follow that passion. For me it was music, but I had to act on that passion to make my dreams come true."

As Stevie wisely advises, it isn't enough to just identify your passion—you must work hard and make difficult decisions to bring that passion to life:

"Lindsay Buckingham and I met and began playing in a band together when we were both very young. Then, as the duo Buckingham Nicks, we made our first album together, but that first album didn't really sell well. There was a point when it looked like it simply might not happen for us. So I had to decide whether to keep going against the odds or give it up and do something safer and more reasonable. We all face those kinds of decisions at some point. Fortunately, my amazing parents remained supportive as I began to worry it might not happen for me."

"When I had just three months left to try and make it, I found myself in Aspen, Colorado, reflecting about where I'd come from and where I was going. Out of that reflection came some of the best songs I ever wrote, including "Landslide." Then out of the blue, Mick Fleetwood heard the Buckingham Nicks record and made an offer for Lindsay, and then both of us, to join Fleetwood Mac. Our egos could easily have led us to say no—to keep trying to make it on our own. But joining such a great group turned out to be what brought us to the world."

Fleetwood Mac, and Stevie's prolific solo career, have produced over 50 hit songs and sold over 140 million albums. Along with her fellow Fleetwood Mac band members, Stevie was inducted into the Rock and Roll Hall of Fame in 1998. Stevie says it was one of her proudest moments.

Even though the journey wasn't always easy, Stevie Nicks found success, balance, and learned to ground herself in her life and career. When someone has overcome great obstacles, we can learn a lot from their journey. Stevie Nicks teaches us important lessons on the dangers of the ego, and the importance of being grounded.

STEVIE'S EMPOWERING THOUGHT: *"If you're lucky enough to figure out what you are meant to do with your life, follow that passion."*

DO IT DAILY:

▸ *Keep your feet firmly planted on the ground.* Don't let your ego run out of control and convince you that you're better than anyone else.

▸ *Don't be afraid of the tough decisions.* Trust your instincts and listen to your heart, not to those things that distract you from your inner-voice!

Ringo Starr

THE BEATLES, ROCK AND ROLL HALL OF FAME

Ringo's Journey:

BROKEN HOME → SICKLY CHILD → BEATLES DRUMMER

As a rock icon, and pivotal member of The Beatles, Ringo Starr is a living legend. Throughout his life and career, Starr has proven that he is a worthy messenger of peace and love. Although the historical movement of peace and love started and gained steam in the 60s, it remains one of the most timeless and important qualities. Ringo Starr firmly believes that we could all benefit from cherishing one another and focusing on living a life filled with humanity and mutual respect towards each other. We are all in this together, and peace and love are character traits we should all not only embody, but pass along to future generations as well.

Ringo Starr was part of the most totally "Fab" success story of all time, and the greatest rock band of all time: The Beatles. More than forty years after the Fab Four went their own ways, Ringo Starr continues to write, record, and perform music regularly, while continuing to spread his signature positive message of peace and love.

As Ringo explains, *"The way I see it, 'Peace & Love' has always been a very good and necessary message. It's always been part of the power of*

The Beatles. And it's a message that people still need to hear even all these years later."

Born Richard Starkey Jr., on July 7, 1940, Ringo has seen a great deal in his time. He went through some pretty tough times growing up on the "other side of Liverpool." As a young man, he experienced rock stardom in the biggest way possible, along with his friends and fellow Beatles - John Lennon, George Harrison, and Paul McCartney. He then became a major solo success story in his own right with acclaimed and bestselling albums like 1973's *Ringo* and 1974's *Goodnight Vienna*.

Following his memorable screen debut alongside his band mates in Richard Lester's *A Hard Day's Night*, Ringo became something of a movie star too. He appeared in films such as 1973's *That'll Be the Day* and 1981's *Caveman,* in which he met and fell in love with his co-star—and future wife—Barbara Bach.

By the middle eighties, however, Ringo's own stardom was in serious decline thanks in large part to a period of excess and alcoholism. But in 1988, he sought help, cleaned up his act, and got back on the road with his first-ever tour as "Ringo Starr & His All-Starr Band."

Soon the All-Starr Band tour became a more or less biannual summer event—an ever-changing super-group featuring Ringo singing and playing, with a little help from new and old musical friends. Performing live for fans—for the first time on a regular basis since The Beatles stopped touring in 1966—proved to be a meaningful and positive change for Ringo.

"For too long a time, I forgot who I was and what I do. The truth is I'm a drummer, and a drummer should drum, or else he'll get himself into trouble—which is exactly what I did."

Ringo also returned to the recording studio, issuing a new album every couple of years. Starting with the acclaimed *Time Takes Time* comeback album in 1992, he has continued to grow as a singer-songwriter on subsequent recordings like *Vertical Man* (1998), *Ringo Rama* (2003), *Choose Love* (2005), *Liverpool 8* (2008), and *Y Not* (2010).

Y Not was the first album he produced himself, and it even features Ringo sharing vocals with his old friend and band mate Paul McCartney on a moving song called "Walk with You." As Ringo explains with a laugh, *"Why not work with the best?"*

In 2012, Ringo released *Ringo 2012* featuring nine tracks, including new versions of "Wings" and "Step Lightly." Also in 2012, Ringo assembled his twelfth All-Starr Band, which toured through the United States, Canada, New Zealand, Australia, Japan, Mexico, and South America. The live DVD *Ringo at the Ryman* was recorded with this band on Ringo's birthday, July 7, 2012.

In June 2013, The Grammy Museum opened "Ringo: Peace & Love," a record-breaking undertaking that hosted more than ninety thousand visitors as the first major exhibit to focus on a drummer. The exhibit remained open for nine months. In September that same year, Ringo was awarded the prestigious French Medal of Honor, being appointed Commander of Arts & Letters in recognition of his musical and artistic contributions.

Photograph, a limited-edition collection of never-before-seen material, including exclusive images from Ringo's own personal archives, was published in December 2013.

On January 20, 2014, the David Lynch Foundation awarded the "Lifetime of Peace & Love Award" to Ringo. One week later, Ringo Starr and Paul McCartney appeared together again at the 56th Annual Grammy Awards in 2014. The appearance by the pair of musical legends was part of the 50th anniversary celebration of The Beatles on *The Ed Sullivan Show*. A few days later they performed together again at a taping of *The Night That Changed America: A Grammy Salute to The Beatles*, which aired on February 9, 2014, on CBS—the anniversary of the historical show that launched their U.S. career.

In 2015, Ringo Starr was inducted into Rock and Roll Hall of Fame as a solo artist.

For Ringo, music continues to be a powerful form of therapy and a kind of musical audio-biography as well:

"Music is my best way of telling my story—three or four minutes at a time."

Famously charming, Ringo says that the biggest obstacles he has overcome in his life have been largely of his own making. When asked, he thought for a moment and responded:

"The biggest obstacle in my own life? Well, the biggest obstacle in my life has been getting over myself. For instance, I know if I get up and walk into the sun, it will be great. But I end up bashing my head into the wall sometimes. We all do it. So getting over myself is my biggest obstacle."

That's the same sort of positive, life-affirming, no-nonsense message that comes through loud and clear in much of Ringo Starr's most recent music. As he explained:

"There's a song on my album, Y Not, *called 'Can't Do It Wrong.' I wrote it with a man named Gary Burr from Nashville. The song says, 'As long as I'm doing it/I can't do it wrong.' That's a line I had, and it's basically another way of saying the same thing—that we have to get out of our own way. And if we can do that, and stop making things harder for ourselves, I think we'll all be much better off."*

"Don't be your own worst enemy. Be your own best friend. As long as it's for love and for peace, then I'm okay. That's the sentiment I'm

always trying to send out to the world: peace and love. That was the
message we were handing out to the world with The Beatles—and I
think you could say it went pretty well."

Ringo paused and offered in that famous Liverpool accent: *"So does that*
answer your question?"

Yes, it does, Ringo—with peace and love. Help spread Ringo's message in
your own life by showing others your love, and pioneering a life of peace.
Only then can we come together and create a world where we support one
another and elevate humanity as a whole.

RINGO'S EMPOWERING THOUGHT: *"We have to get out of our*
own way. And if we can do that, and stop making things harder for
ourselves, I think we'll all be much better off. Don't be your own worst
enemy. Be your own best friend."

DO IT DAILY:

▸   *Be true to who you are.* Never abandon your personal message.
     No matter what comes your way, work hard to remain dedicated
     to that which you hold close to your heart.

▸   *Remember peace and love.* Do you believe in Ringo's message? If
     so, use his life and work as an example of how to spread peace and
     love in your own life and the lives of others.

Seth McFarlane

FAMILY GUY CREATOR

Seth's Journey:

FIRST JOB PAID $5 A WEEK → TV'S YOUNGEST EXECUTIVE PRODUCER → 2X
EMMY WINNER

Seth MacFarlane continues to wow the entertainment industry with his zany, hilarious, and sometimes controversial humor. It is no surprise that many consider him to be an innovator. Through his story, we can learn not only how to be innovators, but also how to follow through with our visions and achieve them through dedication, creativity and commitment.

Innovation is the process of coming up with a new method, idea, or product. In the realm of popular culture, Seth MacFarlane offered the world an unbelievably exciting way to be entertained. He reinvented cartoons and combined them with witty and whimsical comedy that could resonate with all ages. He always has been, and always will be considered an innovator in the entertainment and television industry.

Looking back, I'm still somewhat amazed that my company had the opportunity to do the first in-person art-signing gallery event through the Fox Animation Art Program with *Family Guy* creator Seth MacFarlane.

At the time, Seth, age twenty-four, was television's youngest executive producer, and *Family Guy* was still in its infancy.

Family Guy was new to primetime, and despite good fan support it was struggling due to its constantly changing time slot. We had a great relationship with Fox Studios, representing their *Simpsons* artwork. Fox had asked us if we were interested in hosting a *Family Guy* art event with Seth. The answer was an easy *yes*—we believed that what we saw in *Family Guy's* "fanatic" fan base would outlast the naysayers and all the controversy to become a success.

Seth flew in from California to our gallery on Long Island. The admiration and respect from supporters who came out to see him provided a powerful message: *Family Guy* would be here for years to come.

While out to dinner with Seth, I asked him about his youth and about how he was handling all the peaks and valleys of the animated series. As he spoke, I could immediately sense his calm confidence:

"I really don't let the ups and downs bother me. I believe in what we are doing. We have a great group of writers, voice talent, and animators. I always wanted to be on primetime, and Fox seems to be the perfect fit. My goal was always about making the characters like real people with all their imperfections."

Born in 1973, Seth grew up in Kent, Connecticut. His dad was a teacher and his mother was an academic administrator.

Seth chatted with our clients about how, as a very young boy, he used to draw Woody Woodpecker, Fred Flintstone, and other cartoon characters. He spoke of how he was inspired by comedic legend Jackie Gleason, whose comedy was about bringing laughs. Seth revealed what may have been the source of his calm demeanor: *"From early on my parents did not put pressure on me—always encouraging, but no pressure."*

Seth understood the frustration his fans experienced over the series being moved from Sunday to Thursday nights. He explained, *"I think Fox may have been a little too aggressive. We were on Sunday nights after* The Simpsons, *and within a few months they changed our time to go against the highly rated sitcom* Friends *on Thursday nights. People had a hard time finding us."* Moving a time slot can equal a death sentence for a TV series; however, Seth's confidence and optimism were never in doubt.

In an interview with the Biography Channel, Seth revealed his devotion to his craft, his fortitude, and the boldness he had from an early age: *"When I was old enough to ask questions, I was asking, 'How are cartoons made; how do I do one of these?'"*

Amazingly, Seth was only eight when he landed his first paying job. He earned five dollars a week for his comic strip *Walter Crouton* for the *Kent Good Times Dispatch*.

Soon after he graduated from the Rhode Island School of Design, where he studied animation, Seth joined the legendary animation studio Hanna-Barbera. He was still working with Hanna-Barbera when he had the idea for *Family Guy*, and confidentially approached the Fox Broadcasting Company.

They told Seth, "If you can do a pilot for us for like, fifty thousand dollars, we'll give you a shot at a series." (Typically, costs to produce a half-hour episode for a primetime animated show can exceed one million dollars.)

"Obviously I said, 'Yeah, I'll do it,' not knowing whether I could or not. I spent about six months with no sleep and no life—just drawing like crazy in my kitchen and doing this pilot."

At the end of the six months, Seth presented the show to Fox executives and they loved it. They ordered thirteen episodes of *Family Guy*. Seth's style, talent, innovation, and dedication resulted in his becoming television's youngest executive producer.

Without Seth's sense of faith and enthusiasm for what he was doing, *Family Guy* may never have reached the heights it has. Debuting in 1999, *Family Guy* has been canceled twice—but that "fanatical" fan support and huge rerun ratings left Fox with no choice but to put the series back on the air.

The *Family Guy* franchise is now a billion-dollar-plus industry. Seth has won two primetime Emmy Awards and continues to be one of the highest-paid television writers, having signed a deal worth over one hundred million dollars in 2008. Seth still enjoys featuring as the voice of three main characters from Quahog, Rhode Island: Peter, Stewie, and Brian Griffin.

The success of *Family Guy* has led to many outside projects for MacFarlane including *American Dad!*, and *The Cleveland Show*, as well as writing, directing, and producing his first live-action feature film, *Ted* (2012), starring Mark Wahlberg as a grown man who hangs around with his talking childhood teddy bear. *Ted* is the highest-grossing original R-rated comedy of all time. The film also received an Academy Award nomination for Best Original Song. Universal Studios released a sequel titled *Ted 2* in 2015.

In March 2014, Seth became the executive producer (and provided some of the voices for the animated portions) of *Cosmos: A Spacetime Odyssey*, an update of the 1980's *Cosmos* series written and hosted by Carl Sagan.

The entertainment industry recognized Seth's success by inviting him to host the 85th Academy Awards in 2013.

Seth came close to never realizing his success. On the morning of September 11, 2001, he was scheduled to return to Los Angeles on American Airlines Flight 11 from Boston. He arrived at Logan International Airport about ten minutes late, and the gates were already closed. The flight departed without him, and fifteen minutes later Flight 11 was hijacked. At 8:46 a.m. it was flown into the North Tower of the World Trade Center. In an interview with *TVShowsonDVD.com* in 2003, Seth put it all in perspective:

"... I didn't really know that I was in any danger until after it was over, so I never had that panic moment. After the fact, it was sobering, but people have a lot of close calls; you're crossing the street and you almost get hit by a car ... This one just happened to be related to something massive. I really can't let it affect me because I'm a comedy writer. I have to put that in the back of my head."

Seth's dedication, innovation and commitment to his work are the qualities that helped push him towards success. He did not let any defeats or detours get in the way of going after what he believed was worth the fight—these tenacious habits no doubt contribute to his role as a contemporary innovator. We can use his life, and brilliant mind, as examples for how we too can turn our greatest innovations into realities. As Seth MacFarlane did, work to always be on the forefront of whatever you do, innovating and functioning to be on the cutting edge of what's to come.

SETH'S EMPOWERING THOUGHT: *"I really don't let the ups and downs bother me. I believe in what we are doing."*

DO IT DAILY:

▶ *Combine your innovation with commitment and perseverance.* When you have a vision, stick with it until it becomes a reality. Give it everything you've got.

▶ *Don't let setbacks get in the way of actualizing your vision.* There will be ups and downs, and close calls, on the pathway to success. Stay true and believe in yourself.

Kid Rock

RAP ARTIST

Kid Rock's Journey:

DRUG DEALER → SINGLE FATHER → SIX PLATINUM RECORDS

Life hasn't always been ideal for rapper Kid Rock, but he has learned that being grateful is the way to handle life's adversity. Through gratitude, he changes obstacles into blessings. By living a life full of gratitude, you too can take the things that seem like setbacks, and use them to get closer to your goals.

Robert James "Bob" Ritchie—better known as "Kid Rock"—is an American singer-songwriter and musician credited with five Grammy Award nominations and six Platinum records, selling more than 23.5 million albums. However, if you look back at his career, much of his best work either got off to a slow start or went almost entirely unnoticed.

Kid Rock is a fascinating individual with a unique personality. He is a loving single father who gives free concerts for troops in combat zones and substantially supports military families. Listening to him, it is almost impossible to believe that in his teens he sold drugs out of a carwash. This interview brings to light that he is a defiantly gracious, bottom-line guy with style.

"You've got to be careful what you consider an obstacle in your life. What I once thought could be the biggest obstacle in my life turned out to be the greatest thing that ever happened to me and one of my biggest lessons."

Kid Rock is talking about a truly life-changing moment—a turning point that forced him to really become a man.

"I worried that it was going to screw up my life, but it became the most educational and important thing!"

"See, back when I was still pretty much a kid myself, my son basically showed up on my doorstep when he was six years old. The truth of the matter is that you don't have a lot of choices at a point like that. Sometimes life makes choices for you, and your choice is in how well you handle it."

"I had a kid, and he needed someone to look out for him and raise him. So I really became a parent. Fortunately, as unprepared as I may have been, I had a good support system backing me up. I had enough family and true friends who stood by me—and with me—and they helped me figure things out in my own way. Somehow, with a lot of help from people like my sister, we all came through it together."

Kid Rock continued:

"If you're a parent, you know how having a kid changes everything. Everything in life takes on a different meaning. For me, and I'm sure for a lot of people, everything in life takes on a whole lot more meaning. So raising my son as a single father has become a huge part of my life and reality, and the seriousness of being a dad probably saved me from making even more mistakes than I had already made. Whatever I got caught up in, I always knew I had this great kid at home, and he was counting on me. It kept me from getting in even more trouble along the way."

"I was lucky to have so much help from the people who love me and my son. That taught me a big lesson that I've had to learn a lot of times and in a lot of ways."

"My advice is to keep the people you love and trust around you as much as you possibly can. Surround yourself with people who will always have your back no matter what."

"I had to learn it again a few years ago when I took my kid to California and kind of 'lost my way' in that celebrity world for a while. The truth is that I belong in Detroit. That's where I was made, and that's where I have people who have truly given a damn about me—even before anyone else knew my name. It's great to have fans, but you've got to know who your true friends are. Now, I know I'm not the usual spokesman for traditional family values, but that's what I've learned so far."

"Life will hand you challenges. Eventually, it gets to us all and gives us things to handle. But I'm living proof that those challenges can change your life for the better and save your soul—and even save your ass."

"My son means the world to me. Being a single father hasn't always been easy, but great things aren't usually easy. Being a single dad did more for me than I could ever have imagined. It's kept me grounded. It's kept my priorities in order in a world where so many people have their priorities completely out of whack."

In between recording and touring, Kid Rock is a steadfast, loyal supporter of the United States military. He gave proceeds of a concert to the families affected by the bombing of the *USS Cole* in 2000. He has quietly made numerous trips with the USO—and on his own—to play concerts for soldiers overseas in Iraq, Afghanistan, and Kuwait. He even made his album *Born Free* available to military members as a free download. Rock is grateful for everything in his life—the good and the bad—and it is this quality that has taught him life's greatest lessons, and undoubtedly contributed to his success. Take Rock's journey and advice to heart, and open yourself to gratitude—you will soon see that riches abound.

KID ROCK'S EMPOWERING THOUGHT: *"Life will hand you challenges. Eventually, it gets to us all and gives us things to handle. But I'm living proof that those challenges can change your life for the better and save your soul—and even save your ass."*

DO IT DAILY:

▸ *Build a strong support system.* Value and cultivate those relationships. Keep your loved ones close by your side.

▸ *Be grateful for your life.* Learning to accept and appreciate the good and the bad is how we learn to change setbacks into blessings.

Muhammad Ali

3X HEAVYWEIGHT BOXING CHAMPION

Ali's Journey:

BULLIED → ACTIVIST → "THE GREATEST"

Muhammad Ali is an international household name. He is known worldwide for being fearless inside the ring. But what many don't know is that he was equally as fearless outside the ring.

It was easily one of the more surreal moments in my life: I was just finishing up an art signing with Muhammad Ali at his hotel room in 2011, along with his wife, Lonnie, and his manager. We sat for hours as Ali signed piece after piece. I couldn't help but wonder why, with his declining physical condition, he would still take the time to sign artwork for fans. As Lonnie relaxed and read her book, she put it simply: "He still loves it."

Ali rarely picked up his head or took a break. It was difficult for me to comprehend—until the moment when he finished signing the very last piece. Then I saw the payoff. He looked up and gave us that famous bigger-than-life Ali smile. You could see he did indeed enjoy and love what he was doing.

When it was over, I was asked to help the champ to his car: What an honor and a privilege. As we walked, Ali leaned into my body for support, and I could feel the power and strength he still possessed. Physically he wasn't the man he once was, but his life's spirit was still easily felt.

Over the years, whenever I've had the opportunity to be with Muhammad Ali, I have always found him to be warm, generous, and insightful—always looking to accommodate others.

Muhammad Ali (born Cassius Marcellus Clay Jr., on January 17, 1942) earned his nickname, "The Greatest," by becoming one of the greatest boxers ever to fight. In his career, Ali fought several historic boxing matches against other boxing greats: Sonny Liston, Joe Frazier, Floyd Paterson, Ken Norton, George Foreman, and Larry Holmes, to name a few. He won gold in the 1960 Rome Olympic Games, and when he was only twenty-two he won his first heavyweight championship against Liston. He went on to become the first three-time World Heavyweight Champion in history.

I fondly remember the priceless pre-match hype between Ali, his opponents, and sports journalist Howard Cosell. Who could ever forget the way Ali described his own fighting style:

"I float like a butterfly and sting like a bee! I'm so mean I make medicine sick. I'm so fast that last night I turned off the light switch in my hotel room and was in bed before the room was dark."

Ali had a career like none other; he was crowned "Sportsman of the Century" by *Sports Illustrated* and is one of the few athletes that crossed over from sports figure to world icon.

All of us, at one point in our lives, need to decide what we believe—and possibly risk much for it. Too often we back down because of uncertainty regarding the outcome, or because of the personal price we may have to pay. I think we can learn much more by focusing on what Ali was willing to sacrifice and lose for the principles and values he held so closely. Vilified by some and idolized by others, he was willing to go to jail and give up one of the most coveted awards—the World Heavyweight Boxing Championship—because of his objection to America's involvement in Vietnam. Even though he had to give up the title, he gained much more virtue because he stuck to his values. As Ali said himself, *"He who is not courageous enough to take risks will accomplish nothing in life."*

The outspoken Muhammad Ali was a polarizing and controversial figure, particularly early in his career. He came to the forefront of boxing during one of the most tumultuous eras in modern history. The 1960s will forever be remembered for the counterculture movements. Activism was in full swing. Student protests focused on civil rights, women's rights, and the Vietnam War. Daily headlines featured wide-ranging controversial stories like burning draft cards, the British Invasion led by The Beatles, the assassinations of President Kennedy, Malcolm X, and Dr. Martin Luther King Jr., whose "I Have a Dream" speech characterized a decade like no other.

Ali changed his name from Cassius Clay after joining the Nation of Islam in 1964. Then in 1967, the heavyweight champion refused induction into the U.S. Army in Houston, Texas, on the grounds that he was a "conscientious objector" to the war in Vietnam.

Ali was not alone in rejecting the American military action in Vietnam. Many fled to Canada to avoid the war. Though I was just a little kid at that time, I still remember one of my neighbors who served. He was just a teenager himself when he came home from the war with half his face blown away.

Ali was one of the first to take a stand for what he believed. His opposition to the Vietnam War and his support of civil rights were loud and strong:

"No, I am not going ten thousand miles to help murder, kill, and burn other people to simply help continue the domination of white slave-masters over dark people the world over. This is the day and age when such evil injustice must come to an end."

"I ain't got no quarrel with them Viet Cong. No Viet Cong ever called me nigger! I know I got it made while the masses of black people are catchin' hell, but as long as they ain't free, I ain't free."

These remarks resonated with many. Ali's message motivated many people to continue their pursuit of racial justice. Words can be strong, and few could sum things up like Muhammad Ali:

"Hating people because of their color is wrong. And it doesn't matter which color does the hating. It's just plain wrong."

Ali was arrested and found guilty of draft evasion. He barely avoided a prison sentence, and was stripped of his title, had his boxing license suspended, and did not fight again for over three years. His appeal worked its way up to the U.S. Supreme Court where, in 1971, the justices overturned Ali's conviction in an 8-0 decision (Thurgood Marshall abstained from the vote).

Seven years after the government took away his title, Ali knocked out George Foreman to become the Heavyweight World Champion once again—quite the accomplishment for a young boy from Louisville, Kentucky, who started boxing in 1954 as an 89-pound, 12-year-old.

In 1984, Muhammad Ali was diagnosed with Parkinson's disease. Some believed it was genetic; others claimed it was caused by the trauma from boxing. Whatever the cause, this disease did not change Ali's style and demeanor towards life—he was, and always will be, a fighter.

Ali was inducted into the International Boxing Hall of Fame and received the Arthur Ashe Courage Award in 1997. His boxing gloves are preserved in the Smithsonian Institution's National Museum of American History.

After retiring from boxing, Ali devoted himself to humanitarian efforts around the world, fighting world hunger and poverty and supporting education efforts. He has helped to provide more than twenty-two million meals to feed the hungry. Ali's philosophy on helping others: *"Service to others is the rent you pay for your room here on earth."*

In your own efforts to fight through adversity and reach your own potential, consider the following Muhammad Ali quotes:

"I hated every minute of training, but I said, 'Don't quit. Suffer now and live the rest of your life as a champion.'"

"I never thought of losing, but now that it's happened, the only thing is to do it right. That's my obligation to all the people who believe in me. We all have to take defeats in life."

"If they can make penicillin out of moldy bread, they can sure make something out of you."

"Only a man who knows what it is like to be defeated can reach down to the bottom of his soul and come up with the extra ounce of power it takes to win when the match is even."

Muhammad Ali is truly an incredible man who is fearless both inside and outside the ring. Let his attitude, personality, and strength be a beacon to you during hard times or when faced with fear. You too can be fearless, if you dedicate your life to fighting for the right things.

ALI'S EMPOWERING THOUGHT: *"The fight is won or lost far away from witnesses—behind the lines, in the gym, and out there on the road, long before I dance under those lights."*

DO IT DAILY:

▶ *Be fearless and true to your principles, and stay strong throughout your journey.* Stick to your values even if it means having to give up prestige or acclaim; in the end, you will win far more by way of virtue and morality.

▶ *Never give up the fight for what you desire.* Whether you are in an arena, or behind a desk, keep striving to reach your goals and fulfill your true potential.

Ann Rosenheck

HOLOCAUST SURVIVOR

Ann's Journey:

NAZI CONCENTRATION CAMP → FAMILY MEMBERS PUT TO DEATH →
LIVING A BEAUTIFUL LIFE

Character is defined as "the mental and moral qualities distinctive of an individual." We all hope to live a life that is saturated in high grades of character. Honesty, strength, high-morals, and positivity are just a few of the words we'd hope people use to describe our character. But the truth is that not all character is created equal. There are some people that just have a special set of qualities that define their inner-fabric and set them apart from the rest. Holocaust survivor Ann Rosenheck is one of those people.

She is a holocaust survivor who has had to live with the grief and guilt associated with surviving a tragedy that took over ninety family members. It takes an incredible strength of character to deal with such an experience. We can gain a lifetime of wisdom from Ann and her dynamic life.

Ann was thirteen years old when the Nazis marched in to occupy her small Czechoslovakian town nestled in the Carpathian Mountains. It was 1944, and she was the youngest of five children when her entire family was removed from their home and forced into the ghetto. Shortly thereafter, they were on their way to the infamous concentration camp at Auschwitz. She recalled:

"Josef Mengele, the notorious Angel of Death, told me to go left and directed the rest of my family to go to the right. I walked to the left—to the barracks—but my family was led straight into the gas chamber."

While at Auschwitz, Ann remembers *"waking up every day and thanking God for letting me live through another night."*

The Holocaust took the lives of her mother, father, grandmother, brother, sister, and over ninety other family members. The Nazis eventually moved Ann to Dachau, another infamous death camp, where she was forced to work in a munitions plant until American forces liberated the camp on April 29, 1945.

"I remember when I saw that first American soldier—then I knew what it meant to be liberated." Within a few years, Ann immigrated to the United States, where she lived with an aunt and uncle.

Six million European Jewish people lost their lives in World War II at the hands of Adolf Hitler and his Nazi regime. Over one million children, two million women, and three million Jewish men were murdered. But it didn't stop there. The total number of Holocaust victims was between eleven million and seventeen million people, including Soviet prisoners of war, Polish and Soviet civilians, homosexuals, people with disabilities, Jehovah's Witnesses, and other political and religious opponents of Hitler.

While researching this book, I decided to contact the Holocaust Memorial of the Greater Miami Jewish Federation, hoping to arrange an interview with a Holocaust survivor. Someone who had seen the worst of humanity and survived would certainly have incredible strength, character and inspiration to share that could benefit all of us as we face our own daily challenges.

The federation arranged an interview with Ann Rosenheck, a wonderful, caring woman with a perspective and attitude that are nothing less than *inspiring*.

My interest in Ann Rosenheck and others who survived the Holocaust was fueled by my own personal experiences. I myself grew up on the "wrong side of the tracks" in a very racist area. I know it sounds crazy, but this story really did happen to me while growing up in an American middle-class suburb.

I was constantly picked on—always called names like *Jew bagel, dirty Jew, kike,* or *lampshade* (a racial taunt referring to the horrific Nazi practice of using prisoners' skin in the death camps to make literal lampshades). As a young kid, I assumed that was "just the way it was."

My family and I were big fans of pets—from dogs and cats to even rabbits. One morning I woke up to go to school and was confronted by a truly heinous act. Someone—we never knew if it was kids or adults—had taken our rabbits from their cages, cut their heads off, and used the rabbits' blood to draw swastikas, the symbol of Nazi hatred, all over our house.

As I grew up, being bullied because I was Jewish was something I dealt with all the time. In the long run, I believe it made me stronger.

At our interview, Ann explained why she agreed to meet with me:

"Too many survivors never forgive themselves or others. But bitterness is very ugly; you need to get over things in life. You can't just hold onto them. What has happened yesterday happened yesterday. If you let yourself, there is always a way to find happiness and peace."

"I lost my parents as a child—I miss their love. But when I came to America and, at eighteen, married a man I knew as a child, and was

reunited with my brother, I began to go on with my life, and it was a beautiful life."

On dealing with adversity Ann emphasizes, *"Believe in something. Believe in God—today may be bad—but God will help you tomorrow."*

Today, Ann remains as optimistic as ever. She lectures around the country, recounting the horrors she experienced, hoping that through education such an event will never happen again. Ann's strength of character is truly incredible, and her ability to let go of the past and enjoy the present is positively inspiring.

ANN'S EMPOWERING THOUGHT: *"What has happened yesterday happened yesterday. If you let yourself, there is always a way to find happiness and peace."*

DO IT DAILY:

▶ *Life has a way of being difficult.* Keep a healthy dose of faith, optimism, and hope to help get you through each day.

▶ *Let go of the past.* Focus on the present and release that which no longer serves you.

Joe Namath

Joe's Journey:

SON OF A STEEL WORKER → UNIV. OF ALABAMA QUARTERBACK → SUPER BOWL III MVP

Confidence is one of those traits that can keep you focused, driven, determined, and completely capable of overcoming anything in your path. It is through confidence that you trust in yourself and believe you can reach your goals, no matter how substantial they may be. Confidence will get you far in life. No one knows this better than New York Jets legend "Broadway Joe" Namath. Through his story, we can learn the importance of confidence and the many far reaching benefits it can bring.

"We're gonna win the game. I guarantee it!" That outrageously bold prediction by Joe Namath has become legendary throughout all sports.

My work has given me opportunities to meet celebrities and heroes who I—along with millions of other people—watched and admired as a kid. I am privileged to talk with them about what it was like to achieve such great success. Joe Namath is one of those individuals, and having a chance to spend time him was almost surreal.

Few have had life experiences to match those of Joe Namath—the son of a steel worker growing up in Beaver Falls, Pennsylvania, who went on to become Alabama's Crimson Tide quarterback, and lead them to their 1964 National Championship. He then played professional football and was named MVP when his team, the New York Jets, won the Super Bowl in 1969.

My chance to get to know Joe came when we arranged a private signing in our Florida art gallery. Joe's easygoing confidence was evident. He showed that same self-assurance he had more than forty years ago when his underdog New York Jets beat Coach Don Shula, Hall-of-Fame quarterback Johnny Unitas, and their Baltimore Colts in Super Bowl III.

Super Bowl III was unique in many ways. It featured the championship game between the American Football League (AFL) and the National Football League (NFL), and was the first to officially bear the name *Super Bowl*. Legendary entertainer Bob Hope hosted the pregame, saluting American astronauts for their first successful orbit of the moon.

The Jets' win over the Colts is still considered one of the greatest upsets in American sports history and was instrumental in helping merge the two leagues in 1970.

Joe's demeanor is a lesson in confidence for us all. He and his team backed up his "guarantee," and Joe set himself apart as football's first true media superstar, affectionately known as "Broadway Joe."

As we spoke, he told me there were only two things he did not like in his career—losing and getting hurt. *"I loved the game and still wish I could play,"* he said. Nevertheless, he assured me that he *"relishes each and every day and has an abundance of gratitude for all those who have touched [his] life."*

Joe had only kind words for his Super Bowl III opponent, Johnny Unitas: *"He is my hero. It was my honor to play against Johnny."*

His emotions surfaced as he told me, *"Life can throw lots at you—good, bad, and ugly. I am grateful for all I have and grateful to love and be loved, because that is what really counts."*

Joe has had his share of setbacks, from troubled relationships to battles with alcoholism, but he has always managed to reinvent himself. Joe is a man unwilling to give up, and in 2007—more than forty years since he played college football—he completed his BA degree from the University of Alabama at the age of sixty-four. Talk about inspiration!

Joe was a standout athlete and could have played basketball, baseball, or football. He received offers from several Major League Baseball teams, including the Mets and the Yankees. Lucky for us, Joe chose football— and as they say, the rest is history.

Alabama's legendary coach Bear Bryant once stated that his decision to recruit Joe Namath was "…the best coaching decision I ever made" and that Joe was "the greatest athlete I ever coached."

The year 1969 was unquestionably a good year for New York: the New York Knicks, the New York Mets, and the New York Jets all won professional championships that year, but the memorable performance of "Broadway Joe" Namath will always make him stand out as a champion among champions.

Confidence can help to overcome enormous adversity. It helps you to turn down the noise of the naysayers, and allows you to sing a song that motivates you, drives you, and pushes you towards your goals. It was Joe's confidence and easy-going personality that helped him shine on and off the field. Being confident brings an unparalleled positivity into your life that will help you and others reach goals most will only dream of.

JOE'S EMPOWERING THOUGHT: *"When you have confidence, you can have a lot of fun. And when you have fun, you can do amazing things."*

DO IT DAILY:

▸ *Look around.* You will see the many reasons to be grateful each and every day. Appreciate all aspects of your life and always take the time to pause and truly take it all in.

▸ *Exude confidence in all you do.* Believe in yourself and beautiful things will follow.

Tony Bennett

Tony's Journey:

LOST FATHER AT AGE 10 → SINGING WAITER → 17 GRAMMYS
AND TWO EMMYS

Tony Bennett's long career as a musician has forced him to keep up with an ever-changing industry. With the world's taste in music constantly changing, he has had to learn how to reinvent himself—but he never sacrificed his style. There will be times in your life when you too will need to evolve, but that doesn't mean you have to betray who you really are. Staying true to yourself is one of the biggest lessons of reinvention.

A good friend arranged this *Common Thread* interview with legendary singer Tony Bennett. Tony's responses were rich with wisdom and hold a message to be carried for a lifetime.

Bennett was born August 3, 1926, into a poor family in Astoria, Queens, New York. The Great Depression and the death of his father (when Tony was only ten) made their circumstances more difficult. He recalls that at age sixteen he had to *"hit the pavement and look for work, doing amateur shows and working as a singing waiter under the stage name 'Joe Bari.'"*

In 1944, Tony was drafted into the Army infantry. *"After being discharged,"* he said, *"I was living on a dime a day—literally."* But about five years later things began to turn around for him.

Actress and nightclub singer Pearl Bailey discovered Tony in Greenwich Village, and legendary comedian Bob Hope hired him in 1949, advising him to adopt the name *Tony Bennett* (a shortened version of his last name, Benedetto). Bob Hope put him in his road show, and Tony told *Billboard* in 1997, *"I've been on the road ever since."*

Tony signed with Columbia Records in 1950 and started working with record producer Mitch Miller. It was there he recorded what was to become his signature song, "I Left My Heart in San Francisco." Over the years Tony has collected seventeen Grammys (plus a Grammy Lifetime Achievement Award), two Emmys, and was named a Kennedy Center Honoree. He has sold more than fifty million records worldwide.

Despite his success, life has not always been easy for Tony. He moved to California in the late 1970s and quickly began using cocaine and marijuana; drugs had become an integral part of the celebrity party scene. A near-death experience from a cocaine overdose in 1979 left him passed out in the bathtub. According to Tony, this experience is what straightened him out.

With renewed energy, Tony was able to revitalize his music career, which had floundered under rock and roll's dominance in the music industry. He was at a loss as to how to sustain his career while the public's taste in popular music shifted away from his classic, standards-based style.

Tony weathered these troubles, and he credits his son Danny, who became his manager, with making many of the key decisions that resulted in a complete career makeover. Danny put his father on television—on the animated series *The Simpsons*, on talk shows with David Letterman, and on *MTV Unplugged*.

To mark his eightieth birthday in 2006, Tony released *Tony Bennett Duets: An American Classic*, recorded with a collection of stars including Barbra Streisand, Elton John, Elvis Costello, Bono, and Sting. Tony released *Duets II* in the fall of 2011, and his work with Lady Gaga on "The Lady Is a Tramp" proved to be one of its highlights. The album also featured another distinctive track—the late Amy Winehouse's final recording. She and Tony sang together on "Body and Soul." Their collaboration won a Grammy Award for Best Pop Performance by a Duo or Group in 2012.

Tony Bennett has always championed social and charitable projects that captured his heart. He has lent his name and fame to the American Civil Rights movement—in fact, he participated in the iconic Selma to Montgomery (Alabama) march with Dr. Martin Luther King Jr. in 1965. In recognition of his support of the movement, he was inducted into Atlanta's International Civil Rights Walk of Fame in 2007.

Tony refuses to completely alter his style to stay contemporary for the big record companies. In a 2010 newspaper interview he said, *"I don't follow the latest fashions; I never sing a song that's badly written."* While constantly reinventing himself, he has maintained an artistic integrity that he learned long ago from the singer he most idolized: Frank Sinatra.

"The first time I met Frank Sinatra, he said something to me that has stayed with me my entire life and has helped sustain my career. I was just getting established as a singer in the early 1950s, and Sinatra was doing an engagement at the Paramount Theatre in New York. I had been just hired as the summer replacement for Perry Como on his Kraft Music Hall television show."

"I was still new at show business, and I was nervous as hell. But I thought I'd take a chance and seek Sinatra's advice since he was the singer I idolized. Without incident, I just went backstage and showed up at his dressing room. The Frank Sinatra I met was quite different from the one I had expected—he could not have been nicer to me."

"I asked him, 'How do you handle being nervous on stage?'"

"He said, 'It's good to be nervous. People like it when you're nervous because it shows you care. If you don't care, why should they?'"

"He then gave me the best advice I had ever been given: to stay away from cheap songs. 'Only sing quality songs,' he said."

"I've followed that advice for over fifty years."

As Tony exemplifies, it is possible to reinvent your career while staying true to yourself. There will be times when you need to make changes to keep up with the world around you, but don't let those changes go against your core beliefs.

TONY'S EMPOWERING THOUGHT: **"Stay true to yourself, and the rest of it will take care of itself."**

DO IT DAILY:

▸ *Don't be too proud or too stubborn to seek advice from others.* Learning from others is a wonderful gift—find some guidance.

▸ *Stay true to yourself.* Even when you have to make changes in your life, remember who you are and how you want to be remembered.

"Smokin' Joe" Frazier

WORLD CHAMPION BOXER

Joe's Journey:

SON OF A SHARECROPPER → OLYMPIC GOLD MEDALIST → HEAVYWEIGHT CHAMPION

"Smokin' Joe" Frazier overcame many obstacles and opponents in his life and career due to his unyielding tenacity. We all need to possess the determination and persistence exemplified by Frazier if we want to meet with success. Tenacity is a personality trait or common thread often observed with high achievers. If you are looking to meet with success, look no further than Smokin' Joe for a lesson in tenacity.

I was lucky to grow up during the "Golden Age" of boxing in the 1970s when greats such as Sugar Ray Leonard, Roberto Duran, Thomas "The Hit Man" Hearns, "Marvelous Marvin" Hagler, Ernie Shavers, Larry Holmes, Ken Norton, George Foreman, Muhammad Ali, and of course Joseph William Frazier, better known as "Smokin' Joe," were center stage in the world of boxing.

The son of a South Carolina sharecropper, Joe was one of twelve children in a family that survived by working the land they leased for a share of its crops and harvest. He was raised in the rural community of Laurel Bay where they not only grew crops, but also made bootleg corn liquor to help pay for family necessities.

As the story goes, Joe's uncle watched him work and grow on that leased farm and commented almost incidentally, "That boy there—that boy is gonna be another Joe Louis!" A passing comment by a family member may go almost unnoticed in the course of a person's life, but sometimes a little positive encouragement can inspire him or her to reach great heights. For young Joe Frazier, his uncle's observation ignited his burning competitive desire.

The very next day, Joe recalls in his autobiography, he filled an old burlap sack with rags, corncobs, a brick, and Spanish moss. He hung the makeshift heavy bag from an oak tree in the backyard. *"For the next six or seven years—damn near every day—I'd hit that heavy bag for an hour at a time. I'd wrap my hands with a necktie of my Daddy's, or a stocking of my Momma's or sister's, and get to it."*

Joe became a boxer almost by accident. He first went to a gym in hopes of getting into shape, but soon he started taking boxing more seriously and eventually became one of the best amateur heavyweights in the nation.

Joe turned his outstanding amateur career into one that captured Golden Gloves Heavyweight Championships in 1962, 1963, and 1964 and earned a gold medal at the 1964 Summer Games in Tokyo. His professional boxing career lasted more than a decade, including three fights with Muhammad Ali, leading to the Undisputed World Heavyweight Championship. Anybody who has ever seen Joe Frazier's bobbing and weaving style with relentless pressure to land one of the most devastating left hooks in boxing history, couldn't help but become an instant fan.

I've been fortunate to sit and talk with Joe on several occasions, but the most memorable was probably the time we sat in the back of a limo on the way to a guest appearance on the *Howard Stern Show* that my company arranged.

It was obvious that Joe had never lost the competitive fire in his belly, and he was still seeking a sense of justice and a chance to set the record straight about his epic rivalry with Muhammad Ali. Twenty-five years after his "trilogy" with Ali, he still had much to say. He reminded me that he petitioned U.S. President Richard Nixon to have Ali's boxing rights reinstated after Ali's famous refusal to enter the military so they could fight.

Joe spoke at length about his third fight with Ali, but he concluded with: *"Hey, maybe I lost the decision, but look at Ali now and you can see that I was the real winner of our fights."* Joe was referring to Ali's physical condition, believed to be caused by a combination of boxing and Parkinson's disease.

Joe had little interest in talking about his first fight with Ali. The bout took place in 1971 at Madison Square Garden and was promoted as the "fight of the century"—both Joe and Muhammad came to the fight undefeated. Joe broke Ali's jaw halfway through the fight and won in a fifteen-round decision. But Joe cared more about what the history books would say about the fight.

Joe was deeply affected by the way Ali had spoken about him in public: *"Ali had called me ugly, ignorant, and a gorilla; that just doesn't disappear. However, it motivated me to do my best."*

Joe was considered a small heavyweight, but he turned what some thought was a liability into an asset. In an *Esquire* magazine interview, he stated:

> *"I wasn't a big guy. People thought the big guys would eat me up. But it was the other way around. I loved to fight the big guys. The way I fight, it's not me beatin' the man; I make the man whip himself. Only one big guy I didn't like to fight: That was George. Fightin' George Foreman is like being in the street with an eighteen-wheeler comin' at you."*

After the Howard Stern interview, we brought Joe to our gallery for a public signing event. The line reached around the block. Joe was over fifty years old at the time, but he was still a solid piece of steel. I brought my own heavy bag to our event so that Joe could put on a little show for our clients. The thunder of each blow he landed on that bag left the crowd in awe.

Joe Frazier and Muhammad Ali's fight trilogy—long considered one of the greatest boxing rivalries of all time—is really one of the greatest contests across *all* sports lines. Joe won the first fight; Ali won the second, so the stage was set for what famously became known as the "Thrilla in Manila"—the championship bout fought in the Philippines in 1975.

According to the reports, in the ring that night Ali said to Joe, "They said you were through, Joe." Joe shot back, "They lied, pretty boy." After fourteen grueling rounds, trainer Eddie Futch stopped the fight because both of Joe's eyes were swollen shut. Joe Frazier shouted to his trainer, "I want him, boss," but Futch wouldn't change his mind. He told Joe, "It's all over. No one will forget what you did here today." Ali won the battle, but he said afterward that it was the "…closest thing to dying that I know of."

Perhaps Ali's comment about dying is more of what Joe was referring to when he told me that he was the "real winner" of their fights. Joe was a tenacious competitor, and his conversation always revolved around being a competitor:

"You need to want it more than the other guy when you are in the ring; it doesn't lie. And nobody wanted it more than me."

Ali took two out of their three fights, but together Joe and Ali brought out the best in each other. Common wisdom may consider Ali to be the greatest boxer of all time, but as Joe—ever the competitor—said many times in public:

"Ali always said I would be nothing without him. But what would he have been without me?"

Joe Frazier's overall record was thirty-two wins, four losses, and one draw. Twenty-seven of those wins were by knockout. His public career went beyond boxing: he made a cameo appearance in the movie *Rocky*, was featured on an episode of *The Simpsons*, appeared on *Celebrity Apprentice*, and toured the world with his musical group, Joe Frazier and the Knockouts.

Joe mentored and trained up-and-coming fighters at his Philadelphia gym, and he was an inductee of both the International Boxing Hall of Fame and the World Boxing Hall of Fame.

Sadly, our last scheduled event with Joe in 2011 never took place. He was diagnosed with liver cancer in September and passed away less than three months later. Upon hearing of his death, Muhammad Ali said, "The world has lost a great champion. I will always remember Joe with respect and admiration."

"Smokin' Joe" Frazier's life is a prime example of tenacity. We can learn from his determination and virtue to create a pattern of persistent tenacity in our own lives.

JOE'S EMPOWERING THOUGHT: *"You can map out a fight plan or a life plan, but when the action starts, it may not go the way you planned, and you're down to your reflexes—that means your [preparation]. That's where your roadwork shows. If you cheated on that in the dark of the morning, well, you're going to get found out now, under the bright lights."*

DO IT DAILY:

▸ *Have a consistent mindset to turn the naysayers' comments into a motivating tool.* Use competition and what they say and think of you to up your game so you will win your game.

▸ *Adopt a tenacious attitude toward reaching your goals.* A mindset of non-stop effort and relentless determination are often the key ingredients between winning and losing.

Bill Rancic

ENTREPRENEUR

Bill's Journey:

BELOW-AVERAGE STUDENT → MANY DOUBTERS → FIRST WINNER OF
NBC'S THE APPRENTICE

Optimism is one of those qualities that can help you to overcome an enormous amount of adversity. Maintaining a positive attitude is the type of common thread you'll see with most of the participants in this book. They hold their heads high, keep smiling even when it may seem difficult, and do their best to spread positivity and encouragement to those with whom they come into contact. Optimism is almost a necessity when it comes to building a successful personal life and career. It keeps you moving forward, accomplishing, and overcoming most anything in your path.

In 2004, a quarter of a million people applied as contestants for a new NBC TV show called *The Apprentice*. The reality show was the brainchild of *Survivor* mega-producer Mark Burnett. Advertised as the "ultimate job interview," it was hosted by controversial business mogul Donald Trump. The winner would receive a $250,000 contract running one of Trump's companies. Each week a variety of businesspeople competed against each other, and at the conclusion of the episode, Trump would eliminate a contestant with his signature phrase: *"You're fired."*

As a contestant, Bill Rancic never heard those words. He told me, "I saw an opportunity when a friend of mine received a random fax looking for 'young entrepreneurs.' It turned out to be for *The Apprentice*. I was excited, to say the least, but I found out later that I was the last one picked for the show." Bill ended up becoming the first reality TV star to be hired on national television.

Besides being a gifted entrepreneur, Bill is extremely generous and sensitive, a person more than happy to share insights that can help others fulfill their dreams. He is remembered on the show for his positive attitude and big smile.

"I believe I had an advantage growing up—my parents were both schoolteachers, and they always encouraged me to try different things. It was fine to make mistakes, and that built confidence for me. Unfortunately we don't see enough of that today. My message is you have to know what failure is to truly appreciate success."

"I was always motivated to make money. I was reading the Robb Report *when I was only ten years old. I went to a private school where I was a below-average student, but when I attended public school, I was above average. That opened my eyes, and I began to realize that my education would play a key part in my success."*

"After high school I started a pretty successful cleaning business. It helped me realize that I enjoyed all the aspects of running a business. From there I came up with the first ever 'Cigar of the Month Club' in 1995. In the first thirty days we had one thousand customers—after one year we had over ten thousand! I was stunned."

"It kind of puts a smile on my face. I recall my sixth-grade teacher telling me that I would never make it to college; my eighth-grade basketball coach kicked me off the team because of my grades. Those events had a powerful effect on me, and I've used them as fuel throughout my life. People have always told me I couldn't accomplish things. Even on

The Apprentice, *I wasn't supposed to win. It was supposed to be a Harvard guy. And that's the story of my life—but it's okay because it keeps me moving forward.*"

"*It's important to remind yourself constantly of your goals, to find different ways to motivate yourself. Surround yourself with pictures of things you want. So many people are afraid they will fail, so they don't even try. Anxiety goes hand-in-hand with fear and makes it worse. If something doesn't work out the first time, learn from your mistakes and you'll come back stronger the next time.*"

"*Too many people hit the snooze button ten times when their alarm goes off in the morning. All people have wants, but only a few have enough passion and motivation to pursue them. You will only get out of it what you put into it. Try to focus on time management. I habitually try to work on things I enjoy doing—like public speaking. Chances are, if people concentrate on what they like to do, they'll be much more successful.*"

Bill's advice included this:

"*Don't have any regrets. You never want to look back and say 'What if?' Make every day count. Try to experience everything in life and embrace it all. You are in control of your destiny. I thank God for everything I have. If you let fear paralyze you, it will become a habit that prevents you from living the life you want.*"

"*For young entrepreneurs my advice is this: walk it like you talk it. Actions speak louder than words. Take risks, but manage those risks. Agility is the key to success—look at all the ways you can get a job done. Take the blinders off. And above all, help others along the way.*"

After winning *The Apprentice*, Bill went on to become a high-demand speaker, and now he co-hosts a nationally syndicated daily news-magazine show, *America Now*, with Leeza Gibbons. He also co-executive produced his own top-rated reality TV show, *Giuliana and Bill*, with his wife, Giuliana. The show chronicled the couple's struggle to have a baby and, happily, in 2012 they became the parents of a baby boy born through surrogacy—Edward Duke Rancic. His optimism was truly tested during this difficult journey, but even then his perspective on life rose to the top.

Bill's insight and passion for what he does has touched many. He splits his time between writing *New York Times* bestsellers, coaching kids on how to succeed in business, and rebuilding lives in poverty-stricken countries like Haiti. Bill is the real deal; he doesn't just "talk the talk"—he is constantly giving back. Donating 100 percent of the royalties from his bestseller, *Beyond the Lemonade Stand,* to children's charities says it all. He hopes to instill this sense of positivity and generosity into the world, knowing that if we all walk the talk, big differences can occur.

BILL'S EMPOWERING THOUGHT: *"Don't have any regrets. You never want to look back and say 'What if?' Make every day count. Try to experience everything in life and embrace it all."*

DO IT DAILY:

▸ *Envision your success.* Create a "vision board" to view each day of all that you desire as a useful tool to help you stay focused on your goals and dreams. Maintain it, update it, and check off the accomplishments and milestones as they are reached.

▸ *Focus on your attitude.* More times than not, your attitude will define you. People will remember how you carry yourself and what you add to the room. Strive to be remembered as optimistic and uplifting.

Karrie Webb

Karrie's Journey:

SMALL TOWN GIRL → MENTAL STRENGTH → WORLD GOLF HALL OF FAME

If you want to succeed, you will have to be disciplined. This means you will have to dedicate yourself to your craft, and commit to practicing, practicing and practicing some more, even on the days when you just don't feel like it. Karrie Webb has mastered the art of discipline. She shared her philosophy with me, *"Even now if I don't feel like practicing, I still do. Anyone who achieves must have that frame of mind."*

Karrie Ann Webb holds the crown as Australia's most successful female golfer. On the LPGA tour, she has won thirty-nine times—more than any other active player. During her rookie season, twenty-one-year-old Karrie became the youngest winner ever of the women's British Open. That same year she was also named the Ladies European Tour Rookie of the Year. Karrie became the first female golfer to earn more than one million dollars in a single season.

Karrie could not have been more charming as we spoke about what it takes not only to win, but also to stay on top and compete with the best in the world for almost twenty years.

"I still have that inner drive to achieve. My love and desire to play golf gets me through all the hard work."

"I grew up in the small town of Ayr, Queensland, with less than eight thousand people. I began training with a family friend, Kelvin Haller, who was my first mentor and coach. It still makes me laugh—I used to tell people I wanted to be a professional golfer, and they would look at me like I was a bit crazy. They would ask me what I really wanted to do. Sometimes I'd come up with any old answer, but in the back of my mind I always knew I would make golf my career."

"When I was twelve, my parents took me to see golfing great Greg Norman — a fellow 'Aussie'— play in a tournament. I truly fell in love with golf, and even at my young age I had no doubt I would do all that was needed to be the best I could."

"Practicing golf can be a grind—a bore. So I've always had a big advantage over my competition because of my mental toughness. Plenty of other golfers are better athletes than me, but few have my mindset of doing all it takes to be the best. I was given a gift not only to play golf, but also to be mentally strong."

"I still train six to eight hours a day; if I didn't love what I do, that could never happen!"

"But it's not just about showing up. For me to achieve what I did in my early twenties wouldn't have occurred without a strong work ethic."

"I never get sick of the game. What I wanted to achieve in the long run made all the necessary commitment and hard work a non-issue."

"When I was young, my goal was breaking 90…then 80…then par. Then I set my eye on winning the biggest tournaments in the LPGA. Now my goal is to compete at the 2016 Summer Olympics in Rio de Janeiro, Brazil, repre-

senting my country of Australia where golf has not been played at the Olympics since 1904."

"There have been times when things didn't go my way. When I stopped winning, I was unable to figure out what had changed. I couldn't recognize any process I had followed earlier—something that I could look back on and regain to help me get back on track. I worked with some great sports physiologists, and they helped me realize that I did indeed have a process that had worked for me in the past. We worked on my pre-shot routine, and I realized I was not as fluid as I used to be. We used visualization to help me be more relaxed, and I learned to trust my setup and swing again."

"It was reinforced to me that golf isn't a 'reaction' sport. Once you get your skill set down, golf is reduced to a mental game. There is no doubt that golf is 90 percent mental and only about 10 percent physical."

"I believe what holds people back is their fear of failure—their fear of letting people down. I also see that some people want the reward, but they're not willing to put the work into it."

Karrie explained the "must do" things for up-and-coming golfers—especially in pressure situations: to achieve success in golf, as in anything, you must treat it as a full-time job and be disciplined.

"You must love the game. The work is hard, and if the love isn't there, then the work will not be there."

"Believe in yourself, and be honest with yourself. Understand what your weakness is, but don't get too comfortable only doing what you're good at. When you get to the driving range, work on your weakness first."

"Don't be afraid to fail—sometimes success is failure! You may have to deal with a loss, but that's better than regretting that you didn't at least get out there and try."

"I myself get disappointed when I see a great talent who isn't willing to go the extra mile. Don't make that mistake."

"When facing a 'must hit' drive or putt, I really don't feel any more pressure than normal. I've been there before; I've put in my hard work, so I just keep calm and focus on my pre-shot routine. For me a pressure situation is actually comforting: I'm in my comfort zone where all the hard work finally pays off."

Now an LPGA legend, Karrie was the youngest member admitted to the World Golf Hall of Fame. She's been named Rolex Player of the Year, *twice*, and in 1997 she was recognized as the best female golfer at the ESPY Awards. Karrie was the youngest winner of the LPGA Career Grand Slam and Super Grand Slam, winning every major championship in women's golf over the course of her career.

Karrie's ever-impressive discipline is what led to her success as a pro golfer. Adopting a similar discipline will be no small task, but it will be necessary to advance you closer to your goals.

KARRIE'S EMPOWERING THOUGHT: *Karrie still lives by her parents' creed: "Put your head down and work your tail off."*

DO IT DAILY:

▸ *Don't be afraid to fail.* Develop a strong mindset that says there is no such thing as failure—only setbacks that can be learned from and take you to the next level.

▸ *Embrace discipline.* Focus on your goal and give it everything you've got. Never let your competition win because they were more disciplined than you.

Mel Fisher

SUNKEN TREASURE HUNTER

Mel's Journey:

CHICKEN FARMER → PERSONAL TRAGEDY → $450-MILLION DISCOVERY

Persistence is that never give up quality so many of the greatest possess. In fact, it is one of the most important and consistent common threads we see throughout this book. Without persistence, many of the people between these pages would never have reached the pinnacles they surmounted. Mel Fisher was one of those persistent people who was just unwilling to take no for an answer and always gave 100% and beyond.

"Today's the day!" That was Mel Fisher's motto *and* his mindset. With a bigger-than-life personality, this former chicken farmer set his mind to a goal and poured his efforts into a sixteen-year quest to bring up from the sea a long lost Spanish treasure ship called *Nuestra Señora de Atocha*. The *Atocha* was lost off the Florida Keys in 1622 on its journey from the Old World of Spain to the New World of the Americas. He was told it couldn't be done, if even found, but as usual, Mel stayed persistent until he proved everyone wrong.

Mel's dreams of becoming a treasure hunter started as a child when he read Robert Louis Stevenson's *Treasure Island*. As an adult, Mel's fascination with treasure led him to Spain to pour over worm-eaten antique treasure maps.

As a pioneer of undersea treasure hunting, Mel faced many challenges and obstacles along the way. He experienced personal tragedy when his oldest son Dirk, along with Dirk's wife Angel and diver Rick Gage, died after their boat capsized during their search for the Atocha in 1975.

Still, Mel and his wife Deo—along with the rest of his family—stayed the course. Then on July 20, 1985, Mel discovered the "mother lode" that had been lying on the ocean floor for more than 360 years. The Atocha was found 35 miles off the shore of Key West, Florida, in only 35 feet of water.

The haul included 40 tons of gold, hundreds of thousands of silver coins known as "pieces of eight," golden doubloons, rare porcelain, Colombian emeralds, and other antiquities. The total value exceeded $450 million. Mel famously said, "Once you see the bottom of the ocean paved with gold, you never forget it!"

The *Atocha* was by far the greatest sunken treasure ever discovered at the time, and the story catapulted Mel Fisher onto the world stage when it was featured in a *National Geographic* TV documentary.

But fate threw Mel another curveball: the State of Florida moved in and levied millions of dollars in legal fees by claiming ownership of the treasure. After a legal battle, the US Supreme Court confirmed Mel's ownership of the recovered treasure—with a provision that Mel's company donate 20 percent of the artifacts to the State of Florida.

This was the point at which I first met Mel. I was only twenty-six and in the early days of my business. I remember watching Mel's journey on television and quickly noticed how determined he was to reach his goal— a goal few of us could ever imagine. I always remembered he was steadfast and determined to get the job done.

Back then, I was looking to grow my business and believed there must be collectors out there who would want to own a "piece of history" from Mel's sunken treasure haul. So I decided to call Mel and see if I could strike a deal with him to offer the public some of the treasure he had found. When I called his office in Key West—much to my surprise—Mel himself answered the phone! We had a short conversation about potential business opportunities that concluded with Mel saying, "If you're ever in this area, give me a call and we can get together."

That was all it took for me; I saw an opportunity that could not be passed up. From one persistent man to another.

Within days I booked a flight and called Mel to tell him I was going to be in Key West with some friends and asked if I could stop by and see him. It was truly amazing. One day I was watching this remarkable man on TV, and a few days later I was in his office talking business face-to-face. I learned an important lesson here: *If you see an opportunity, don't sit back. Make the call!*

Mel and I clicked right away. In the midst of discussing a possible business venture, Mel interrupted himself mid-sentence to say, "Do you want to get some soup?" It was only ten o'clock on a Saturday morning.

I thought it a little strange, but who was I to say no to Mel Fisher? So we took a walk to the local drinking establishment where I learned that Mel's definition of "soup" was a double "151" rum and Coke! To say the least, Mel and I got along just fine as he went on to recount some fantastic stories of his explorations.

He emphasized: *"Never give up on your dreams. Always believe in what you do—even when things don't go as you planned."*

A couple of hours later we had cut a deal for my company to represent Mel Fisher's personal collection of treasures and offer it for sale to the public. It was amazing to watch Mel swing into action: he was faxing our agreement back and forth with his lawyer in Washington—and I didn't even know what a fax machine was back then. Mel was way ahead of his time not only in treasure hunting, but also as a businessman and public figure. Very few could compete with Mel on all these levels.

Our relationship lasted many years. We sold lots of treasure for him. I'm still amazed when I remember him letting me enter his museum to select items for our clients—literally climbing over gold and silver bars to make our selections. He was always gracious, signing letters to authenticate the treasures purchased by our clients stating that they came from his private collection.

Sadly, Mel passed away in 1998 at the age of seventy-seven. His now famous motto, *"Today's the day,"* was the attitude—the mindset—that kept him focused and inspired people during good times, and fueled their determination to carry on when the going got tough.

MEL'S EMPOWERING THOUGHT: *"Always believe in what you do—even when things don't go as you planned."*

DO IT DAILY:

- *Persistency pushes you to forget the past and focus on the future.* Adopt Mel's motto and mindset as your own: *Today's your day!* You never know when that small push or additional effort will help you reach your goals. So keep pushing forward.

- *Don't ever give up the hunt.* Following Mel's lead, we are often looking for a needle in a haystack. But the simple act of persistence will often give us the fuel we need to find exactly what we are looking for.

Dennis Eckersley

BASEBALL HALL OF FAME PITCHER

Dennis's Journey:

YOUNG SUPERSTAR → ALCOHOLISM → MLB ALL-CENTURY TEAM

If you asked most people how they would like to be viewed in life, "courageous" would be a pretty common answer. Courage is the will to face fears, and then set them aside, knowing that you can and you will overcome. Dennis Eckersley is one of those people who have always remained courageous, even in the face of difficult experiences.

My dad, a lifelong Brooklyn Dodgers fan, was fuming when the news broke about his beloved Dodgers moving to Los Angeles in 1957. There was no way he would ever switch his loyalty to the American League and become a Yankees fan, so he wound up migrating to the new National League expansion team that arrived in town in 1962—the New York Mets.

Like any good son, that made me a Mets fan as well. My two sisters, Bonnie and Marla, followed suit. It was very unlikely that we would take much notice of a pitcher playing for the Oakland Athletics, an American League team on the other side of the country. But Dennis Eckersley commanded a lot of attention from baseball fans everywhere.

Dennis was simply one of the most dominating closers ever to step on the mound. You couldn't help but respect and admire his skills—even as you felt that sickening sensation as you watched him step in as a reliever to stop your favorite team in its tracks.

"Eck" was drafted right out of high school, he made it to the big leagues by the time he was twenty. His twenty-three-year career (1975-1998) found him playing for the Cleveland Indians, the Boston Red Sox, the Chicago Cubs, the Oakland Athletics, and the St. Louis Cardinals.

Named American League Rookie Pitcher of the Year in 1975, he went on to post a no-hitter against the California Angels in 1977. A decade later his Oakland A's swept the Red Sox in the 1988 American League Championship Series. Dennis was credited with saves in all four games.

The very next year, the A's swept the San Francisco Giants in the 1989 World Series. Dennis helped secure the victory in game two and earned the save in the final game four. In the entire 1990 season, he gave up just five earned runs, resulting in a season earned run average of a mere 0.61. In 1992 he not only won the American League Cy Young Award, but was also named the league's Most Valuable Player.

Dennis Eckersley was the first of only two pitchers in all of Major League Baseball history to record both a twenty-win season *and* a fifty-save season in the same career. Interviewing a baseball star with a résumé like that was a great honor for me. Even as he spoke, I remembered watching the lanky, longhaired pitcher throw that signature "live" fastball that shut down hitter after hitter. But at the time of our meeting, when he was in his fifties, Dennis provided one of the most open and candid interviews I conducted.

Telling his story gave Dennis more than a chance to vent. More importantly, he wanted to offer hope to others so that they too could overcome. He proved himself a real standup guy as he spoke honestly about the dark times he lived through and how he finally moved forward into a more peaceful sense of being. He surprised me by asking if I had interviewed others who—like him—didn't enjoy their careers:

"When I think back, I could have cried because I didn't really enjoy the game. There was always so much pressure—it was so intense, I couldn't enjoy myself. I think fans always assume the players on the field are happy, but for me it just wasn't so."

Dennis recognized the importance of his father's involvement at the beginning:

"I wasn't a great player early on, but Dad took the time to play with us. He was very involved and took the time to teach us. I always wanted to keep up with my older brother. That turned out to be a real benefit, because we had instant competition."

He spoke openly about his personal life and how it affected him both off and on the field:

*"I was married at eighteen, and it helped keep me in line—it kept me out of trouble. But when I was twenty-two, things really got bad for me. I was traded to the Boston Red Sox and my wife left me for another player. **I have to be honest with you: I was personally devastated. I was crushed when my marriage ended—so I put all my energy into my profession.**"*

He found his motivation and the drive to keep going in spite of his failed marriage:

*"I had a little girl only two years old. I had to keep focused for her and her wellbeing. **I tried to use what happened to me and turn it around to something positive. I kept a chip on my shoulder—and that helped keep me focused each day. I could have gone real bad, but I would not let it defeat me—no way, not me!**"*

With this same kind of remarkable honesty, Dennis shared his insights about his struggles with alcohol:

"I hit bottom shortly before the Cubs traded me to Oakland. I was in complete denial about my alcohol abuse. Believe me when I tell you self-denial is a killer! But I knew I had to do something different—alcoholism runs in my family. I needed to get sober. My turning point was when I finally accepted the fact that I was an alcoholic. I was scared, but I turned to Alcoholics Anonymous and went into rehab for a while. So when I went to Oakland I was clean and sober."

Gaining control over his drinking helped prepare Dennis to accept a major change in his career at Oakland.

"I had been a starter for twelve years, but my manager, Tony La Russa, and my pitching coach, Dave Duncan, convinced me to become a reliever. I accepted what they wanted me to do, and it was like being reborn."

Dennis reflected on what made the difference in his life—how he was able to overcome the obstacles and become a big-league sensation:

"I always had the passion for the game because I wanted to be the best I could. Therefore, doing the necessary things to prepare for the game was easy for me. I had that extra drive that separates successful people from others. I don't know any great athlete who doesn't have drive and a major passion—it's a must."

"Being a relief pitcher is like always having to jump out of the plane to continue to prove yourself. I was a very anxious guy as a closer. The fear I felt came across as confidence, but deep down inside I was afraid to fail. Even highly talented people question themselves."

"People are held back from reaching their goals because of their fear of failure. They get tentative—and that doesn't work. You have to truly

believe in yourself. You can't fake it. Fear motivated me. Fear made me better. The thought of not doing well got my attention, so I always kept the pressure on myself. Even when I was inducted into the Hall of Fame, I didn't think I deserved it."

But others did.

In 2005, the Oakland Athletics officially retired Dennis Eckersley's uniform number (43). Fremont, California's Washington High School, his alma mater, renamed its baseball field in his honor. He was named to the Major League Baseball All-Century Team and inducted into the Hall of Fame in January 2004. Upon retirement Dennis had appeared in more games (1,071) than any previous pitcher in MLB history, recording 390 saves.

Dennis is one of those remarkable, successful people who picked up the pieces and rebuilt his life on more than one occasion. As we finished up our conversation, I thanked him for his openness and honesty in sharing his life story. He offered his parting thoughts about his message of hope and overcoming:

"Beyond your goals, enjoy the memories of your life and appreciate the moment. The way to live is to be honest within yourself so you can make clear decisions."

"My advice to others is about acceptance in your life. When things happen to you, do all you need to do so you'll have no regrets. No half steps; go all in. Give it all you have."

For me, the most impressive part about Dennis was his honesty. It was that honesty that was indicative of his courage. He was courageous and willing to open up to help others and share some of the darkest and most emotional parts of his life with me, knowing they would be shared with the world.

DENNIS'S EMPOWERING THOUGHT: *"I could have gone real bad, but I would not let it defeat me—no way, not me!"*

DO IT DAILY:

- ▸ *Courage is making the most of your life.* Yesterday is gone, tomorrow who knows? Appreciate and love each and every day. Find the courage to make the moments count, always working to smile and laugh with those you love.

- ▸ *Fear is temporary; courage should be a constant.* Don't let fear stop you from dreaming big. Don't let it prevent you from taking chances. Fear will eventually subside, but maintaining your courage can carry you through it all.

Leonard Marshall

3X ALL PRO NFL PLAYER

Leonard's Journey:

EXPERIENCED RACISM → LIMITED ROLE MODELS → 2X SUPER BOWL
CHAMPION

NFL great Leonard Marshall didn't grow up in the best neighborhood or have the best role models, however, Leonard did not let his lack of support slow him down. He knew if he wanted to achieve his dreams he would have to give beyond 100 percent, and that is exactly what he did. We often give too little or don't put in the effort necessary to reach our goals, and instead we just settle for the easier route resulting in mediocrity. If you dream big, and want to live large, then look no further for a role model than Leonard Marshall.

As a kid growing up in New York, my Sunday afternoons were all about watching New York Giants football with my dad. I've always loved and played football. Football became for me a mirror of life. The game teaches and reinforces all sorts of values: dedication, integrity, hard work, winning and losing—and so much more.

As a defensive lineman myself, I was constantly transfixed by the performance of the Big Blue's defensive end, number 70, Leonard Marshall. His intensity and sheer physicality impressed me throughout his career in the

NFL. Leonard was not only a great player, but also he consistently displayed a high level of sportsmanship.

As an adult, I met Leonard in Florida and we became fast friends. I soon realized that it was indeed his strong character that makes him who he is—both on and off the playing field.

He played twelve storied seasons in the NFL, during which he was selected All-Pro three times, and won two Super Bowl championships with the Giants—Super Bowl XXI and Super Bowl XXV. Who could ever forget his devastating hit on legendary San Francisco 49er quarterback Joe Montana during the 1990 NFC championship game?

Marshall recently completed a book about that memorable 1990 season and Super Bowl XXV. *When the Cheering Stops: Bill Parcells, the 1990 New York Giants and the Price of Greatness*, with CBSsports.com writer William Bendetson, not only chronicles the highlights of that season, but also intertwines them with the stories of what has happened to numerous players in the last twenty years, revealing some of the difficulties retired players face.

Since I've had the opportunity to know Leonard as a friend, I can say that he truly has a heart of gold. His passion for those who have suffered from playing football motivated him to create and manage The Game Plan Foundation, an organization that helps retired football players deal with the many injuries they received during their playing days.

It's hard to believe that this mountain of a man was once told by his teacher, "You won't amount to anything." But Leonard didn't believe it—he says of the experience, *"Since then, any negative thing I hear only motivates me more. What that teacher said still motivates me every single day to be the best that I can be."*

Leonard has always possessed an insatiable appetite to succeed, and that drive and passion has helped him overcome many obstacles. This passion is a common thread that ties him to the other personalities in this book.

Marshall grew up in South Louisiana in a rural town of only 450 people: *"It was a drug-infested, crime-ridden community with few acceptable role models. It was challenging to say the least."*

He learned early on to take something positive away from every situation: ***"I focused on looking around and seeing the guy I did not want to become rather than the guy I wanted to be. I didn't want to become the guy on the corner—the bum with his hand out, looking for excuses rather than solutions. You're not always going to pick yourself up. But picking yourself up just one more time than you got knocked down is a mark of a true champion."***

Leonard's motivating one-liners and mantras make you feel like you can do anything:

"Tough times don't last, tough people do."

"Forget about everybody else's life, focus on yours."

"Never be the guy who says, 'I can't!'"

Leonard's critical turning point came while attending Louisiana State University. During his freshman year his teammate and friend, Lawrence Williams, got kicked off the team for bad behavior. That awakened in Leonard a desire to stay on the straight and narrow. He explains, *"It woke me up, and I learned that you are only as good as the people you surround yourself with. If you're with shit, you will be shit."*

Leonard persevered and was ultimately named LSU's most valuable defensive player in 1982 by legendary coach, Bear Bryant. Leonard found great satisfaction in this accomplishment because his very own father—a tremendous football player in his own right—wasn't allowed to play for LSU because of the color of his skin.

Some would use racism like that experienced by Leonard's family as an excuse, but for Leonard it only served to motivate him, providing an impetus for his unrelenting desire to succeed on the field.

"My dad instilled drive and determination in me. He showed me who I did not want to be, and he showed me what he envisioned for me in my life. You can't be too sensitive. Being thick-skinned is an important aspect of character building."

Leonard Marshall believes strongly that it is fear, and only fear, that stops people from achieving their goals.

He advises, *"Fear should drive you, not determine you."*

He recited to me a line that his old Giants' coach Bill Parcells used to tell him: *"Put a chip on your shoulder and dare people to knock it off."*

In early 2014, ESPN's *Outside the Lines* reported that Leonard, along with pro football Hall of Famer Tony Dorsett, had been diagnosed with chronic traumatic encephalopathy, a degenerative condition many scientists say is caused by head trauma; it is linked to depression and dementia.

Always striving to be his best, despite what life throws at him, Leonard Marshall attributes his great attitude to what he has learned from his friends and loved ones—the people who have cared about *him* for who he is, not for what he has achieved or accumulated. Leonard's dedication and passion are what fueled him to go beyond 100 percent, and achieve great success, which is one of the common threads and traits amongst the greatest around.

LEONARD'S EMPOWERING THOUGHT: *"Whatever you're going to do, do it like it's the last time you're gonna do it!"*

DO IT DAILY:

▸ ***Beat the odds by turning around negative situations to be used as massive motivating tools.*** Don't let negativity slow you down; instead, use it to push even harder and farther.

▸ ***True success requires true commitment.*** Commit yourself to reaching your goals, and give beyond 100 percent of what others, and even you, thought was possible.

Grace Slick

Grace's Journey:

FIGHTING THE ESTABLISHMENT → JEFFERSON AIRPLANE/STARSHIP →
FINE ARTIST

What a wonderful opportunity our company had when we featured artwork from Grace Slick, a true rock and roll icon. Her unique understanding of the world is simply fascinating. Grace is the personification of a lightning bolt—bizarre, beautiful, and charged with electricity.

A member of the Rock and Roll Hall of Fame, Grace Slick is known for her vibrato voice and musical chops featured on hits like "White Rabbit" and "Somebody to Love." Her voice is what helped give Jefferson Airplane and Jefferson Starship their characteristic sound. No doubt, her songs will be listened to by future generations to come. Her legacy, like that of her close friend and contemporary Janis Joplin, makes her one of the most prominent female rock musicians of all time.

Growing up, Grace's musical influences included Mick Jagger and The Rolling Stones.

She explained:

"The Rolling Stones—now that is rock and roll! They command the stage. To be a rocker you don't need to be a great singer, but you do need to have great stage presence. And that's what the Stones had. As far as The Beatles were concerned...I remember seeing The Beatles on TV singing 'I Want to Hold Your Hand'—too cutesy for me."

As Grace spoke of her experiences during one of the most creative musical times in history, she demonstrated a very clear understanding of the era:

"My generation decided individuality was the way to go. We were talking about peace and freedom—trying to make an impact and alter the status quo. We were too naïve to think it couldn't happen."

"I met Jimi Hendrix in Monterey in 1967, and I was in awe. Jimi represented what we were doing and what we were all about—bringing in different races. Few could represent their art form like Jimi. I loved his clothes and his performances."

"Even though I wasn't a Grateful Dead fan, Jerry Garcia became one of my closest friends. Jerry was such an interesting individual. He had a gift: he could listen and understand people when they spoke."

"As far as Janis Joplin...I just loved Janis. She was strong, funny, and up for almost anything: sex, drugs, rock and roll—and that's what we did. We were very similar backstage. They called us 'Fire and Ice.'"

Grace's love of art brings her full circle: *"I visited the de Young Museum in San Francisco when I was about four, and I've been hooked ever since. I loved Rembrandt and other classics."*

After retiring from music, Grace began painting and drawing. She uses acrylic paints, pen and ink, pastels and pencil.

"I very much enjoy doing renditions of my fellow musicians, like Janis and Jerry. I also enjoy the white rabbit from Alice in Wonderland. *I really iden-*

*tify with her story. I was a kid in the 1950s, a very rigid time. **Going into the '60s for me was like going down the rabbit hole of curiosity.***"

As a youngster she was a fashion model. In her book, *Somebody to Love? A Rock-and-Roll Memoir*, she talks of her bouts with alcohol, LSD, and marijuana.

Despite these self-imposed obstacles, Grace can teach us a great lesson of continuing to move forward, as she has never stopped pursing her dreams as a musician, painter, and author.

Over the years, Grace has shared with others her own philosophical thoughts:

"Everybody's got issues. Get a life and get over it! Sometimes life is hard."

"I don't miss anything about the 1960s, not really. I did it. It's like asking, 'Do you miss the fourth grade?' I loved the fourth grade when I was in it, but I don't want to do it again."

"Through literacy you can begin to see the universe. Through music you can reach anybody. Between the two there is you—unstoppable!"

"When you get older, it's not what you did that you regret—it's what you didn't do."

When I asked Grace how the "revolution" is going forty years later, she responded: *"We are getting there, but still there's a long way to go."*

It is Grace's electric energy and unique personality that helped propel her career as a musician and artist. You can learn from Grace's super-charged love of life, and channel your own inner lightning bolt to help illuminate your path to success.

GRACE'S EMPOWERING THOUGHT: *"Everybody's got issues. Get a life and get over it! Sometimes life is hard."*

DO IT DAILY:

▸ ***Don't dwell on your past regrets or let them define you.*** Continue to learn, continue to evolve, and continue to move forward.

▸ ***Fight the Status quo.*** It's not always necessary to conform to society's "norm." Take ownership and create the world you desire.

Mike Eruzione

CAPTAIN 1980 "MIRACLE ON ICE" OLYMPIC HOCKEY TEAM

Mike's Journey:

DAD WORKED THREE JOBS → IGNORED BY HOCKEY RECRUITERS → OLYM-
PIC GOLD MEDAL

One of the prevailing common threads in this book is that success depends on doing whatever it takes—Mike Eruzione is yet another perfect example of the work ethic necessary to be excellent.

Michael "Ritz" "Rizzo" Eruzione made history in one of the biggest sport upsets of the twentieth century: he captained the 1980 US Winter Olympic hockey team that defeated the highly favored Soviets, and won the gold medal in the epic "Miracle on Ice" championship game. In fact, Mike scored the winning goal against the Soviets.

He retired from competition after the Olympics, despite contract offers from the New York Rangers, saying that he'd reached the pinnacle of achievement already. He served as a technical consultant for the 1981 film *Miracle on Ice* and went on to become a television commentator, covering five Olympic games for ABC and CBS.

In 1999, *Sports Illustrated* named the "Miracle on Ice" the Top Sports Moment of the 20th Century. Mike beat the odds to get to that historic game. He grew up playing hockey in Winthrop, Massachusetts, and was part of a large Italian-American family. As we spoke, Mike recalled:

"I faced plenty of obstacles growing up. My dad was a bartender and also worked in a sewage plant. Finances were always a concern. I grew up with my parents, cousins, aunts, and uncles all living in the same house."

"As a hockey player I was not highly recruited at all. People told me I was an OK player, but not Division One material. That didn't matter to me. I believed in myself and always had confidence."

"When I was a senior in high school I only weighed 150 pounds. When someone doubted me, it only motivated me further. That included coaches. The more coaches yelled at me, the harder I worked."

"It was tough for me at my first college. I had a coach who didn't believe in me—he even forgot my name! So I transferred to Boston University where I was lucky to come under Coach Jack Parker's wing. He became head hockey coach just as I arrived, and he helped me a lot. I led the team in goal-scoring my freshman year. Coach Parker even called me 'Pete Rose on skates.'"

"The bottom line is that if you want to be successful you need to do whatever it takes. Believe me, my dad worked three jobs! Do you think he wanted to? No way!"

"You need to develop an attitude that recognizes that you are in control of your own destiny. You can't worry about what other people think. For me it was about practicing. That's the key to succeeding at athletics, school, or business. It comes down to this: if you are not prepared, you will not be successful."

"I figure what holds people back is a lack of confidence or a lack of work. Lots of people out there have great talent and abilities, but talent and ability isn't enough. You must combine talent and ability with a tremendous work ethic."

"To up-and-coming athletes, I would say, 'Have fun, work hard, and believe in yourself.'"

"My dad told me something that I have always kept in mind: 'If you understand the value of work, someday you'll be successful. It might not be next month or next year, but what you accomplish will be because of the hard work, not because you were lucky, or it was a fluke or a miracle. It boils down to hard work.'"

When asked about his big win at the Olympics, Mike responded:

"Winning the gold medal was great—any achievement should be satisfying. However, there is still more to achieve. Take each day as it comes, and do a good job no matter what the challenge is. Enjoy life!"

In 2013, Mike's 1980 "Miracle on Ice" Olympic Game-worn jersey sold at auction for $650,000 and his hockey stick for $262,000—a true testament to his excellence. If you want to attain excellence like so many others in this book, you have to be ready to put in the effort. True and lasting success comes to those who work hard and recognize the value of giving nothing short of full effort.

MIKE'S EMPOWERING THOUGHT: *"Your attitude should be that you are in control of your own destiny, and you can't worry about what other people think."*

DO IT DAILY:

▸ *Practicing is the key to succeeding at athletics, school, or business.* Be prepared, and you will be prepared to win.

▸ *Have a strong inner self-belief system.* Even when others doubt your ability, believe in yourself and you will be well on your way to proving them wrong.

Jerry Schilling

ELVIS PRESLEY'S BEST FRIEND

Jerry's Journey:

FOOTBALL WITH ELVIS AT 12 → IN THE SHADOW OF THE KING → MAKING IT ON HIS OWN

Self-worth is crucial to realizing your dreams. But self-worth doesn't come easy for some, which is why Jerry Shilling's life is such a great lesson in learning our own value.

"Your mother died when you were a year old. You never had a home. I want to be the one to give it to you." Elvis Presley said these words to Jerry Schilling. It is no wonder that Jerry described Elvis as *"the most unselfish human being I ever met."*

Jerry was only twelve years old when he first met Elvis back in 1954, but many years later his emotion—and love—for the "king of rock and roll" was evident as he described that first encounter to me.

He still remembers the exact date: Sunday, July 11. Jerry was watching Elvis and his friends play a game of football on the local playground of a very poor neighborhood in North Memphis when they invited him to join in.

Imagine this: nineteen-year-old Elvis Presley was playing quarterback. He threw the ball to young Jerry. Jerry made the catch and ended up playing football with Elvis every Sunday for the next couple of years. Not long after, Elvis asked Jerry to join his team of bodyguards, now referred to as the "Memphis Mafia."

Over the years Jerry was there in the recording studio, on film sets, backstage, and on tour. He acted as Elvis's stunt double and personal aide, among other responsibilities. Most importantly, he became a trusted friend and confidante to The King.

I met Jerry Schilling while my company was producing artwork under a licensing agreement with Elvis Presley Enterprises. Jerry had so many stories about Elvis that he could have talked for days—even weeks! From his unique perspective he described what he called *"a real human side of Elvis that not many people saw. He became bigger than life to most people, and he earned it."*

Elvis was born in a two-room house in Tupelo, Mississippi, on January 8, 1935. His talent, good looks, and charisma, as well as his humor, sound, and style, made him a worldwide sensation. He starred in thirty-three successful films and sold over one billion records globally.

Living in the shadow of Elvis and never realizing his own dreams and aspirations became an unacceptable reality for Jerry. And he was very forthcoming about why he needed to go his own way:

"The hardest thing I ever did was to leave Elvis Presley. I left him because I felt like I had to make it on my own. So it wasn't so much about getting away from Elvis as it was about proving things to myself."

"I wanted to pursue my own dreams of films, managing, editing, and more. I felt like I had the potential, but if I didn't leave Elvis, I was sure I would have had regrets."

"I guess the lesson here for others is that no matter what, getting out of your comfort zone is always going to be necessary if you want to achieve your innermost dreams."

"I took a chance and walked away from a job that most people would envy. It could have meant losing a great friend, but if I hadn't taken that chance, the thought of not knowing if I could be successful on my own would have always haunted me."

Jerry did indeed make it on his own—as a tour manager helping to guide the careers of "The Piano Man" Billy Joel, the Beach Boys, and Jerry Lee Lewis. For a short time he even managed Elvis's daughter, Lisa Marie, and he co-edited *Elvis on Tour* with Martin Scorsese.

Listening to Jerry was like leafing through a personal photo album. Among his favorite moments, Jerry shared the following:

Barbra Streisand offered Elvis the starring role in *A Star Is Born*. Elvis wanted it, but management turned it down.
To get in shape for his 1968 comeback, Elvis trained in the martial arts and eventually earned his eighth-degree black belt.
Elvis was always up and ready for the show: Nervous yes, but anxiety? Never.
He and Elvis would "Indian wrestle" as a warm-up to get ready for shows. When Elvis put on his stage wardrobe, it was like a fighter preparing to go into the ring.
Elvis was actually very disciplined. He used meditation to help him prepare for the day.
He was able to travel the world with Elvis, meeting famous and powerful people from The Beatles to President Nixon.

"I never made a lot of money, and I don't owe any money. But when I look back, I don't have any regrets. I have great respect, and I'll always try to preserve Elvis's memories. I still live in the same house he gave

me, and I wear the ring he gave me. We remained friends until his death in 1977."

In his book, *Me and a Guy Named Elvis*, Jerry Schilling portrayed his friend as a deep, unassuming person who grew to great heights. And yet he always remained a genuine friend who cared.

Jerry took a risk and has no regrets. He had the best of both worlds: helping a dear friend reach the very pinnacle of fame, and having a rewarding career of his own. If Jerry hadn't realized his own self-worth, he never would have taken that risk. Because he believed in himself, he was able to reach new heights and achieve his own personal goals.

When I visited Graceland I paid my respects to Elvis Presley, his parents Gladys and Vernon Presley, and his grandmother, all buried there in the Meditation Garden. I discovered that Graceland can evoke a flood of emotion when you realize that Elvis was more than a movie star or an amazing voice. Beneath that public figure was a real person whose life was tragically cut short.

JERRY'S EMPOWERING THOUGHT: *"It could have meant losing a great friend, but if I hadn't taken that chance, the thought of not knowing if I could be successful on my own would have always haunted me."*

DO IT DAILY:

▸ *Live your own dreams with no regrets.* Don't rely on the dreams of others to define who you are and what you can achieve.

▸ *Know your self-worth.* You will struggle in life if you don't believe you are capable and worthy of success.

Randy Couture

MIXED MARTIAL ARTS LEGEND

Randy's Journey:

CUT FROM WRESTLING TEAM → U.S. ARMY → UFC CHAMPION
AFTER AGE 40

You may have noticed that a common thread in this book is passion and dedication—finding what you love and giving it all you've got. To go even further, you will need to have a special kind of heart. Mixed Martial Arts legend Randy Couture is a man with the heart of a lion, and we can follow his example when it comes to our burning desire to achieve our dreams.

When I review Randy Couture's awards, triumphs, and career, it is humbling to have been able to sit with him on several occasions and hear what he believes it takes to be a champion. We discussed the mindset he uses day in and day out to put him at the top of his game and to become the ultimate warrior.

Randy's career as a competitor in the UFC is second to none: he became a three-time UFC Heavyweight Champion and two-time UFC Light Heavyweight Champion. Over his tenure, Randy had fifteen title fights and was the first to hold championships in two different weight divisions. He's the fourth member nominated to the UFC Hall of Fame and the only athlete in UFC history to win a championship *after* becoming a Hall of Fame member.

One of MMA's original superstars, Randy retired from the UFC in 2006 after nine years of fighting. He announced his return one-year later in 2007, feeling he had more to accomplish—and he came back a better fighter. No one else has won a UFC championship over the age of forty: Randy Couture did it four times.

Born in Everett, Washington, Randy Couture came from a family situation that was less than ideal. His dad was rarely in his life, and his mom worked long days to support the family.

Although an athlete, Randy did not make his first wrestling team and had to go up two weight classes to eventually make the squad. However, he went on to attend Oklahoma State University, where he was a three-time NCAA Division I All-American.

After college he joined the Army, eventually attaining the rank of sergeant in the 101st Airborne Division. Randy was a young father whose first apartment for his family was behind a junkyard; joining the Army would provide financial security for his wife and child.

He demonstrated his ability to turn a hopeless, unfair situation into an opportunity when he applied for tryouts with the Army's freestyle wrestling team, and got a rude awakening. Due to a clerical error, he was listed to compete in Greco-Roman wrestling, a discipline he had never trained in. Ever the dauntless competitor, he persevered. Even with no experience, he went to the tryouts and made the team. After leaving the Army, Randy continued his Greco-Roman wrestling and became a three-time Olympic team alternate (1988, 1992, and 1996).

In 1997, at the age of thirty-three, Randy made his debut in the UFC's Octagon cage as a heavyweight. In those early days there were few rules.

Senator John McCain famously compared the sport to "human cockfighting" and said MMA should be outlawed.

Weighing close to two hundred pounds, Randy won his bout in less than one minute; he was up against a fighter who tipped the scale at more than three hundred pounds. Before the fight, Randy's opponent predicted that he would "rip off Randy's arm."

Over the next fourteen years, Randy's heart and determination helped him become a standout as he competed at the highest level of MMA. He defeated the likes of Chuck Liddell, Vitor Belfort, and Tito Ortiz.

As a fan—and amateur martial arts competitor since my mid-twenties—I remember watching Randy in the early days of the UFC. His fighting ability was extraordinary, of course, but he also impressed me with the respect and class he showed for the sport and his opponents.

I spent time with Randy both at his gym, Xtreme Couture, in Las Vegas and later at South Florida's first *Beyond the Cage* MMA Expo that my team and I promoted.

When it was time to choose a guest of honor—someone respected by the world of MMA fans—Randy was our obvious choice. We couldn't have asked for a more accommodating celebrity. Fans lined up for hours, and Randy spent time with each person, taking photos and signing autographs.

Our event featured jiu-jitsu tournaments, and Randy agreed to do a one-hour MMA training seminar. His seminar lasted more than two hours! Randy's philosophy is simple: *"If you are going to do something, do it right."*

Despite his nickname, The Natural, Randy doesn't give much credence to the concept that he's a "natural" at any sport:

"I will take an athlete who is willing to work and have the self-discipline needed to compete over a 'natural talent' anytime. That's what it's all about—that's how I did it."

Like others in this book who have achieved great success, Randy says many people have difficulty getting out of their own way:

"People are held back from achieving their potential for a plethora of reasons, but ultimately it boils down to choice. We forget that everything is a choice and we have the freedom to decide what we do and what we want to commit to."

"I believe I was able to find everything, including the people I needed to help me make the most of the gifts God gave me."

Ask Randy what habits you should develop—what you should do each and every day—and you'll get a passionate response:

"Every day frame everything positively. Every day visualize success. Every day set small goals to get where you want to be—get 1 percent better every day!"

"If you love something, stand your ground. Stick with it! Losses are more important than wins because they are a gut check for what went wrong. You have to change something to have a better outcome next time."

I asked Randy what he thinks about during his fight-training process. He described it this way:

"When I have an upcoming fight, I see my opponent as a problem I have to solve and prepare accordingly."

MMA is an action-reaction sport, and Randy explains, *"There's not a lot of time to think. You need to depend on your preparation and training."*

Before his last fight, Randy told me:

"I am passionate about my sport. I know [my career] is coming to an end, but I want to go out on my terms."

Randy continues to be one of the all-time MMA favorites. Throughout his career he was often viewed as the underdog in many of his fights, but he became widely respected as one of the most resilient fighters. He had an overpowering will to win and an unsurpassed ability to bring other fighters to their breaking points.

The multifaceted fighter revealed a softer side in a 2012 interview with Maxim.com—namely that he is an avid fan and writer of poetry. *"I spent most of my life containing emotion so it wouldn't impair my performance. That's why the poems started coming out of me,"* he said.

Ever evolving, Randy is currently pursuing an acting career. He appeared on an episode of the History Channel's *The Human Weapon* and as part of the Season 19 cast of ABC's *Dancing with the Stars*.

In 2013, Spike TV announced a multi-year creative partnership with Randy. One of the projects birthed out of that partnership was *Fight Master: Bellator MMA*. The second, which aired in August 2014, was *Gym Rescue*, a series in the vein of Spike's *Bar Rescue* and *Tattoo Rescue*.

His movie appearances include the villain Sargon in *The Scorpion King 2: Rise of the Warrior* (2008), the 2011 film *Setup* with 50 Cent and Bruce Willis, the lead role in the 2012 action film *Hijacked*, and the character Toll Road in *The Expendables* movies.

Toll Road is the film's demolitions expert and is also an expert in grappling combat—the perfect role for the MMA legend. Randy loved Sylvester Stallone's movie *Rambo* and was privileged to work alongside him during *The Expendables* film series. Sly co-wrote, directed, and starred in the first film in 2010 and commented that Randy was the "toughest guy in the cast."

MMA fans in particular welcomed the release of *The Expendables 3* in 2014 when female UFC undefeated champ Ronda Rousey joined the cast, which also features Randy and Sly, along with Antonio Banderas, Jet Li, Wesley Snipes, Dolph Lundgren, Kelsey Grammer, Terry Crews, Mel Gibson, Harrison Ford, and Arnold Schwarzenegger.

Randy Couture's lion heart is something to be admired. His extraordinary life and career would not have been possible without his courage and determination. Take Randy's life as an example, and open your own heart to a world of possibilities. Dream big, love furiously, and fight for what you believe.

RANDY'S EMPOWERING THOUGHT: *"To me nothing is so big that you can't get over it if you are committed."*

DO IT DAILY:

▸ *Take extreme action to beat out the competition.* Remember that talent isn't everything—hard work, passion, and preparation are equally (if not more) important than talent.

▸ *Have the heart of a lion.* Just as a lion is king of the jungle, maintaining a lion heart filled with commitment and determination will beat out most challenges that come your way.

Dan Caldwell

Dan's Journey:

DRIVE-BY SHOOTINGS → NO "PLAN B" → WORLD-RECOGNIZED BRAND

One of the common threads in this book is overcoming challenges to trail blaze a path to success. In order to do this, you need to be a game changer. That means you need to find new, innovative ways to keep moving forward and indulge your passion. Dan Caldwell is a game changer, and his personal and professional success serve as an example of what we all can achieve.

Imagine investing $200 in something you love and watching it grow to over $200 million in just ten years. That's exactly what Dan Caldwell did back in 1997. He and his partners, Charles "Mask" Lewis and Tim "Sky-skrape" Katz, founded TapouT, generally recognized as the first brand to represent the sport of Mixed Martial Arts (MMA).

They had little money, but big hopes and dreams—and a love for what many saw as a brutal sport. In their eyes, MMA was a respectable sport that offered them a real opportunity.

Originally sold out of the trunk of a car, TapouT's line of apparel has grown into a true market force, and is now sold in over twenty thousand stores worldwide. It's a serious competitor with the likes of Nike and Under Armour. TapouT's rise to international success goes hand-in-hand with MMA's own historical rise in the world of sports.

MMA, a full-contact combat sport that allows the use of both striking and grappling techniques, draws on a variety of other combat sports and martial arts. In 1993 it was still illegal in most states, when an eight-man tournament with no weight classes and few rules debuted in Denver as the Ultimate Fighting Championship (later renamed UFC 1: The Beginning).

The age-old question of which martial arts discipline was the most effective finally would be answered. The competitors' fighting styles included boxing, traditional martial arts, kickboxing…and even a 440-pound Sumo wrestler. The answer was "none of the above."

The most unlikely participant shocked the world of combat sports that night, weighing in at only 170 pounds. Brazilian jiu-jitsu artist Royce Gracie easily defeated world-class athletes in other disciplines, achieving most submissions by lying flat on his back inviting his opponent to go for what looked like an easy victory. Royce then used his legs and arms to maneuver his competitor into positions that few had ever seen or experienced. Royce inflicted pain or restricted breathing to such a degree that each opponent would "tap-out," signaling that he was surrendering.

The developers of that first UFC championship planned it as a singular tournament, but it became a huge pay-per-view event that begged for a sequel. So a new sport was born—along with a new vocabulary and a new palette of fighting skills. *Arm bars, triangles, rear-necked chokes, leg locks*, and a host of other techniques were exposed to the mainstream.

One of my favorite descriptions expresses it well: **it's like playing chess with human body parts. If you don't tap-out, your arm or leg can easily snap—*tap or snap!***

Royce won the $50,000 prize, and, more importantly, the name Royce Gracie and the discipline of Brazilian jiu-jitsu became a phenomenon for athletes all over the world.

I remember my own amazement when I watched this historic pay-per-view event. With similar amazement, Dan Caldwell watched the tournament—and fell in love with the sport. But what separated Dan from so many others who watched that night was that he and his co-founders recognized an opportunity. Dan told me, *"There was no real brand for this up-and-coming sport."*

In the early days of MMA there were few rules—no biting, no eye gouging, no groin strikes, and rounds were limited to five minutes. The referee could stop the match only in cases of extreme injury, and matches ended by submission, knockout, or if a fighter's corner man threw in the towel.

Dan and his partners started TapouT with just a few hundred dollars and a commitment to stay true to the sport. He says, **"We were first, and this gave us great credibility."**

To establish a brand and a unique look, they created individual images and names for themselves: "Punkass," "Mask," and "Skyskrape." Feeling that traditional-style logos were too small, Dan told me, *"If we are paying these fighters to wear our brand, we needed to make sure everyone would see it."* This is how the TapouT logo became a visually no-miss brand. They maxed out their credit cards selling their T-shirts out of their cars, at small tables at underground MMA competitions, and at high school jiu-jitsu tournaments.

As MMA's wave built momentum around the world, so did TapouT. They began to pay a few hundred dollars to fighters like Chuck "The Iceman" Liddell to wear their brand on his walkout shirt on his way to the cage. Today's fighters can get *millions* for similar endorsements and paid sponsorships. Dan says of his company's growth:

"One step at a time we grew it into a monster of a company. We were doing a hundred million when our closest competitor was doing less than a million!"

In 2007, Spike TV aired the TapouT television series, featuring the three partners touring the country and looking for new up-and-coming fighters. By 2010, Authentic Brands Group LLC acquired TapouT for $200 million.

As an experienced publisher and distributor of entertainment fine art, I had represented several big brands for years—and since I was already a fan of MMA—I wanted to develop the first fine art line featuring these fighters. I met Dan through a friend, and we sat in TapouT headquarters as he showed me a video roll of sports and celebrity photography by Eric Williams.

I was sold on Eric's work from the moment I saw it. Dan put me in touch with Eric, and we published the art under the brand Beyond the Cage. We wanted to show the fighters more in lifestyle scenes rather than in "blood and guts." Both the fighters and the public enjoyed the art featuring such UFC fighters as Anderson "The Spider" Silva, Georges St-Pierre, "The California Kid" Uriah Faber, Wanderlei "The Axe Murderer" Silva, Chuck "The Iceman" Liddell among others.

Over time, I got to know "Punkass" better, and I soon realized that his story hit home for this book. Dan grew up in San Bernardino, California, which he describes as the murder capital of the United States:

"Drive-by shootings were regular occurrences. We had more murders per capita than any other place in the United States."

"My early life shaped me. I never felt in danger. I had good parents, but not much money."

"I decided to set higher standards for myself—that it was going to be different for me. What I saw showed me what I did not want."

"People are often constricted by their insecurities. I know I personally battled insecurities all of my life, so I know what it does to you. Insecurities will hold you down—and keep you down—if you let them. I lived in a world where I was just never good enough or smart enough. I never thought I could have what those successful people over on the other side of the tracks had!"

"When I finally got the courage to attempt something, I was so worried that I was going to fail that I overcompensated in every way. I would have to research everything I could find on whatever subject I was pursuing. I wanted to make sure I did it better and differently, and with more imagination than anyone else—because I had to!"

"I would live with it, constantly considering how I could better my idea. Once I started to have success in different areas, I began to gain confidence and learned to think less about my insecurities."

"You get this momentum, like a train traveling down the tracks. When the train starts moving a simple piece of scrap metal on the tracks could stop it, but once it starts to gain momentum it's virtually unstoppable!"

"Overcompensating for my personal insecurities has helped me forge ahead in life, blaze trails, and achieve things I never thought possible at one time."

"When chasing a goal, I have always made one commitment—a 'must' that I've always held—to make sure I do something every single day to advance toward my goal. No matter how small, I will never let that day go by without doing at least one thing."

"I constantly educate myself. If I'm in the gym, driving, or running, I am listening to a book, a podcast, or a YouTube video. I'm finding out those things I don't know—that I need to know. I am listening to other leaders or business-men who have written books, so that I can learn from their mistakes. I take some comfort in knowing that I am outworking my competition!"

"I always let myself know, as soon as I am attacking a new goal, that there is no Plan B. Once I start traveling down that path, nothing can stop me! I close all my doors of escape, and I will fight to the death."

"Rejecting the idea of a Plan B helps you adopt a sense of urgency too. In 1519, Hernán Cortés faced overwhelming odds when he landed in Mexico with only five hundred soldiers on his eleven ships. He knew he was going to face an Aztec army of over five hundred thousand men. Aware of his desperate circumstances, he ordered that all the ships be burned! Giving his small army no way to retreat, he demanded, 'Victory, or death with honor!' Those soldiers fought and were victorious in part because there was no Plan B."

"I eliminated my Plan B with my tattoos. I don't tell anyone to get tat-toos, but it was something that worked for me. The tattoos on my hands and neck represent that I can never again go back to a nine-to-five job. That was my burning-the-ships moment!"

"Today I carry a two-hundred-year-old Spanish coin wherever I go. It bears the image of Hernán Cortés, and along with those tattoos it reminds me that I have no Plan B. I must make it!"

"I love that military commercial that shows the soldiers jumping out of air-planes, rappelling from helicopters, and doing some of the coolest things you've ever seen. A voiceover simply says, 'If someone wrote a book about your life, would anyone want to read it?' That's what I want out of my life."

"The miles you must run to get to your goal are never easy—in fact, it's probably the most difficult thing you'll ever do. But do you really want to go through life in mediocrity? We are meant to experience life! Pur-

suing your dreams should not cause you to fear. Rather, the thought of being average should bring you fear, anxiety, and sleepless nights."

"I think everyone wants their life to be meaningful and to have a purpose. So why not chase that idea, invention, or career that excites your soul? After all, what's the worst that can happen: that you'll fail? We all fail! We must fail so that we can learn from those failures."

"I've had so many failures I've stopped counting! But my successes far outweigh my failures. Theodore Roosevelt once said, 'If he fails, at least he fails while daring greatly. So his place shall never be with those cold and timid souls who know neither victory nor defeat!' We owe ourselves that!"

"Often in life we need to move forward, past difficult situations. After my business partner Charles passed in a car accident, I realized there was too much to deal with. I couldn't even think about what I was going to do, or if I could handle it alone, or if I even wanted to. I just knew I had to deal with what was happening right now. We had 160 employees and a booming business. All of that was bigger than me or Charles."

"Later I had some personal issues because I hadn't really dealt with Charles's passing. I ended up having a hard breakdown a few months later when it struck me that my best friend in the world was gone. The one thing that had made me most happy was our collaboration—our endless nights of brainstorming on the business we both loved, and it would never happen again. That's a hard reality!"

"Ultimately, however, I realized that moving forward was something that Charles would have wanted."

"In life we sometimes lose people or experience tragedies, and even though nobody would blame us if we just lay down and quit, that is not an option. There are people depending on us to be strong and to keep moving forward."

"No one said life was going to be easy—not a life worth living anyway!"

Success stories come in many forms. Dan is a living example of someone who refused to allow where he began dictate where he would end up. He is an ambassador for MMA, and the TapouT brand continues his quest to challenge himself as an entrepreneur, actor, and film and TV producer. He is a role model for anybody who thinks they can't!

Dan's personal story is one of the most powerful, motivational, and inspirational stories in the world of business, and he loves sharing it with leaders and professionals. He shares many of the common threads exhibited by others in this book—he overcame his struggles and setbacks because he found his passion and fought hard to succeed. His unique entrepreneurial mind has made him a visionary game changer in the field of MMA. He also has strong feelings about his obligation to speak to tomorrow's leaders—high school and college students, and he loves fulfilling that obligation to inspire today's youth. To learn more about Dan, visit DanCaldwellSpeaks.com and MentorMojo.com.

DAN'S EMPOWERING THOUGHT: *"We cannot let our dreams die from any self-doubt or insecurity; we must stay stronger than our imperfections."*

DO IT DAILY:

▸ *Be on a constant daily search to learn the things or develop the skills you need to achieve.* There are always new ways to strengthen your mind. Seek them out and use them to reach your own pinnacle of success.

▸ *Be a game changer.* Turn your insecurities and limitations into tools for growth. Use your own uniqueness as an asset to separate yourself from others, always working to improve and leave your competition in the dust.

Ron Greschner

NEW YORK RANGER

Ron's Journey:

SLOW ICE SKATER → NHL STAR → GRESCHNER FOUNDATION FOR
AUTISM AWARENESS

NHL maverick Ron Greschner knows the value of going the extra mile. He shares the common thread of grit and determination. Just like Ron, if you have found what you love, and want to take it to the next level, you are going to have to go the extra mile to achieve your dreams.

Ron Greschner played 16 years with the New York Rangers professional hockey team—as a defenseman and a leader. Ron's entire career with his beloved Rangers spans 982 games, 179 goals, 431 assists, and 610 points. He is without a doubt one of the brightest and most likeable stars in NHL history.

"Gresch," as he is fondly called by friends and fans, told me:

"To get into the NHL takes a certain amount of natural ability, but then it comes down to how much you really want it. I was the 32nd overall player selected by the Rangers in 1974."

"The hardest thing about the NHL is staying in the NHL; you have to prove yourself every day, every month, and every year."

"Every game I ever played I was nervous—not scared. I had to play and perform each time I was on the ice. I loved the game; I didn't want to screw up."

"I had tunnel vision and stayed focused on each shift. To prepare, I always studied film of the guys I was facing, and it gave me a competitive edge."

***"Believe me I had plenty of weaknesses. But instead of accepting a weakness, I did my best to turn it around.** Speed was always an issue; most guys were faster than me. So I learned to play smarter. I learned to play the angles. I was able to read plays developing from either end of the ice and to be in the right spot at the right time."*

Ron's love for hockey started at an early age. He had the desire, but coming from a very small town of only 150 people made it difficult to get noticed. But his support at home proved key:

"My mom and dad were great role models. They taught me that whatever you start, you need to finish. They instilled great work habits. I would stay after practice and practice even more."

"When I think back now, I really appreciate my parents more than ever. Whether I played well or not so well, Mom and Dad would treat me the same. I think that had a big impact on my confidence."

"The way I see it, if you get a chance to do something, do it the best you can and it's likely you can achieve plenty in life. People need to know that almost every day you will need to overcome something on your way to success. You have to approach it all with an attitude that says, 'I will not be defeated!'"

"I don't think anybody wanted to play hockey as much as I did. My whole life I wanted to play the game. Hard work, mental focus—I would do anything I had to do to get into the big leagues. Whatever your goal is, you need that to be your attitude."

Reflecting on how people fail to meet their goals and achieve their dreams, Ron believes a fear of failure stops most people:

"They are concerned and afraid that people will look down on them if they fail. My advice is this: what other people think doesn't matter! You need to focus on your play. Do it the best you can, and don't let what others say interfere with your mindset or how you feel about yourself."

Ron advises up-and-coming players that there is no replacement for hard work. He plainly tells them:

"Dedicate yourself to working hard, and stay away from drugs. Whether you agree with your coaches or not, listen to them. The teams that I played with in the seventies could not compete with today's teams, due to the new training methods. If you don't train, you will not be able to compete."

"Develop that never-give-up attitude. You will have failures along the way, but the key thing is to not give up—have perseverance. Take my dad's advice. He always said, 'Make sure you have a good time when you're alive, because you will be dead a lot longer!'"

Hockey is a tough sport requiring a lot of drive, determination, and *heart:*

"I had lots of injuries over my career: broken hand, broken feet—I broke my nose six times! I've had all my teeth knocked out. The way I saw it, a hurt ankle or knocked-out teeth are far from your heart. So even with all my teeth knocked out I would get up and get back on this

ice—I never missed a shift. I don't say that to prove I was a tough guy. It's just that if you want to go big-time, you need to have a big heart."

Ron certainly has a big heart. After retiring from pro hockey, he established the Greschner Foundation to support autism research and awareness. He wisely believes that *"When you reach a certain level, you need to remember where you came from and give back."*

Ron shows us that going the extra mile is a way to ensure success. In your pursuit of your dreams, figure out what you can do to dramatically increase the odds of achievement by going the extra mile.

RON'S EMPOWERING THOUGHT: *"What other people think doesn't matter! You need to focus on your play. Do it the best you can, and don't let what others say interfere with your mindset or how you feel about yourself."*

DO IT DAILY:

▸ *When an opportunity arises, there is no choice—give 110 percent effort!* Often, that additional ten percent or going the extra mile can be the difference between success and failure.

▸ *Don't let fear get in your way.* We all have fears, but we should all work to use the emotion of fear as a way to elevate our game. If you do this, you will compete at a much higher level.

Jim Davis

GARFIELD CREATOR

Jim's Journey:

CHILDHOOD ASTHMA → LOVED TO DRAW → MORE THAN 263 MILLION
DAILY READERS

Jim Davis is a true visionary and an amazing artist. But like the others in this book, he knows that living the best life means putting forth your best in all that you do. Jim is quick to point out that pure talent alone won't help you overcome adversity, but commitment, passion, and a positive attitude will.

Early in my career of publishing and marketing animation artwork, I recognized a few key licenses that could have a significant, positive impact on our business. High on that list was Paws Inc., the corporate home built by entrepreneur and artist Jim Davis and his lazy, fat, lasagna-eating cat named Garfield.

I met Jim's staff at a licensing trade show, and from the outset they couldn't have been a nicer group of people. Nevertheless, it was clear that their due-diligence process would be intense even though my company had experience representing other big name studios. This would be the first time Paws Inc. would ever award a license to an outside company for publishing *Garfield* artwork.

After presenting our business and marketing plans for several months, Paws Inc. granted us a production and distribution license. I soon discovered that at Paws Inc.—as with many successful organizations—it all starts at the top.

I drove through the cornfields of Indiana to reach the world headquarters of Paws Inc., to sit down with Jim Davis and talk about our plans. More than a brilliant artist and cartoonist, he's a man who gives all he has to provide opportunities for others to succeed.

Almost instantly, I could see Jim's genius as he reeled off one great idea after another. Most other studios we dealt with previously (such as Disney or Warner Bros.) no longer enjoyed the personal leadership of their original founders. Having the man who truly understands his brand and why people are so fond of the character he created proved *priceless*.

Audiences and critics alike have shown their fondness for Garfield. Over the years Jim and Garfield have earned four Emmy Awards. In addition, they have earned other prestigious awards, including the 1989 Reuben Award from the National Cartoonist Society for overall excellence in cartooning. The National Arbor Day Foundation presented its Good Steward Award to Jim and Garfield in 1990, and the State of Indiana honored Jim as a Distinguished Hoosier a year later.

Their TV show, *Garfield and Friends*, has run in over 130 countries. Plush toys, books, T-shirts, figurines, and so much more are available for people to enjoy their own little piece of Garfield.

In 2004, Garfield starred in a feature film Jim produced in conjunction with Twentieth Century Fox—*Garfield: The Movie.*

As I worked with Jim and got to know him on a personal level, it became obvious that his story—and his wonderful insights and words of wisdom—belonged in this book. Like the other amazing contributors to this project, Jim did not have success handed to him.

He grew up on a small farm near Fairmount, Indiana, with his family and twenty-five cats. We catch a glimpse of Jim's childhood on the farm in the character of Garfield's owner, Jon Arbuckle, who was also raised on a farm by his parents.

"We grew up with little money, and that was fine because we had plenty of laughter and plenty of room to play. And I developed an imagination as big as the sky."

Having developed asthma as a child, Jim's first mentor was his mom, who said to him one day, "Here's a pencil—now draw!" And draw he did.

"To be honest with you I was not a very good artist at all, but drawing gave me an outlet. Looking back, I guess my biggest hardship wasn't my asthma, it was my lack of talent!"

"In fact, I've come to believe my asthma was more of a benefit than a hindrance, because it gave me opportunity to practice over and over again. I learned early on that artists have to accept that they will have plenty of bad cartoons before they come up with a good one."

In the early 60s, Jim worked for a time at a local advertising agency, but in 1969 he began assisting on Tom Ryan's comic strip, *Tumbleweeds*. He then created his own comic strip, *Gnorm Gnat*, that ran for five years in the *Pendleton [Indiana] Times*, but when he tried to sell it to a national comic strip syndicate, an editor rejected him with: "Your art is good, and your gags are great—but bugs? Nobody can relate to bugs!" After five years—and multiple failed attempts to get *Gnorm Gnat* syndicated—Jim simply ended the strip one day by drawing a giant foot coming from the sky to crush Gnorm!

"Getting into the business was tough—I mean really tough. I could have wallpapered a cathedral with all the rejection letters I received!"

Jim willingly did *anything* to stay in the game to do what he was most passionate about.

On his journey to create *Garfield*, he went from sweeping the floors, to drawing backgrounds for others, to lettering their comic strips. Eventually he focused his attention on developing his iconic original comic strip. He studied and evaluated the market, considering what was already being done. He realized *"There were plenty of dogs out there, like Snoopy and Marmaduke, but no cats!"*

He developed his beloved Garfield character from a grouchy cat he remembered from his early days on the farm. His grandfather, James Garfield Davis, inspired the cat's name.

Jim expresses a unique perspective when he talks about adversity:

"Adversity actually gets me excited. I love the challenges. Hey, when things are going too well, we tend to get fat and happy. 'Fun' is in the adversity!"

"You don't learn much from success. I live for adversity—that's what pulls people together. You learn from it, and it feels great."

Jim traces his success from 1978:

"After two years of working on **Garfield***, 41 newspapers picked up the strip. One Chicago newspaper decided to drop the strip, and it received over 1,300 letters from readers demanding they reinstate* **Garfield***. Since first publishing in 1978, we've become the world's most widely syndicated comic strip. We're read by more than 263 million people in 2,600 newspapers around the world every day."*

He has a great handle on his own mindset:

"When I am in the right mindset, I have a habit of doing lots—getting way ahead of the curve well before something is due. However, when I don't feel like doing something, I simply don't do it. So it's particularly important for me to be both physically and mentally prepared for any project. You can't force a gag. The trick is to have fun with the writing; when people 'get' the gag, they become loyal readers and fans."

"I don't let the pressure get to me. If I did, I'd end up lowering my standards. I prevent that by sticking to the basics and having fun when creating."

"Believe it or not, if something is not going bad, I tell my team, 'Let's create some what-if scenarios to prepare us for the future and keep us from being afraid of failure.'"

When I asked Jim what holds people back, he shared a few things they can—and should—avoid:

"Don't put roadblocks up in front of you; there will be plenty without you creating your own. You must act as your biggest ally."

"Don't get too involved with the details. Focus on starting (and keeping) the process moving."

"Never allow your competition to distract you. Keep moving forward or you will fall behind."

"Don't be paralyzed by a fear of failure. I play golf because it provides me with failure! It's okay to be embarrassed—as long as it gets you closer to your goal."

"Don't be afraid of work. Rather, maintain a good, old-fashioned work ethic. Avoiding work will hold anybody back from reaching his or her true potential."

"Don't set your goals too high—set smaller, achievable ones (complete with timetables). Achieving those goals builds your confidence. Every goal I hit excites me!"

"Whatever you can do or dream you can, begin it. Boldness has genius, power and magic in it." —attributed to German author Johann Wolfgang von Goethe

Jim offers specific advice for up-and-coming artists:

"Your voice will come from your experiences."

"Read, read, read! To be a good comic strip artist you must be a good writer. Art is important, but writing can make or break you. Learn all you can by watching movies and TV, socializing, studying people, and analyzing their behavior. Try different drawing tools and styles. Above all find something different to say—something unique—something that is especially 'you'!"

"I still work twelve to fourteen hours a day because I simply love what I do."

When I asked the renowned artist about retiring, he said, *"I want to live to be very old and continue to write until somebody taps me on the shoulder and says, 'Jim, you're not here anymore!' I want to continue to make people laugh. I certainly enjoy seeing the impact it has on others."*

Jim Davis has a long history of giving back. Along with other acts of generosity, he founded the Professor Garfield Foundation dedicated to supporting children's literacy.

Surrounded by creative ideas and diverse opportunities, Jim clearly knows where his priority lies: *"As long as we take care of the cat, the cat will take care of us!"*

Jim's dedication and wisdom inspire everyone whose life he touches, including mine. I feel fortunate to call him my friend and business colleague. I consider him a mentor who has taught me by his example. His mindset and insight have proven indispensable, and my hope is they will do the same for you. He truly exemplifies, and lives, the best of life.

JIM'S EMPOWERING THOUGHT: *"Adversity actually gets me excited. I love the challenges. Hey, when things are going too well, we tend to get fat and happy. 'Fun' is in the adversity!"*

DO IT DAILY:

▶ *Pursue what you love with a "never-give-up" attitude.* Combine that with commitment and passion, and you will have an edge up on most others.

▶ *Want the best? Give your best.* Life often acts as a mirror-and will reflect whatever stands in front of it. So give the best to get the best in return.

Chris Isaak

Chris' Journey:

SON OF A POTATO-CHIP FACTORY WORKER → STUDENT BODY PRESIDENT → ROCK STAR

If you don't appreciate the ups and downs of life, then you will never be satisfied. Lasting success is contingent upon learning to value all aspects of life—not just the good ones. In addition, we need to develop an appreciation for the people who help us on our journey, so that we can help others progress as well.

"The biggest lessons I've learned in the music business are not really about the music at all—they're about life."

So says Chris Isaak, successful singer, songwriter, bandleader, and actor who worked hard for more than a quarter century, recording international hits like "Wicked Game" and "Baby Did a Bad, Bad Thing." Moreover, he has appeared in movies (*The Silence of the Lambs* and *That Thing You Do!*) and starred in his own Showtime series, *The Chris Isaak Show*. Chris shares some of the wisdom he gained along the way:

"No matter what you do in life, somewhere along the way you need to learn a little about helping out the other guy, about being honest, and

166

about the other kind of qualities you want to see in yourself—otherwise I think you're in big trouble in this world and setting yourself up for, at best, momentary hits and momentary happiness."

"I'm a very lucky guy because one of my heroes became a mentor to me: the late, great Roy Orbison. How amazing is that? Roy inspired me as an artist before I met him, but he inspired me even more when I got to actually work with the man. For a legendary guy, Roy showed a lot of humility."

"He did so many things that I watched and thought, 'That's a lesson I'll try to remember.' For instance, I hadn't had a hit yet when we first met. I wasn't important, and he certainly didn't need to be nice to me. Yet Roy immediately treated me like I was a friend and an equal. And that is something I try to remember to this day: **treat everybody like you would like to be treated. That's not just a music business lesson—that's a great life lesson.**"

"When I met Roy, I was opening for him. 'Wicked Game' had not come out yet, so nobody cared about me at all. But Roy was in the middle of a big comeback, so there was tons of media interest, and everybody would show up to take his picture. Whenever it would be time to take a picture, my brother heard Roy say, 'Go get Chris.' Even though it was him they all wanted in their pictures, Roy put his arm around me to force them to use a picture with me in it too. So the next day in all the papers there were captions with Roy Orbison and my name misspelled!"

"Roy was a classy guy, and that was a big lesson I learned from somebody who was a lot bigger than me."

When Roy Orbison posthumously received the Iconic Riff Award for "Pretty Woman" from the Musicians Hall of Fame in 2014, Chris was honored to present the award.

When Chris started out, he knew nothing about show business, and he didn't know anybody in the business. All he had heard was that *everybody* in show business was crooked. His first producer and manager was Erik

Jacobsen, best known for producing The Lovin' Spoonful's early hits, including "Do You Believe in Magic," "Daydream," and "Summer in the City."

After striking a deal, someone told Chris that he shouldn't have signed that contract. He recalled:

"This became a big turning point for me, because I finally decided to trust somebody in this business. Instead of going around Erik, I went straight to him with my concerns and he said, 'Fine, let's change it—what do you want to do?'"

"I thought, Wow, I'm dealing with an honest and reasonable man here! I learned that the best way to do business isn't to be tricky; it's to be honest. I could have learned the wrong lesson if I had dealt with the wrong guy, but instead I learned a very good lesson in life."

When it comes to the music business, Chris has seen a lot of talented people fall short of reaching their full potential:

"From what I've seen in the music business, what holds people back is either laziness or thinking that the whole thing is just one big party. They forget that getting the best things in life actually takes a little sweat. If you're a musician, leave the partying to the people out in front. Your party is the music. So I never drank and I never got high— that allowed me to focus on the music and on the work."

Chris attributes his success—at least in part—to an honest work ethic he learned by watching his parents as he grew up:

"My dad drove a forklift and Mom was a worker in a potato chip factory. They both got up every morning and went to work—and they loved it."

"All the guys in my band come from working-class backgrounds, and I believe we're all thrilled to have a job we like. So we respect the work, and we respect the people who give us the work."

"The opportunity to make music for people is a pleasure and a gift. We love it so much that in twenty years we've never missed a show. That's a record we take pride in!"

"So I show up for my job, and I smile and work hard because the audience is your boss. If you do a good job, they'll hire you back. Remember, every night is really an audition, and you want to be invited back."

Just because Chris recognizes that making music is his "job," it doesn't mean he recommends being all business and no pleasure:

"Have fun up there! Nobody wants to pay to have their teeth pulled."

Chris has made it a habit to take obstacles in stride by approaching them with a positive attitude. When he looks at what might be considered obstacles, he remembers an old cowboy song he loves. It has a line in it about playing with your troubles "like a toy."

"I always thought my troubles in life were so few that I never even prayed to God about them. There just never were enough to mention. I had my family and my health, and beyond that everything else was groovy."

When Chris first started out, before he knew anybody in show business, he realized that the car he was driving could never get him from the little town of Stockton, California, where he grew up, to Los Angeles, the city of dreams. But he didn't think of it as an obstacle. Rather, he just thought, *"Okay, I can make it to San Francisco."* So he borrowed a friend's car and drove to San Francisco one Wednesday. He sang at a coffeehouse for free, and he thought, *"Boy! I'm in show business now!"*

"That's a wonderful thing about being a beginner: you bring tons of energy and optimism. And you have no idea how high the mountain is because you've never been on top."

Chris told a story about country singer-songwriter/musician Buck Owens. Buck was working with some young guy, helping him with his music career. Then Buck stopped working with him. Someone asked him why, and Buck said it was because the guy didn't want to be a star as much as Buck wanted him to be a star!

"When I hear people say things like 'I could make it—if someone would only introduce me to the right people,' it drives me crazy! I call that the Magic Door Syndrome. I never approached it that way, and I don't advise anybody to stand around waiting for somebody to hand you your dream on a silver platter. You've got to build your own Magic Door, and then step through it with everything you've got."

"The common thread I see among successful people is this: they really want it, and they work hard at it."

Chris sheds light on an important quality—appreciation. We must be appreciative of all that we have in life. Even while you are working to better yourself, appreciate where you are and how far you have come.

CHRIS'S EMPOWERING THOUGHT: *"I show up for my job, and I smile and work hard because the audience is your boss. If you do a good job, they'll hire you back."*

DO IT DAILY:

▸ **Work hard, but don't forget to have fun.** It is true that finding success means putting in some sweat and tears, but it doesn't mean you can't have fun along the way.

▸ ***Develop the mantra: "It's nice to be important, but it's more important to be nice."*** There is no reason why you can't win at the game of life while making people feel great along the way.

David Diehl

ALL PRO NEW YORK GIANT

David's Journey:

LOWER MIDDLE-CLASS → 160TH NFL DRAFT SELECTION → SUPER BOWL CHAMPION

Intensity sometimes carries a negative connotation, but that is not the case with David Diehl. Intensity is what allows David to stand out as a true champion.

There's nothing like going out to dinner with a 6-foot-5 Goliath of a man who weighs over 300 pounds. I'm talking about David Diehl, the New York Giants' left offensive tackle and Pro Bowl player.

Throughout his career, David has received many awards, including the Wellington Mara NFL Man of the Year Award in 2012. He was also honored, along with other members of the New York Giants team, at the White House by President Barack Obama for winning the 2012 Super Bowl.

David shared with me his story of growing up in a lower-middle-class neighborhood in Chicago. His parents were of Croatian descent on his mother's side and German descent on his father's, and he gives them all the credit for his success. So it was one of his biggest losses when his father passed away of a heart attack in 2003, just as David's pro career was getting underway:

"My father passed away just two weeks before my first regular-season game with the Giants. He was only fifty-nine. I was devastated."

"My parents did not push me in any single direction, but they taught me that if you start something you need to finish it. They told me to do what I love and give it all I have."

"I was a fifth-round NFL draft choice in 2003 and was the 160th overall selection. There are many more-gifted athletes than me playing in the NFL, but few have my mental strength. If you want to build anything, you need a strong foundation."

David certainly has a strong physical foundation, but it's his incredible mental strength known around the league that has enabled him to become one of the NFL's elite competitors.

"Before the season I train very hard, watch film, and lift weights so I am totally prepared for getting out there on the field with nothing to worry about. If you're thinking too much you can't be at your fullest potential."

"In my opinion, people don't reach their potential because they hold themselves back. Whether it is fear or self-doubt, the mind can be your biggest weapon and your greatest threat. You have to learn to work outside your comfort zone and override your mind. Preparation will give you that edge."

David's philosophy for success has to do with mental toughness:

"I have never accepted the word no, *and I don't understand the word* can't. *Adversity happens every day, but we have the opportunity to bounce back by being mentally tough and working hard."*

"What makes me tick is my passion to work and accomplish a goal. Everything I have gotten in my life has been through hard work—nothing was ever given to me. I say, 'Believe!' If you do believe, your belief becomes your philosophy and driving force."

"My advice is to pursue your dreams: set goals, have a vision, work hard, and deal head-on with fear and failure. Believe totally that you are in control of your life and your own destiny."

"I think most people, when asked, would choose to be good or great at something over not being good or great. A person may want to be a great NFL player, a great teacher, a great doctor, a great coach, or whatever. Yes, they want to be great, but they don't want to become great! What does that mean? It means they won't pay the price to become great. They won't put in the work and they won't overcome the mindset holding them back."

"I feel most people know how to live a fulfilling life. The problem isn't knowing—it's doing. It's acting. As Russell Crowe said in the film Gladiator, *'At my signal, unleash hell!'"*

David ended the interview with this:

"Winning the Super Bowl didn't define who I am, but it defined who I can become. The birth of my daughter Addison gave me a different purpose in life. She helps me see better; she gives me a vision of what life is really all about."

If you can be intense in the positive and healthy areas of your life and career, you will benefit. Just like being your best, and giving it all you've got, being intense means you are committed to working for your success.

DAVID'S EMPOWERING THOUGHT: *"Pursue your dreams: set goals, have a vision, work hard, and deal head-on with fear and fail-*

ure. Believe totally that you are in control of your life and your own destiny."

DO IT DAILY:

▸ ***Finish what you start.*** No task is too small or too big to push aside. When you make a decision to begin, don't stop until you reach the end.

▸ ***Stay intense.*** Intensity is a gift. It gives you focus, keeps you grounded, and allows you to overcome the enormous adversity life can often serve up.

Evander Holyfield

BOXING ICON

Evander's Journey:

ACADEMIC STRUGGLES → OLYMPIAN → 5X WORLD HEAVYWEIGHT
CHAMPION

Known as one of the most talented heavyweight boxers in professional boxing history, perhaps Evander's strongest muscle has always been his strong heart. For most of the participants in this book, a strong heart is a common thread with which they can all relate. A strong heart moves you in the direction of your dreams, smashing through obstacles in your path and bringing you that much closer to success. Your heart not only pumps blood through your body, it energizes your life and gives you the ability and opportunity to overcome.

Any fan of boxing will tell you that, without question, Evander Holyfield will go down in history as one of the all-time greatest boxers, but he will also be remembered as a person who exemplifies the *warrior* attitude. He said, ***"Boxing—or life—is about what you put into it. If you're not willing to put all you have into something, you will get little out of it."***

Based on my personal experience with him, I can also add that Evander happens to be one of the nicest and most giving athletes around.

Evander was born in Atmore, Alabama, in 1962 and was the youngest of nine children. As a youngster, he moved with his family to Atlanta where he began boxing at just twelve years old.

His achievements are second to none. He had an amateur boxing record of 160 wins and only 14 losses, knocking out 76 opponents. He was the National Golden Gloves Champion and won a bronze medal in the light heavyweight division at the 1984 Summer Olympic Games in Los Angeles.

At the age of twenty-one, Evander turned pro. Known as "The Real Deal," he became the undisputed champion in both the cruiserweight and heavyweight divisions. Evander is the only five-time World Heavyweight Champion with victories over iconic fighters such as George Foreman, Larry Holmes, Riddick Bowe, and "Iron" Mike Tyson (twice).

Evander described his early days to me:

"As a young kid, I came from a very negative world; most would consider where I grew up as the ghetto. I didn't learn how to read and felt very bad about myself. I was very insecure. I never understood why I couldn't read."

"Dad never went to school; Mom only had a sixth-grade education. But Mom always said, 'I am poor, but you are not. You have a chance not to make the mistakes I made.'"

"My mom was a big motivator. She told me that if I would master one thing, I would do well. That one thing for me was boxing. She strongly stressed respect—not to be prejudiced against anybody."

"Even my first coach told me, 'People don't choose their own skin color, so don't ever judge anybody by their color.'"

"When I was fifteen, he told me I could be heavyweight champ of the world. He set me on the right track by reinforcing positives to me. Fact is, most all the people that helped me along the way were white. If I was prejudiced, I never would have gotten the opportunities I've had."

Evander went on to describe his drive to pursue those opportunities and how he developed as a boxer:

"As I've grown older, I have learned that if you love something you can be successful. Many things along the way won't work out, but if you love what you're doing, you can overcome all. In life you can learn anything—you may not be the best, but you can learn. I've always been open to listening to others, following directions, and making sure I did not quit."

"Looking back, I now realize that my biggest asset as a kid was my mother. She always stressed sports and God. I had plenty of whoopings as a kid, but I developed a never-quit attitude early on. Having very little, I just kept practicing until I was better than anyone else. I was brought up with the Word of God. He says, 'Fear not.' And every time I wanted to do something real bad, I prayed, 'Please, Jesus, help me.'"

"When I was a kid, I really didn't enjoy boxing. I could barely get through a three-round fight because I was fighting in the South, and I was rarely given a fair shot at a decision. I let that get to me, and so I didn't pace myself. I just went out there trying to hit as hard as I could, and I often lost my stamina early. When I got older, I was able to travel. I found the fights were judged more fairly, so I learned to pace myself. I learned the importance of relaxing in the ring. And once I learned that, my wind has never been a factor again."

"I learned early on that life is a constant test. It was never about size for me—often I would fight bigger and stronger guys. It never mattered; I was willing to pay the necessary price to be the best. A great boxer knows that somebody will always come along who will hit harder than you, and even be more talented. I learned to develop different

strategies for different fights. There's no single 'master plan' that will beat all styles. Ninety percent of men would love to be boxers, but if you ask them if they're willing to pay the price, you mostly get nervous laughter!"

I remember watching Evander Holyfield fight in the 1984 Summer Olympics in which most people concluded he didn't get a fair deal after a controversial disqualification. His attitude is something to be admired: *"Many people believe I was robbed at the Olympics. The way I see it, you need to take the bitter with the sweet. I think my experiences as a kid not always getting what was 'fair' made me better equipped to handle what happened at the Olympics. My philosophy is don't let someone else steal your joy. Even if you don't get the decision, keep the victory!"*

For all of us who grew up watching Evander fight, I just *had* to ask what was going through his mind during the famous tenth round of his fight against Riddick Bowe, generally considered one of the greatest rounds in heavyweight boxing history. Bowe was a much bigger man, and just about any other fighter would have gone down from the punishment Evander took. But Evander showed incredible heart and demonstrated the warrior's mentality for which he is famous.

He explained: *"I never worried about losing or getting hurt. I just gave it all I had; I put it all on the line. I was saying to myself, 'Don't quit before you get where you want to be!'"*

Next we turned our conversation to what may be one of the most notorious events in boxing—perhaps in all of sporting history. It was 1997. With forty seconds left in the third round of his contest against Mike Tyson, Tyson, who was losing by a large margin, decided to bite Holyfield's ear. He didn't just bite it; he took a chunk out of it! Tyson was immediately disqualified and Evander kept his heavyweight championship belt.

Evander's first reaction as we spoke was laughter: "Funny thing is, when I was a kid and couldn't beat my older brother or sister, I used to bite them so I could win!" He went on, "Tyson bit my ear because of fear. He was frustrated. He was losing, and he was afraid to lose. What he was really saying when he bit me was 'I quit!'"

Evander likes to keep things simple. When he announced his retirement from boxing in 2012, he stated, "The game's been good to me, and I hope I've been good to the game."

Evander is, and always will be, the ultimate warrior. Evander Holyfield is ranked as the greatest cruiserweight of all time by the highly regarded online boxing forum *The Boxing Scene*. He's had endorsement deals with Coca-Cola and Sega Genesis, and he was chosen to carry the Olympic torch for the 1996 games.

EVANDER'S EMPOWERING THOUGHT: *"My philosophy is don't let someone else steal your joy. Even if you don't get the decision, keep the victory."*

DO IT DAILY:

▸ *It's all about the effort.* Don't come up short or be beaten by your competition because of a lack of preparation and effort. Have no limit, no boundaries, and no hesitation in giving every last ounce of effort you have.

▸ *Take the bitter with the sweet.* There will be good times and bad. But always remember that better days are ahead. Weather the storm, remain resilient in the strong winds, and be willing to accept that it may not always go your way, but if you have heart, you can withstand any of life's punches thrown at you.

Snoop Dogg

HIP-HOP AND RAP ARTIST

Snoop's Journey:

GANG MEMBER → CLASS CLOWN → 30 MILLION ALBUMS

We learn them the hard way, and sometimes the easy way. But the lessons life gives us are often more valuable than the easily attained success it offers. If viewed properly, each of these lessons offer an amazing opportunity to learn and educate. We can implement the lessons learned from adversity and use them to better ourselves and move forward in life.

Perhaps you wonder why I would include Snoop Dogg in a book like this. Considering his upbringing and background, who better to send a message to inner city youth that they too can be successful in life? The reality is that Snoop learned an enormous amount about life through dealing with some of life's most difficult situations. But it was learning those lessons in the manner that he did that has given him the perspective that has changed the way he views life.

Most know the side of Snoop associated with his alleged gang membership in the infamous Rollin' 20 Crips on the east side of Long Beach, California, and from his numerous brushes with the law. But the reality is that over the years, Snoop Dogg has grown to become a role model and mentor to those who face the same challenges he once did.

Born Calvin Cordozar Broadus Jr., in 1971, Snoop Dogg has risen from his Long Beach roots to become one of the most successful musicians in recent history. As an award-winning rapper, singer-songwriter, record producer, and actor, he has already left a legacy of music around the world, to the tune of over thirty million albums sold. Snoop has been associated with some of the top recording labels—including Death Row Records, No Limit Records, Priority/Capitol/EMI Records, and Geffen Records.

His father, a Vietnam veteran, singer, and mail carrier, left the family when Snoop was only three months old. His mother gave him his now-famous nickname because she thought he looked like the Snoopy character in the *Peanuts* cartoons.

Snoop's talent was evident at an early age when he began singing and playing the piano at Golgotha Trinity Baptist Church. But it wasn't until he was in the sixth grade that he started rapping.

According to Snoop, *"People thought I was going to be a comedian— not a rapper. I was always the class clown."*

I had the chance to interview Snoop during a press conference where he was promoting his youth football league. Snoop is a certified football coach and avid sports fan (including football, hockey, and baseball).

"Football coaches—not rap stars or musicians—helped make me in the long run. They were my true mentors. I want to give something back—to give these kids something I never had."

"It is very important for kids to have mentors and role models. I try to let each kid get to know me as a person; then he can trust me. They need to have someone they can talk to."

"I asked one kid who wasn't really good enough to be on the team if he wanted to be the water boy. He said yes—and he learned what football was all about.

The next year he was the most valuable player on the team! Now that's what it's all about."

"I want the best for the kids. I want to see who will be the next superstar. You don't need to be the best football player. If you have the heart and desire, you can really enjoy the game and be successful."

"I would tell you to pass this along to your readers: if a kid can have a winning attitude in any sport, or in school, or in anything he tries, he can certainly be a winner!"

This holds true for Snoop's own son. As I was updating the stories for this book, I learned that Snoop's philosophy has paid off. His son Cordell, a high school senior at the time this book went to press, is on the top national recruiting list for college football wide receivers, being recruited by some of the nation's top programs including LSU, Baylor, Notre Dame and Florida State. In February 2015, he committed to playing for UCLA.

Despite the concerns some people have with Snoop, you can see through his better-known quotes that he has tried to empower youth over the years:

"Love goes unappreciated a lot of times, but you still gotta keep giving it."

"It's so easy for a kid to join a gang, to do drugs...we should make it that easy to be involved in football and academics. Sometimes a loss is the best thing that can happen. It can teach you what you should have done—and what you should do next time."

"If it's flipping hamburgers at McDonald's, be the best hamburger flipper in the world. Whatever you do, you have to master your craft."

In 2012, Snoop Dogg announced, in conjunction with his first reggae album, that he was changing his name to *Snoop Lion*. Promoting the album *Reincarnation* on the *Howard Stern Show*, Snoop explained:

"Growing up in the environment I came from, I am not proud of all I did. But it was a learning experience...Snoop Lion is like a transformation for me. My role models and mentors used to be drug dealers and gangsters. Now I am feeding off positive energy. Going to jail showed me a place that I did not want to be."

SNOOP'S EMPOWERING THOUGHT: *"Sometimes a loss is the best thing that can happen. It can teach you what you should have done and what you should do next time."*

DO IT DAILY:

▸ *Go all out.* Whatever it is you do, become a master of your craft. Remember that how you do anything is how you should do everything. Whether big or small, take the time and devote the energy to be the best in all you do.

▸ *Learn from your past to build a better future.* Recognize that mistakes and bad decisions are simply part of the journey. But what you take away from those decisions is what can be the difference in what you can accomplish much later in your life.

Keith Askins

MIAMI HEAT 3X NBA CHAMPION

Keith's Journey:

CHILD OF DIVORCE → VOLUNTEER COACH → 25-YEAR NBA CAREER

The best word to describe Keith Askins is *grounded*. Keith is all about positive beliefs, optimism, developing your problem-solving skills, and cultivating a strong social network, all while remaining grounded and understanding your position in life. His accomplishments could never have been achieved without his dedication and positive mindset. It was that perspective that gave him a level headed approach in life.

Six-foot-seven-inch Keith Askins played basketball for the University of Alabama where his coach, Winfrey "Wimp" Sanderson, told him, "I won't guarantee you'll play, but I *will* guarantee you a good education."

"That was fine with me," recalled Keith. He was grounded enough to recognize the opportunity staring him in the face.

Keith never expected to play in the NBA—he wasn't drafted like most NBA players, but in 1990 the Miami Heat picked him up. "To be honest, not being drafted had very little impact on me because I had plenty of job opportunities outside of basketball."

However, Keith's aggressive play and long-range shooting proved attractive to the newly formed Miami Heat franchise.

"My coach called me one day to tell me about a new expansion team, the Miami Heat. He thought it just might be a good fit for me. He told me, 'You are young and athletic—it just may work.' So I gathered up all I had in the world—a suitcase full of clothes and a few hundred dollars—and I went down to Miami. And now here I am, in my twenty-fourth year with the Heat, as both a player and a coach!"

Able to play multiple positions, this versatile athlete spent his entire career as a reserve and defensive specialist. He accumulated career totals of 1,852 points and 1,428 rebounds. Keith still ranks among Miami's all-time leaders in games played, three-point field goals, total rebounds, steals, and blocked shots.

Keith Askins served as the Heat's captain for four straight seasons, from 1995 through 1999. The club awarded him the team's Leadership Award in both the 1994-95 and 1995-96 seasons.

Immediately after he retired from the NBA, the Heat management demonstrated their confidence in Keith by asking him to serve as an unpaid volunteer coach. They knew he still had much to contribute to the organization. And once again, he was grounded enough to see the opportunity and take full advantage of all it offered.

Keith worked and interacted with some of the most successful players and coaches of all time, including Pat Riley and Erik Spoelstra, LeBron James and Dwayne Wade, while winning three world championships. Keith first joined the coaching staff under Riley halfway through the 1999-2000 season and got promoted to a full-time position a few months later at the start of the following season.

I sat down with Keith right after the Heat's storybook 2012-2013 NBA championship season. The team celebrated 66 wins with only 16 defeats with a record of 15 and 1 in their own division. The Heat put together the second longest winning streak in NBA history with 27 wins that season (the 1971-72 Los Angeles Lakers still hold the record with 33 straight victories).

What a great time to get his insight and wisdom. His team had just demonstrated the power of Keith's core philosophy: ***"We have one mindset, and that mindset is winning!"***

Every team and every player knows the challenge of trying to stay on top of their game:

"We faced plenty of adversity and critics, yet sticking together as a team in all situations kept us from falling apart." Giving his players that grounded attitude was a real difference-maker for his team.

Keith's parents divorced when he was only six. So his grandfather became his role model and mentor:

"My grandfather grew up without a great education. He worked as a janitor for General Motors. I remember him coming home from work and still getting on the tractor to cut the grass and take care of the pigs and goats he had. All my grandfather had was his word and his work ethic. He was the kind of man who, if he said he would do something—believe me—he would do it! He never missed a day of work until the day he was diagnosed with cancer. I believe the fact that he couldn't work bothered him more than the illness itself."

"I learned to never look at anything as a hardship. I never wanted for much. I figured I had clothes on my back, food on the table, and a place to sleep. There is a difference between needing something and wanting something—I had everything I needed."

"When it comes to adversity, I see it as a challenge—a job that needs to get done. I look at it as a process, and I come up with a plan that I

believe to be the most efficient way to handle the situation. I don't want to waste my time or anybody else's time. I've developed the habit of writing down my game plan for dealing with whatever obstacle I may face—and then I attack it!"

"It wasn't always easy. For my first five years as a player I had only a one-year guarantee each year. A player could really resent that kind of pressure, but I think my upbringing taught me not to expect to get something for nothing. Understanding the value of hard work helped me deal with those times. I wasn't going to beat myself up, because I knew it was a business—and my business was to perform."

I asked Keith if he could see a *common thread* running through the success of NBA stars such as LeBron James, Dwayne Wade, and others he has worked with during his twenty-five-plus years in the business. He didn't hesitate in his response:

"You have to be competitive and committed to the cause. Everyone needs a good network of people surrounding them, helping them aim to do better. Success breeds success."

Keith values confidence over strident cockiness. The confidence he finds valuable is demonstrated in players who respect the team and themselves. They care about each other.

"You need to be prepared and be willing to take on whatever comes your way, believing you can do it. I've never met anybody who doesn't believe in God, Allah, or some higher spiritual power achieving a high level of success."

"Remember, we live in a very competitive society. If you drop your guard, somebody is going to knock you out. You need to be able to defend yourself with the right values and work ethics. I believe people don't reach their fullest potential because of their lack of self-esteem. They give up too early. Often they've failed to surround themselves with

the right people. We all need help—someone to give us an opportunity. But we need to take the opportunity and run with it ourselves."

"You can't be thinking you're entitled to something; you need to work hard for it. The only way you win is by knowing that losing hurts real bad—that it hurts so much you refuse to let it happen again. If you feel comfortable with losing and just say 'It's okay,' you have a mindset that will never let you be a winner! The pain of losing has to be a very strong motivator for you."

"Everybody is born with something special about them. But it's up to each person individually to develop it. I've never met a truly successful person who hasn't worked for it. Talent can be wasted if you don't have the right mindset."

KEITH'S EMPOWERING THOUGHT: *"I've developed the habit of writing down my game plan for dealing with whatever obstacle I may face—and then I attack it!"*

DO IT DAILY:

▶ *Stay grounded during life's ups and downs.* Have a winning mindset, commitment, and a positive network of peers who help you remain grounded through the peaks and valleys.

▶ *Opportunities knock in various ways.* Never think you are too good for an opportunity. Successful people are willing to bet on themselves, understanding that if the door is even slightly opened for them, they have a great chance to run right through it.

David Wild

ICONIC WRITER, BEST SELLING AUTHOR

David's Journey:

POOR STUDENT → ROLLING STONE MAGAZINE → GRAMMY AND EMMY
AWARD SHOW WRITER

Sometimes it isn't only talent or intelligence that takes us to the top, but rather sheer focus and superb time management. David Wild is a man who has excelled in these areas, and as a result, his career continues to reach new heights.

Bestselling author David Wild is a contributing editor to *Rolling Stone* magazine, an Emmy-nominated television writer, and the former host of Bravo's acclaimed interview-and-performance TV series, *Musicians*. His published books include *Friends: The Official Companion* (1995) and *Seinfeld: The Totally Unauthorized Tribute* (1998). In 2014, David was a contributor on CNN's *The Sixties: The British Invasion*. Along with others, he provided insights into the influence of the British Invasion on the culture of the 1960s.

He is also one of the most giving people I know, and one of the most diversified personalities featured in this book, and one of the most focused.

David has worked with some of the biggest legends in music. He has written liner notes and essays for dozens of artists, including The Rolling Stones, Bob Dylan, Frank Sinatra, Van Morrison, Randy Newman, Sheryl Crow, Neil Diamond, Van Halen, The Eagles, Fleetwood Mac, Simon & Garfunkel, Aerosmith, AC/DC, and Ringo Starr. He even spent a month on the road with Paul McCartney.

His interactions with celebrated stars are not limited to music icons. He has been associated with some of the world's most influential people, including Tom Hanks, Steven Spielberg, and Michelle Obama, for whom he wrote an inauguration speech. If that weren't enough, David has written for the Grammy Awards since 1999, and for the Emmy Awards since 2005. In 2009, he produced the Biography Channel series *The Chris Isaak Hour*. Currently, he is a blogger for the *Huffington Post*.

Despite these successes, David freely admits, ***"I'm not the most talented, nor the best looking."*** But David certainly has something about him that provides inspiration for up-and-coming artists, authors, or anyone working in the creative fields. Here is a guy who wrote for his school newspaper and grew up to realize his childhood dream to hang out with rock stars and write about their lives.

David believes it helps to have a mentor growing up; he fondly remembers Pulitzer Prize-winning author William Kennedy:

"He got me my first job at Esquire—*gave me my first break. Without that I don't think I would have reached the level of success I have had. I am just not an aggressive person. What up-and-coming young people should do is what I did while at* Esquire*: I would do anything they wanted me to do—no questions asked."*

Surprisingly, there was a time when David's success seemed unlikely:

"Ironically enough, I was a very poor and slow reader when I was growing up. My father helped me by tapping into my interests to find

anything that could help motivate me and bring out my potential. I loved baseball, so anything my Dad could find about baseball he gave me to read. I'd say that is a good lesson for all parents."

"As I got older, I realized that my world was very different from the one my father grew up in—where most people worked for one company, earned a pension, and then retired. I keep thirty to forty jobs going at once. A traditional nine-to-five job—no doubt I would have failed at that."

"People often ask how I handle so many projects at once. It's called 'frontloading.' When I get a project, I don't think much about it. I try to get as much done as I can on each project up front, before I have a chance to make up excuses or lose interest."

"Frontloading can work for anybody. One of my life's greatest achievements was helping put together 'America: A Tribute to Heroes' after 9/11. It should have taken four months to put together, but I did it in four days."

When confronted with the impossible, David's focus and response is different than most:

"Some people just walk away from a challenge. But when I'm challenged, I tend to come up with my best work. People need to work on what holds them back. I believe they are held back from reaching their goals by fear and ego."

"In my experience at **Rolling Stone** *I constantly had people emailing me their work. Most weren't very good, but the ones who were good enough to come in for an interview would blow it—I'd say nine times out of ten—because they couldn't perform due to anxiety caused by their fear."*

"As you pursue your dreams, your mindset should be something I think [tennis great] Jimmy Connors said best: 'I hate to lose more than I love to win!' *Most people dream of being famous, but most people just don't do what it takes."*

Don't let fear or a lack of discipline get in the way of your dreams. If you want to meet with success, you will need to develop your own strategy on what works for you to manage your time and get the job done!

DAVID'S EMPOWERING THOUGHT: *"Do what you love. Do it and don't worry about it—that's the way to go. Don't think about it— just do it."*

DO IT DAILY:

▶ *Stay focused.* When you have a lot on your plate, it is easy to get distracted. Remember to stay committed and disciplined all the way to the finish line.

▶ *Make the most of your time.* We are all gifted with 24 hours in the day. But the way in which we use each of those hours can be the difference in the level of success and the accomplishments that we achieve.

Tom Terwilliger

MISTER AMERICA

Tom's Journey:

LABELED LEARNING DISABLED → OUTLAW BIKER → CHAMPION
BODY-BUILDER

I knew how to set goals and accomplish what I wanted. I wanted to become an outlaw biker and I became one. Now I turned my attention to becoming Mr. America, and in 1986 that's what I became," so said Tom Terwilliger. Much like many of the participants in this book, the common thread of self-evolution and growth is a steadfast belief many of these folks remain focused on.

Tom Terwilliger and I go back to grammar school. Tom is one of those people that you can't forget. As a kid I was a bit on the wild side, but Tom set his own standards. As far back as the sixth grade, Tom showed himself to be a true leader. I remember I used to hang out with him as part of his gang, the Savage Skulls. We would go out and cause havoc around the neighborhood, but I eventually had to quit the gang because I wasn't allowed to be out past nine o'clock!

I was always a bit curious about Tom and his twin brother, Michael. It seemed to me that they followed their own rules. But at the same time, they were also smart, talented artists with abilities to stand out in the crowd and become something special. They were constantly evolving and working to redefine their lives and their goals.

For some reason, the school system made the decision to take Tom and his brother out of the regular fourth grade and put them in "special classes" for mentally challenged kids until they were fifteen years old. When I interviewed Tom for this book he was thankful that I understood what had happened to him more than forty years ago:

"I was hyperactive and had dyslexia. They labeled me 'learning disabled.' It put an emotional scar on me and my self-image. The school did not know what to do with me, so they put me in the special-ed classes. As a result, I believed I was stupid—not good enough—and I was treated like an outcast. I was called a retard. I didn't take it lightly, and I fought back. I became a bully killer."

Don't get the wrong idea; Tom indeed was a handful, feared by most—and for good reason. When he was eight years old, Tom recalled, "I saw the Hells Angels motorcycle club while visiting my grandmother in Manhattan one day, and I liked what I saw. They represented power and instilled fear. As I grew up, I wanted that for myself, and I was inspired to become an outlaw biker." And so he did. His evolution didn't always fit into the societal norm, but it was truly amazing to see a person dedicate himself, and simply evolve into something new and completely different.

Tom had a goal of being infamous and feared, and it turned out that he was good at it. I remember one high school party where there must have been more than one hundred kids in the house. Dressed in his leathers, Tom rode up on his Harley, walked in by himself, and every kid went running for the hills out of fear. It was like a scene from a cartoon—the house was empty within minutes.

Not only did Tom have the demeanor of a rebel, but also he could back it up. His brother Raymond was a New York City police officer and a Kung Fu instructor. He helped make Tom into an exceptional fighter.

Encouraged by Ray, and mentored by champion bodybuilder Tony Pandolfo, Tom began entering bodybuilding tournaments at age sixteen. Yet again, another transformation by a man that continually evolved. Tom says, "At that point in my life, I was on the right track and in an environment of positive people with unlimited hopes." But he would take a few detours along the way:

"At nineteen, I decided to take a month off from bodybuilding. That month turned out to be three years, hanging out with my old biker friends. My self-esteem went way down; I was in the clubhouse partying with some members of a notorious biker gang. When I turned twenty-two, I looked around and realized this was not what I wanted for my life. Right then and there, I walked out of the clubhouse. A few seconds later, somebody pulled the trigger of a double-barrel shotgun in the clubhouse and accidentally blew a hole in the bar right where I had been standing. The blast also blew a hole in the girl who had been standing right next to me. Fortunately, she survived. But, talk about a sign!"

"This was my turning point. Many people do like I did and develop self-doubt that drags them down. All too often we use our obstacles to say, 'I can't do it.' My advice: do not set your bar too high, but you need to get out of your comfort zone and figure out exactly where you are going and how you are going to get there."

"The greater the goal, the greater the challenge. But I knew I was up for it. Having discipline gives you the ability to do the things you don't want to do. You need to know what you want enough to overcome the obstacles you will face along the way. The desire to get what you want has to be stronger than the obstacles you will inevitably face. You need to believe in yourself and believe that you deserve more—that there is

something better out there for you. Believe in God and prayer. Whenever I begin to doubt, Christ always answers."

Tom's bestselling book, *7 Rules of Achievement*, describes the following rules:

Get crystal clear on exactly **what** you want.
Get equally clear on precisely **why** you want it.
Get a clear picture of **where** you are now, your starting point.
Identify the **resources** you have and the resources you need.
Create a clear yardstick or evidence procedure for **measuring progress**.
Create a vivid **internal representation** of the desired outcome.
Take **massive action**.

Tom has truly turned his life around. For more than thirty years he has been an ambassador for fitness and healthy living. He's a bestselling author, an international speaker and host, and his work as co-director and producer of the nationally syndicated television show *Muscle Sport USA*, on the FOX Network, has earned him a prestigious Telly Award.

Tom, along with his wife, fitness model Dawn Terwilliger (Mrs. Metropolitan 2009), hosted and co-produced the radio talk show *One on One with Terwilliger Fitness*. Working with celebrities like Regis Philbin, Cindy Crawford, Eddie Murphy, and Howard Stern, Tom clearly demonstrates how somebody who was far off-course can become an inspiration and role model for people around the world and ultimately help others reach their own limitless potential.

TOM'S EMPOWERING THOUGHT: *"You need to believe in yourself and believe that you deserve more—that there is something better out there for you."*

DO IT DAILY:

▸ ***Always dedicate yourself to relentless self-evolution.*** Get clear on what you want and why you want it, identify your resources, measure your progress, visualize it, and then take massive action.

▸ ***It's never too late to change.*** Change can be small or it can be large. But it can never be too late. The time is always right for change. Make your personal development and your personal evolution a lifelong responsibility and a gift to yourself.

Charles Fazzino

POP ARTIST

Charles' Journey:

INVESTED $10 IN HIMSELF → SOLD ART AT STREET FAIRS → GALLERIES WORLDWIDE

The fantastic people featured in this book are all, in some form or another, self-starters. Meaning, they are all dedicated and share the common thread of being creators and delivering on something new and exciting. It is not always easy to be the innovator and originator. But being a self-starter is truly a special skillset that puts many of these people on the cutting edge and cusp of something big.

"All artists—including me—were told the worst way you can choose to make a living is as an artist." Those were the words of Charles Fazzino, entrepreneur and lifelong self-starter.

Fast forward to today: Charles Fazzino has been one of the most successful pop artists in the world for more than thirty years. His whimsical and detailed 3D fine art prints and originals are unparalleled and exhibited or offered for sale in hundreds of fine art galleries and museums around the world. Charles has been commissioned to create artwork for major events and organizations including The Super Bowl, Grammy Awards, Major

League Baseball, The Daytime Emmy Awards, National Hockey League and The Olympics.

Collectors of his artwork include Paul McCartney, Presidents Bill Clinton and George Bush, Derek Jeter, Mariano Rivera, Keith Urban, Morgan Freeman, Joe Torre, Tom Brady, Ellen Degeneres, Richard Petty, and Warren Buffett, to just name a few.

My company was honored to carry Charles's artwork, and I had the pleasure of getting to know him well. He is a humble man who always seems to have two feet planted firmly on the ground.

"I had plenty of people trying to discourage me. I had my own fears about getting out of my comfort zone. Now when I do get out of my comfort zone, it seems to bring out my best. Over the years I have learned that when people tell me I can't do things, all it does is motivate me."

"My mom was a Finnish sculptor and my dad was an Italian shoe designer. As far as school went, I never did well. It was a terrible time for me, so art became a way for me to build my self-esteem. I was a seventh-grader when I took my first art class, and I was literally terrible as an artist—but I had the motivation."

"I finished art school in the late 1970s, graduating from the School of Visual Arts in New York City. I was very independent. My mom was an artist, so I wanted to show her that I could be one as well. At age twenty-four, I exhibited my flat artwork at some street fairs. At one of those fairs, I walked into an art supply store and saw some older people sitting around a table, just spending their day enjoying and creating art. It cost me just ten dollars to sit in with them and take the opportunity to learn what they were doing."

"I thought their 3D technique would work well with my artwork, so I made a few pieces, framed them up in a simple box, and went back to

Washington Square Park where I offered to sell them for fifty dollars each. People started buying them and that did wonders for my self-esteem!"

"I have always kept that motivation—fear is a good motivator. Believe it or not, I still fear that I'll end up back on the street trying to sell my art. I don't believe great artists are born; they are created. Even though there are many talented artists in the world, I think most are held back by their fear of failure, their fear that others won't appreciate their art."

"As an artist, you need to become a businessperson as well. I wanted to branch out and combine my art with big brands. I accomplished that, and when I look back, I recognize that my artwork really reflects what life and pop culture was like at the time. I tell aspiring artists, 'If you want to do art for your heart, take art courses; if you want to do art for a living, then take business courses.'"

That ten-dollar investment Charles made in himself to learn something new has produced millions of dollars—and a legacy that makes him part of the next generation of iconic pop-culture artists, following in the footsteps of innovators like Andy Warhol, Keith Haring, and Roy Lichtenstein. Across his career and his life, Charles has always been viewed as a self-starter. No matter what he has accomplished, the one constant is that he devotes himself to the goal and religiously works to build it. And that is exactly where self-starters begin.

CHARLES'S EMPOWERING THOUGHT: *"Now when I do get out of my comfort zone, it seems to bring out my best."*

DO IT DAILY:

▶ *Self-starters take it one step at a time.* Invest in yourself by starting small, taking action, and recognizing that each step will lead to another. The culmination of those steps will eventually become the journey that moves you to your goals.

▸ ***The biggest returns are the ones you'll get from yourself.*** Self-starters aren't situation specific. Whether it be as an artist, businessman, or any other profession, self-starters transcend scenarios to take that common thread approach of innovating and inventing from the moment they begin their journeys.

Joe Walsh

Joe's Journey:

SCHOOL CHOIR → STAGE FRIGHT → GRAMMY AWARD WINNER

It is said that extraordinary things don't happen when we are in our comfort zone, which means we have to face our fears, push ourselves, and learn to embrace the unknown. Joe Walsh, the Eagles' superstar guitarist, knows this better than most.

Life's been good to Joe Walsh (so far!). He's the enduring guitar god who has spent his life making music not only as a solo artist, but also with great bands like The James Gang; his most famous gig, of course, was with rock history's legendary The Eagles.

For all the life he's lived, however, Joe has never forgotten one early fan who played a key role in helping him build that life:

"My first mentor was my high school music teacher. Mr. MacClellan was in charge of the choir, and he was probably the first person to see something in me. Mr. MacClellan introduced me to the Madrigal Choir and gave me a lot to do in the music department outside of class. He even asked me to do administrative office work for him. He paid a lot of attention to me and encouraged me to go ahead and become a musician."

"Mr. MacClellan taught me much that helped me prepare for my eventual career as a singer and a musician. But the most important thing he gave me was the fact that someone who knew something told me that I had some talent. **He said it was okay for me to follow my dream—never mind what the world or my parents told me."**

"Many, many years later, I had a chance to bring Mr. MacClellan to an Eagles concert. I'm not too sure that Mr. MacClellan actually approved of the kind of music I was making, but he still told me I did it really, really well."

What advice would Joe Walsh share with someone who dreams of following in his musical footsteps?

"I would tell a young musician starting out today: first, learn every Beatles song—every one top to bottom. Why not learn from the best? Learn all the guitar parts; learn every word and every one of those harmony parts. This will make you a better musician. It will teach you the crafts of great writing, playing, and singing if you study those guys."

"The second thing: play your instrument every day as if nothing else mattered. For that time you're playing, never mind your homework, never mind your job. If you're going to be a musician, play your instrument as much as you can every day. If that's what you want to do with your life, do it. Don't 'kind of' do it—do it. Don't do it a little bit at a time and assume you'll get better. Just get better."

"The third thing: get in front of people and play. Perform wherever and whenever you can. Play for free. Play as much as you can for as many people as you can because you cannot become a legend in your parents' garage!"

"For me, the biggest obstacle I faced in becoming a musician was stage fright—that absolute total fear of being in front of people doing anything. The way to overcome that fear is to play in front of people every chance you get. And that's exactly what I did. I got up and played for

free at church dances, at high school sock hops, at coffeehouses—any-where, for anyone who would have me."

"Gradually—as the number of people I was playing for grew—I got more and more comfortable with it. It actually was a great rush to play for anyone, but initially my terror got in the way of me actually doing it. Don't let your fear get the best of you."

Sheer determination and a driving work ethic aren't enough, according to Joe. He encourages artists to cultivate a good attitude as well:

"Whatever you do, try to go into it with a very positive attitude, but be realistic. The way you perceive things can be totally different from what is really going on. Be careful, because you may form attitudes and general positions which will get in the way of achieving what you want."

"We tend to invent problems and issues that don't exist. If your way of thinking leaves you with an inability to have an open mind, it can be a terrible obstacle to achieving anything—especially as a musician or an artist. You have to be in touch with reality to write about it."

"You also have to be thankful and recognize when things go right in life. One turning point for me came with The Eagles when the 'Hotel California' album first came out. I think we were in Chicago, and we walked out on stage and there was a two-minute standing ovation—before we even played a note! I remember thinking, **This is about as good as it gets—to be loved that much, and you haven't even done anything.***"*

"But I guess we had done something; we just never imagined when we were making 'Hotel California' that we would affect as many people on the planet as we did. To have that album impact that many people around the world is amazing—it's a real privilege. For me, The Beatles did that. For instance, the song 'In My Life' still inspires me in my life."

"Hotel California" topped the Billboard Hot 100 singles chart for one week in May 1977 and peaked at number 10 on the Adult Contemporary charts. Three months after its release, the Recording Industry Association of America (RIAA) certified the single Gold, representing one million copies sold. The Eagles also won the 1977 Grammy Award for Record of the Year for "Hotel California" at the 20th Grammy Awards in 1978. The song was certified Platinum (Digital Sales Award) in 2009 by the RIAA for sales of one million digital downloads.

And what does Joe do when things *don't* go his way? The famously funny Joe Walsh advises:

"Whatever obstacles you face, a sense of humor can help a lot. It's the best way to go. There are so many things that can get you upset in this world that it's just ridiculous when you think about it. And the best way to deal with all that is to realize that in the end, it's all a big distraction from doing what we're supposed to be doing—which is to breathe."

"Then the best thing to do is to make a joke about it, because sometimes the basic absurdity of life becomes too ridiculous to comprehend seriously. All that said, life has been good—no, life has been great to me—and I wouldn't change a thing!"

As Joe's life shows, getting out of your comfort zone can lead to extraordinary things. And when the going gets extra tough, a jovial personality and perspective can help us stay positive and stay grateful.

JOE'S EMPOWERING THOUGHT: *"For me, the biggest obstacle I faced in becoming a musician was stage fright—that absolute total fear of being in front of people doing anything. The way to overcome that fear is to play in front of people every chance you get."*

DO IT DAILY:

- ▸ ***Practice your passion.*** When you find what you love, do that thing every day with attention and care.

- ▸ ***Laughter is the best medicine.*** When you are dealing with hard times, humor will help carry the burden.

Bill Germanakos

THE BIGGEST LOSER WINNER SEASON 4

Bill's Journey:

5'8", 334-LB. COUCH POTATO → $250,000 WEIGHT LOSS WINNER

Family, friends, career, and even losing weight; we are all committed to something. But the most successful people in the world and the true difference makers are those that choose to be extremely committed to their goals. Commitment propels you to improvement, betterment, and higher levels of success. It is to the common thread of commitment that the participants in this book credit much of what they accomplished. For Bill Germanakos, it was that commitment that turned a couch potato into a $250,000 weight loss winner.

"Inspiration is important but motivation is a must." Bill was honest and emotional when we spoke in his Lynbrook, Long Island, home:

"I went to Six Flags amusement park and was asked to leave the rollercoaster because the seat belt would not fit over my belly. I cannot begin to tell you the embarrassment I felt. It was my ah-ha moment when my daughter leaned over and whispered 'It's okay, Daddy, I still love you.' It was then that I knew something had to change."

"I was 5'8" and weighed 335 pounds. The doctor said I was morbidly obese and would likely die before I was 60. I realized I was following in the footsteps of my dad, who passed when he was only 57 years old. He always struggled with his weight."

"I was somewhat heavy as a young child but very athletic as a teen. While in college on a lacrosse scholarship, I was injured, and at the age of 18 had to have major knee surgery. I got very depressed and became a couch potato—I gained 75 pounds in one semester."

"By 26, I weighed 285 pounds. But I hit my top weight when I turned 40—tipping the scales at 335 pounds! My blood pressure and cholesterol were through the roof. I was pre-diabetic and at severe cardiac risk."

"Then my life changed with the opportunity to be on NBC's reality weight loss show The Biggest Loser. *Funny thing is, I didn't even apply to the show. It was my twin brother Jim who applied for both season three and four, and once he mentioned he had a twin they decided to bring both of us into the competition. For me, being on the show was like being in jail. I really missed my family, but I was determined to change my life, given such a rare opportunity."*

"I had all the incentive I needed—I wanted to walk both of my daughters down the aisle at their weddings but was heading in the wrong direction. *Was I prepared for the competition on the show?* ***Let me put it this way: both my parents' families were from Sparta, Greece, so I am 100 percent Spartan. The phrase we live by is 'You either win or die trying.'"***

"I was one of 18 contestants on the fourth season. I lost 164 pounds—more than 49 percent of my starting weight—reaching 170 pounds. I won the first prize of $250,000."

"Perhaps one of the biggest issues people deal with is how to lose weight and keep it off. While many of us continue to try fad diets, we never actually get educated about how to live a healthy lifestyle. My attitude was to turn myself

over to the professionals on the show—to put the onus on them to teach me how to lose weight the right way. I vowed that I'd do whatever they said to do, and would work harder than anyone else in order to stay on the ranch."

"Self-doubt is a main reason why people have a hard time losing weight. They lack the confidence to realize what they are capable of. Fad diets don't work; a lifestyle change does. You can't let yourself feel defeated. It just takes hard work and the willingness to get out of your comfort zone.

"As far as I'm concerned, anything you want to accomplish in life requires people that will stick with you and will support you and your efforts. Weight loss, like anything else, takes a willingness to make sacrifices."

"Chasing your goals cannot be something you do only when the rest of your life allows for it. Rather, the pursuit of your dreams should be something you dedicate yourself to on a daily basis. As my brother Jim says, 'The hardest part of any self-improvement plan is overcoming the inevitable stumbles along the way. It's okay to fall down, as long as you get up and continue forward.'"

"Have a plan! Just saying that you want to lose weight doesn't mean it will happen. Lay the groundwork to success by detailing exactly how you will reach your goals. Then get to a doctor for guidance and ask for a referral to a professional, registered dietician. You have to STOP MAKING EXCUSES! If you don't like running, try walking. If you don't like lifting weights, try 'hot yoga.' If you can't afford a trainer, buy an exercise video you can follow in the privacy of your home. You see? There's a good answer for every excuse."

"My dad always said, 'If you want to get something done, you first have to get it started.' These are the words I try to live by. If today was a bad day, start again tomorrow. Don't let a minor setback ruin all your hard work, and always remember that the best pound lost is the first pound. My goal now is to

help enlighten others with my knowledge, while not forgetting what I learned to be happy and healthy for the rest of my life."

"My desire is to 'pay it forward,' to become 'half the man so I can be twice the man,' and to give back to family, friends and my career."

Bill went on to work in the corporate wellness field and is a professional motivational speaker. He has acted as a "wellness ambassador" and spokesman for several large companies and organizations, and is a frequent guest on well-known shows such as *Dr. Oz*, *The Ellen DeGeneres Show*, and *The Today Show*. To say the least, Bill's commitment and dedication to making a substantial life change has not only changed the trajectory of his life, it likely saved it.

BILL'S EMPOWERING THOUGHT: **"Every one of us comes from the same place. Success doesn't happen by accident. You should have a solid plan in place and always consider the recipe for success to be: inspiration, motivation, education, dedication, and perspiration!"**

DO IT DAILY:

▶   **Remain committed even when it's easy to quit.** Stay the course, and failure will never overtake you. Commitment can overcome any obstacle or challenge in your path.

▶   **Grow your commitment.** Every day is an opportunity to develop your commitment to your goals. Do so through being passionate, purposeful, and driven. These are the fundamental pillars of success.

Jeff Idelson

BASEBALL HALL OF FAME PRESIDENT

Jeff's Journey:

POPCORN VENDOR → HOT DOG VENDOR → EPICENTER OF BASEBALL
HISTORY

We've all heard of the domino effect. It is the practical experience of starting the motion of one domino that eventually knocks over another, and then another, and so on and so forth, until all the dominos have been laid to rest. Success is the same way. Sometimes it just takes that one domino to start the momentum in your journey. Putting that one single piece in motion can have a monumental impact on your life. For Jeff Idelson, president of the Baseball Hall of Fame, the domino effect played a pretty important role in the advancement of his career. Jeff's personal story recounts his successful climb up the corporate ladder with the Boston Red Sox organization.

He eventually went on to become the sixth president of the Baseball Hall of Fame and has rubbed shoulders with some of the greatest heroes ever to play the game. He has spent time with them, observed them, and gotten to know many of them in ways few can boast about. Jeff's insight into what makes them tick may seem somewhat elementary, but it only proves that basics really do count.

Jeff himself had a passion for the game from a very early age. As we spoke, his love of America's favorite pastime was evident:

"I went to my first baseball game when I was five and caught 'baseball fever.' I never looked back—I was willing to do anything just to be a part of the game. I started out working as a popcorn vendor at Boston's Fenway Park, then I worked my way up to ice cream, finally making my way to the top of the food chain for vendors—hotdogs! In 1986, five days after graduating from Connecticut College, I was presented with the opportunity to be the public relations intern with the Boston Red Sox. And thus my career was born."

It was Jeff's first job as a popcorn vendor that ignited the flame. That flame burned and burned and burned. It was never extinguished and only gained heat. New York was Jeff's next stop. The New York Yankees hired him to be the club's assistant director of media relations and publicity, and he quickly ascended to director. Prior to joining the Baseball Hall of Fame, Jeff served as senior press officer/assistant vice president for the 1994 World Cup organizing committee. Later that year he went to work for the Baseball Hall of Fame as its director of public relations and promotions. He rose through the Hall of Fame organization, eventually becoming its president in 2008, where he now oversees three million historic documents and forty thousand artifacts at the epicenter of baseball history. From one domino to another, Jeff kept the momentum going in the right direction.

Reflecting back on his career, Jeff advises people to follow the same passion he learned from his father:

"Enjoy every day. Don't miss the essence of life. My dad taught me passion, value, hard work, and an appreciation for people pursuing their dreams."

"One thing I have learned from some of the greats is that there is no replacement for discipline, perseverance, and confidence. Game day should just be about execution, because success isn't possible if you're

not properly prepared. For many athletes it's all about keeping in the right frame of mind. I run thirty miles a week. Running keeps me in the right mindset; it helps me think of each day as a journey."

"The Hall-of-Famers that I have come to know have plenty in common. They trust themselves. They let fear of failure motivate them. They understand that they will fail sometimes; they learn from it and adjust. *There's a well-known saying in baseball that Buck Showalter first shared with me: 'Players show their true colors in times of adversity, and so does everyone else.'"*

"Hall of Fame members have overcome adversity. Their solid character reveals them as great teammates. Yes, athletes at this level are born with talent, but that doesn't mean much if you don't work your butt off. And believe me, that is exactly what these guys have done. If you're busy worrying about something else in your life, then it's hard to realize your full potential."

At the end of our interview Jeff shared one of his favorite quotes with me, which serves as a great reminder to us all. It comes from Jackie Robinson, the first African-American to play Major League Baseball:

"A life is not important except in the impact it has on another life."

In Jeff's life, the dominos starting falling quickly and at an early age. He found his passion and was driven to take it one step at a time. He recognized it would take time, but eventually the momentum took over and everything fell into place. We all have the pieces in our lives; it is just a matter of organizing them and recognizing that each one will play a pivotal role in our journey.

JEFF'S EMPOWERING THOUGHT: *"The words of Bill Veeck Jr., the longtime Major League Baseball franchise owner, provide a great lesson on how to reach your goals: 'Take your work very seriously, go for broke, and give it all you have.'"*

DO IT DAILY:

▶ ***Recognize the value in building momentum.*** If you truly want to rise to the top, be willing to start at the bottom. Each and every experience will open the door to a new opportunity.

▶ ***Put the dominos in place.*** The most successful people in the world plan for the future. Each domino is one step in the right direction. So take the time to plan your journey to achieve your goals. And then the momentum will eventually take over.

Jeff Henderson

CELEBRITY CHEF

Jeff's Journey:

DRUG DEALER → PRISON → CAESAR'S PALACE

We all need fortitude. You know, the strength to not only manage adversity, but also overcome it. Fortitude can be mental or physical, it can be personal or professional, and it can help you to handle the small obstacles, or conquer the large ones. But you'll find that the most successful people around all possess a certain amount of fortitude. They have nurtured it and allowed it to grow over time. Fortitude is a difference-maker and common thread for all successful people.

"I needed prison to discover myself" were the first words I heard from Jeff Henderson, better known as "Chef Jeff" to his many loyal fans and followers. Jeff hosted the Food Network TV show *The Chef Jeff Project* in 2008. The show was aimed at helping young adults with challenging backgrounds complete projects in the hope of winning a scholarship to culinary school.

Since that show, Chef Jeff has gone on to become a *New York Times* bestselling author and popular public speaker. He also hosts a YouTube series called "In the Kitchen" and launched a cooking show, *Family Style with Chef Jeff*, which focuses on the impact of good choices in the kitchen.

Another show, *Flip My Food*, went into syndication in 2014. In each episode, Chef Jeff meets up with people across the country to show them how to "flip" their favorite food into a more appetizing and healthier dining experience.

Jeff spoke of growing up in the ghetto of central Los Angeles:

"My mom and grandparents helped raise me and my sister with little help. My dad never taught me responsibility, and I developed a criminal mentality. Early on I went to jail multiple times, and I was stabbed in the chest by a rival gang when I was just sixteen. Never doing well in school, I graduated with a certificate of completion and a 1.0 average."

*"We moved to San Diego, and I started selling drugs. In a short time I was making thirty-five thousand dollars a week dealing crack cocaine. In 1987, I was arrested by the San Diego Drug Task Force and charged with distributing illegal narcotics—I was found guilty. **I thought my life was over. I spent the next ten years in prison.**"*

But it was his fortitude and willingness to pay his debt to society and then bounce back that put Jeff on the fast track to rebuilding a successful life.

*"**There is an art to doing time: you have to learn how to deal with it. Either it will control you or you will control you. Either way, I will tell you right here and now that prison saved my life!** I had plenty of time to reflect back on my youth. Nobody ever told me I was smart so I always thought I was inferior. I had a victim mentality—thought I was owed something. I blamed everyone for my shortcomings."*

*"In prison my job was a dishwasher. From there I moved to the kitchen. As I worked in the kitchen and thought about my past, I increasingly beat myself down with regret—and I dreamed of being a free man. **I began to see the value of education. I accepted responsibility for my past. I looked at**"*

how others were negatively affected by drugs. I started to read about my heritage, and I discovered there was plenty to be proud of."

"In the kitchen, food and cooking became very important to me. It put me around bright minds—people I respected as mentors, people with the right mindset. **Now, instead of cooking cocaine on the streets, I was cooking for fifteen hundred convicts three times a day."**

"After prison I moved to Las Vegas; I wanted to become an executive chef. I had to overcome the stigma of being a convicted felon, but I learned to smile, and I worked hard to build up my résumé. I became the first African-American at Caesar's Palace to be named Chef de Cuisine, *and in 2001 the Tasting Institute of America named me Chef of the Year. I'm in the right place now, and I enjoy helping others avoid making the same mistakes I did."*

Jeff has written several books, including his bestselling autobiography, *Cooked: My Journey from the Streets to the Stove.* He has been featured on *Oprah,* CNN, *NBC Today, Good Morning America, ABC World News,* and *The Talk.* Continually on the speaking circuit, he helps others by sharing his experiences and success in prisons, schools, and other venues throughout the country. Jeff is all about giving back and trying to inspire others:

"I want to inspire and motivate lives. Food is a celebration of life, and I'm able to use it to help create opportunities for gang members, drug dealers, and the homeless."

Jeff's endless fortitude is what helped him turn his lengthy prison sentence into a learning experience and opportunity. Prison took a lot away from him, but it gave him perspective and helped to develop the inner strength, or fortitude, he needed to rebound and build a successful career. It is that fortitude that pushes him ahead of the pack and inspires his goals of making a difference in the lives of others.

JEFF'S EMPOWERING THOUGHT: **"Sacrifice all for your dream, and believe in yourself with passion. We can't let our fear of failure be** *greater than our desire to achieve. At the end of the day it's all about the choices you make."*

DO IT DAILY:

▸   *Your life is what you make of it.* Taking responsibility for your actions is the first step in shaping your life. Remember that life is a gift and you aren't owed anything other than an opportunity to do great things.

▸   *Exhibit fortitude in all that you do.* Courage, bravery, determination and resilience are just a few of the ingredients for fortitude. A heavy dose of each will no doubt put you on the right path.

Marty Balin

JEFFERSON AIRPLANE, ROCK AND ROLL
HALL OF FAME

Marty's Journey:

AUTISM → REJECTED → "VOICE OF AN ANGEL"

Belief isn't always the easiest trait to sustain. Maintaining that steadfast determination and just knowing, deep inside your heart and soul, that you are headed in the right direction can often be challenging. Marty Balin's ability to believe in his talents and his journey is truly inspiring.

Getting to know Rock and Roll Hall of Fame inductee Marty Balin, a founding member and lead vocalist for Jefferson Airplane/Starship, is like getting to know rock and roll history from the inside out.

A mutual friend introduced me to Marty, and as an art publisher I immediately recognized Marty not only as a music legend but also as an extremely talented artist. Marty and I sat down to discuss producing limited-edition prints of his artwork. We decided to unveil his art at a private concert for our staff and clients. I got to introduce this legend onstage—an unforgettable memory for me.

I was a little too young to attend the historic Woodstock Festival, the Monterey Pop Festival, or the Altamont Speedway Free Festival, so I felt especially fortunate when Marty—the man with the "voice of an angel"—shared his firsthand stories and personal insights from these iconic times with me.

Some would think Marty's laid-back attitude would prevent him from giving direct insight on why some people succeed and others don't. But Marty shared some specific recommendations to pass along to anyone dealing with whatever issues stand in their way.

"First of all, I was diagnosed with autism as a child and struggled with it while growing up. I loved music, but my biggest obstacle was people telling me that I did not have what it takes to be a successful musician."

"I was a folksinger at the time, but I wanted to play electric. I wanted to 'electrify' the folk sound. I wanted to play with electric guitars and drums, but when I mentioned that notion in clubs where I played, the owners would say, 'We wouldn't have you play here, not with that electric stuff.'"

But Marty believed in his mission and knew he could preserve his goals and manifest them into a reality. His reality. It was 1962 in San Francisco and Marty was leading a folk music quartet called The Town Criers. Marty wasn't one to just sit back and accept what others told him he couldn't do:

"I had no interest in listening to the naysayers. I decided to open my own club in 1965. I was twenty-three years old when I renovated an old pizza shop. We called the new nightclub The Matrix."

The club became an important place in the formative years of the San Francisco rock music scene. Legendary bands such as Jefferson Airplane, The Grateful Dead, Steve Miller, Santana, and The Doors played there.

Marty co-founded Jefferson Airplane and sang as one of its lead vocalists from 1965 to 1971. Despite being immersed in the drug culture of the time, Marty has some fond memories of those years. His favorite memory of Woodstock, for example, is playing cards backstage with Janis Joplin, Jimi Hendrix, and Pete Townshend of The Who.

Marty's deep belief in himself shines through:

"People need to have self-confidence and take chances. I always believed in myself. I love to sing and dance—make a fool of myself. My advice is to be willing to reveal yourself. Put it out there, follow your intuition, and stay focused."

"What helps keep me focused is creating a to-do list in my mind. I always need to accomplish things. I like the fact that I deliver. I take pride in delivering what I promise. God gave us all certain talents; use them and you will be happy. If you don't, it's likely you won't be happy. You might fail—and that's okay. But if you pursue your dream, it can come true."

When asked why he thinks people have a hard time reaching their goals, Marty explained:

"People don't get the encouragement from others they should. I suppose it has a lot to do with your upbringing, your family and your parents."

In 1974, Paul Kantner asked Marty to write some songs for his new group, Jefferson Starship, and in 1975 he penned one of the band's biggest hits, "Miracles."

"I wrote 'Miracles' about my girlfriend at the time—and also about the miraculous powers of Sai Baba [a spiritual saint and miracle worker whose teachings were an eclectic blend of Hindu and Muslim beliefs]. *I went to Puttaparthi with her and saw Sai Baba. We journeyed through the South*

Indian desert to the village; the song emerged from that experience. When I wrote 'Miracles,' I had my love for my girlfriend and my love for Sai Baba, two very different forms of love running through me. So the song is about both of them. I picked up my guitar and started singing, 'If only you believe, if only you believe like I believe, we'll get by.' The words flowed one after another, along with the music. I got the song written down in one draft, on a sheet of yellow paper."

At the end of 1978, after several major hits with Jefferson Starship, including "Miracles," "With Your Love," "Count on Me," and "Runaway," Marty left the band to focus on other projects. He likened his philosophy about music to Michelangelo's view of art:

"Michelangelo claimed that he did not create a sculpture. Rather, the form was contained within the block of marble; he merely removed the excess, revealing the work of art. I feel the same way about music, and about all the projects I'm involved in. The projects do themselves; the music comes through me."

The same vision Marty had when he launched Jefferson Airplane is present today. In fact, nearly everything he has worked on over the years has been fueled by his vision of art and music: they are vehicles for expressing a positive message.

"I still have the same attitude. I still love the positive, uplifting songs, and I believe in songs with those qualities. I believe that music can help change the world for the better."

MARTY'S EMPOWERING THOUGHT: **"You might fail—and that's okay. But if you pursue your dream, it can come true."**

DO IT DAILY:

▶ **Believe in miracles!** They happen every single day: small ones, large ones, and life-altering ones. So long as you believe that you can make a huge impact on the world, you can absolutely become a miracle-maker.

▸ ***Let your beliefs guide your life.*** Don't compromise who you are or where you came from. Remain steadfast in that which moves you to action and no matter what you are told, remember that your strong belief-system should guide you in the direction of your goals.

Gary Carter

BASEBALL HALL OF FAME

Gary's Journey:

MOTHERLESS AT 12 → TWENTY SURGERIES → 11X ALL-STAR

Competition...some people simply live for it. We call those people "competitors." They live their lives filled with the notion that the only way to live is by giving all they have. They don't quit, they are always looking to improve, and they are willing to embrace the challenges around them and outlast the opposition. Competitors rise to the occasion and get the job done.

It's no wonder that Gary "Kid" Carter ended up in baseball's Hall of Fame; he had a "hall-of-fame" attitude. Gary's constant smile and love for the game earned him the moniker "Kid." But from behind that smile emerged one of the fiercest, most competitive players ever to set foot on the field. He told me that from the very get-go in his rookie year, he *"tried to win every sprint, and hit every pitch out of the park."* In his life, both on and off the field, Gary was always willing to go the extra mile.

I remember first seeing Gary as an outstanding catcher and hitter for the Montreal Expos in 1975—but when he joined the New York Mets in 1985, he was one of *us!* I grew up on Long Island in a family of Mets fans.

I loved playing baseball as a catcher, so having Gary as part of the Mets team was pure pleasure for me.

On April 9, 1985, in his first game as a Met, Gary hit a tenth-inning homerun to give the Mets a 6-5 opening-day victory over the St. Louis Cardinals. The Mets won ninety-eight games that season, and Gary hit a career high thirty-two homeruns and drove in one hundred runs.

I only wish my dad—probably the most die-hard Mets fan ever—was still alive when I spoke with Gary. I asked him about overcoming adversity and what he believed it takes to reach your goals. Gary provided insights drawn from his twenty-one-plus-year career as a major league player. His stats are impressive: Rookie of the Year, three-time Gold Glove winner, Eleven-time All-Star, more than 300 homeruns, 1986 World Series champion, and a Baseball Hall of Fame inductee in 2003.

As I interviewed Gary, I realized that he has an amazing ability to focus—something he clearly used to prepare himself mentally before going onto the field. There was never a game where he didn't give it his all.

Gary's young life was marred when his thirty-seven-year-old mother passed away due to leukemia when he was only twelve. He recalled that he never really got a chance to say goodbye to her:

"Each day I had to get up, get dressed, go to school, and do my homework by myself. Even though my dad played both mom and dad, he was a working guy. I had to get on with my life—no choice. I remember it like it was yesterday. It made me want to get better at sports and fulfill my dream of getting into the big leagues. I just loved sports. I always wanted to be a professional athlete as far back as I can remember. After my mom passed, sports kept me on the right track and out of trouble."

Gary fondly remembered how his dad and older brother influenced him while he was growing up:

"Everything my brother did I just wanted to do better. I was born with talent, but I loved the competition! I was always motivated to be the best. When I was a rookie drafted by the Expos, it was for shortstop— not as a catcher. The Expos converted me to catcher. To be honest I wasn't very good at first, but I had the drive to make sure I got better and stayed in the big leagues. I never thought of being a Hall-of-Fame player; my focus was on my goals and success. If I didn't make it, what else would I have done? I saw that it wasn't always the most talented player that made it; it was always about desire and enthusiasm. I always wanted to win—all the time."

Gary was very specific about why he believes people don't reach their full potential—and he has a definite message he wants to pass on:

"I believe what holds people back from reaching their goals is fear of not succeeding—a fear of failure. You can fail seven out of ten times in baseball and still be considered one of the greatest! The key thing you need is always to push on. God has a plan for all of us; we just need to recognize it."

"Nothing will ever come easy. It's a matter of how much you want it. You want to be an example. I looked to Johnny Bench and Pete Rose. You've got to love the way they played: 100 percent all the time. When I'm out there, I'm just going to give it all I have."

It didn't come easy for Gary. He spoke about the many surgeries he underwent during his career:

"Without my desire, enthusiasm, and love of the game, my twelve knee operations and a shoulder operation, two ankle surgeries and two broken thumbs would have kept me from being in the game as long as I was. The inner drive to overcome all challenges motivated me. I always loved to play in front of large crowds, and I never wanted to make the last out. I never wanted to be a trivia question with a bad ending."

"I accomplished everything I wanted to, and I would never turn the clock back even if I could. It all boils down to choices. We all have just one life to live, so we need to look in the mirror and ask, 'How do I want to be remembered?' I always believed that the Lord defines me and that 'I can do all things through Christ who strengthens me.'"

Sadly, Gary was diagnosed with malignant brain tumors in May 2011 after complaining of headaches and forgetfulness. On February 16, 2012, at the age of fifty-seven, Gary died of brain cancer.

But his positive and energetic attitude will always live on. He was an active philanthropist. The Gary Carter Foundation helps support underprivileged schoolchildren in Palm Beach County, Florida. The vision of the foundation, now run by Gary's wife Sandy, is to seek to "better the physical, mental and spiritual well-being of children"—a fitting legacy for a wonderful human being and a talented baseball player. Gary will always be remembered for being competitive and outworking and outlasting the competition on and off the field.

GARY'S EMPOWERING THOUGHT: *"I never thought of being a Hall-of-Fame player; my focus was on my goals and success. If I didn't make it, what else would I have done? I saw that it wasn't always the most talented player that made it; it was always about desire and enthusiasm. I always wanted to win—all the time."*

DO IT DAILY:

▸ *Give it your all in all that you do.* You have just one life to live, so live it well. Look in the mirror and ask, "How do I want to be remembered?" And then answer that question by giving 100% dedication and effort.

▸ *Be competitive.* Maintain a consistent, competitive attitude that will outlast all your opponents.

Ann Marie Saccurato

WOMEN'S WORLD CHAMPION BOXER

Ann Marie's Journey:

ABUSIVE UPBRINGING → LIFE-THREATENING INJURIES → WORLD
BOXING CHAMPION

What keeps me competitive? When people say I can't!" That is just a glimpse into the attitude and warrior mentality of world champion boxer Ann Marie Saccurato. Her warrior mentality has propelled her forward, and positioned her as one of the most feared and respected boxers of her time. If you're looking for a roadmap to change tragedy into triumph, or to convert a negative life situation into something positive, you'll find inspiration in the journey of female boxing champion Ann Marie Saccurato.

Ann Marie helped pioneer the sport of boxing for women. She won many titles including 2001 New York and US National Golden Gloves, three WBC Lightweight World Championships, Biggest KO of the Year, Most Inspirational Boxer Award, Road Warrior of the Year, and many more. One of her fights was named "Fight of the Year," and she was also listed among the Top 10 pound-for-pound boxers in the world.

Without question, Ann Marie is a true warrior, both physically and (more importantly) mentally. I got to know her first as a professional athlete, and then later as a friend.

Watching her train is like watching a Spartan in action: strong, graceful, and confident. Talking to her is pure inspiration.

Ann Marie overcame tremendous odds just to be with us today.

"Growing up wasn't easy. My family was completely dysfunctional. My father was abusive toward my mother and left us with no money. He told us he 'wanted us out on the streets selling pencils to survive.' There were no role models for me."

"But I was born a fighter. It lives in me, so I did whatever I needed to follow my dreams. My mom did what she could to take care of us, and my brother is as much a fighter as I. Through food stamps, no heat, power being shut off, and more, we became the people and the fighters we are today, and I am so grateful for it all. It has only given me strength and made me hunger for more. Now I can pass it all on to whatever lives I touch."

Her struggles didn't end with her childhood. While returning from a volleyball competition at the Empire State Games in 1995, Ann Marie was a passenger in a devastating car accident. The driver of the vehicle was killed, and Ann Marie suffered a punctured lung, a broken pelvis and hip, two broken legs, a shattered arm, broken ribs, and severe nerve damage. She was not expected to live through the night. But warriors never quit and she fought her way back to health.

Ann Marie explained how she not only survived, but also overcame such overwhelming odds to become an even greater athlete:

"I was eighteen when I was in that terrible car accident—the doctors told me I would never play sports again. To me that was simply unac-

ceptable. Even as a kid I always knew something special was inside of me. Everybody's born with a certain amount of drive, and I was lucky to be born with warrior strength inside of me—probably more than most. I was not going to let a car accident or anything else get in the way of doing what I loved: being an athlete."

"The accident was actually the reason I started boxing. I spent months in rehab and I needed something to challenge me, so I took a boxing fitness class to cross train. I started working with a coach and loved the competition and the workout. As time went on, I got stronger and better. Then a friend of mine sent me an application for the New York Golden Gloves. I saw it as an opportunity. I said to myself, 'Can I do this?'"

"I entered the tournament. I didn't win the first year, but I redoubled my efforts and training and did win the following year. From there I didn't look back: I fought as often as I could and was on my way to winning a world title. I was an amateur for two years then turned pro in 2002."

"We all have an inner drive that we need to tap into. Are you truly committed? Are you willing to sacrifice things in your life to achieve your goals, or do you want it just handed to you? Are you willing to keep on learning? Because once you stop learning you're dead! Are you going to use negative outside influences as excuses and let them get in your way, or are you going to stay true to yourself and your goals?"

"Let's be honest, society has a strange way of knocking you down if it can. My attitude is to spit in the eye of adversity! Don't get me wrong: you won't win every time—nobody does. But if you don't come out on top even when you gave all you had, you should still be proud! Just ask yourself what you should do differently next time and move on."

Ann Marie stresses focus and determination when pursuing your goals:

"My advice: you will run into plenty of obstacles in life. They are to challenge you and make you stronger. They are tests, and you are only given what you can overcome. They will prepare you for what is to come in your life. Learn from them. Learn from all your losses. Learn from all your wins."

True warriors are those that face challenges and use them to motivate and elevate their game. And that is exactly what Ann Marie has done throughout her life.

"Don't let money drive you; let your passion drive you. Hey, when I was fighting for the title, I would get up at 4 a.m., do my strength work and sparring, and then train others so I could pay my rent. My training camp would last for months. Fighting for the world title offered a payoff of just five thousand dollars. Believe me, it was not about the money. It was for the love of the sport."

"Life is an amazing journey so live each day and the dreams within you to the fullest, because each breath you take is one you cannot get back. Every dream you wish can and will come true if you believe in it, know it, and go after it. Each victory you achieve is another life you inspire. Each loss you suffer is for you to learn and grow stronger. Look to leave a legacy; know your purpose. Life is a gift, and the greatest gift you can give is to spread love and inspire another."

ANN MARIE'S EMPOWERING THOUGHT: *"Life is an amazing journey so live each day and the dreams within you to the fullest, because each breath you take is one you cannot get back."*

DO IT DAILY:

▸ *Spread the warrior mentality.* Work to spread the warrior mentality to others. Warriors breed warriors and it is all of our responsibilities to uplift and elevate those around us.

▶ ***Sustain the warrior attitude.*** Set specific goals—the more specific your goal, the more likely you will achieve it. If you want to be a true warrior, then spit in the face of adversity!

Moti Horenstein

Moti's Journey:

ISRAELI SPECIAL FORCES COMMANDO → LANDSCAPER → DEADLIEST
WARRIOR

In life, we all have to fight to survive. Survival can take form in many different ways, but for Moti Horenstein, survival was simple: life or death. Survival may not take the same form for each of us, but the reality is that we fight every day to survive and succeed. It may not be life or death, but we survive adversity, challenges, obstacles, and plenty of other difficult situations.

The Israeli Army is known throughout the world as one of the most advanced and effective military operations in existence. In the arena of military combat, Moti Horenstein is the elite of the elite. As an Israeli Special Forces commando officer, he served in the Lebanese war from 1983 to 1986. During his military career, Moti served as a crisis response team paratrooper, as a firearms and weapons trainer, and later as a counter-terrorism expert teaching tactical and psychological preparation. He has frequently served as a consultant and instructor for the United States Military and for police forces around the country. He teaches people to survive in unbelievably challenging and tasking situations.

234

I got to know Moti while training at a friend's karate dojo (training school). When you first meet Moti, he is simply a wonderful person with a great big smile, but don't be fooled! "Grand Master" Horenstein was featured on the hit TV show *The Deadliest Warrior*. He started martial arts at age five and has risen to ninth-degree black belt, and now he's a professional martial artist.

Moti holds six world champion titles in six different martial arts disciplines. In April 2008, he was listed in the *Guinness Book of World Records* for "Most Baseball Bats Broken in One Minute." He split thirty-eight bats—and cracked an additional eleven—with his powerful roundhouse kick. He has had over four hundred fights against the best competition in the world.

Moti was more than willing to share his experiences to help others achieve their goals and dreams:

"For me the reality of being drafted into the Israeli Army was an unbelievable shock. I was a boy in high school, and then suddenly I was in a real war with real guns and tanks trying to kill me. My life as a kid was over. I lost a lot of friends in the war—not just acquaintances. These were my friends from when I was four and five years old. Like a lot of kids growing up, I got into my fair share of trouble, but the war straightened me out."

"I had to fight to live, so I gave it all I had. Fortunately I had some training under my belt in martial arts, and soon they put me in the Special Forces, and eventually I became a Special Forces instructor. The memories of war and death stay with me all the time. But I have tried to take such a negative situation and turn it into a positive one. So even when I am totally exhausted, I push harder and harder for those who didn't make it."

This is the epitome of a survivor's mentality: the will to live. In 1989, Moti moved from Israel to America. He found work as a landscaper and a bouncer:

"It was very tough for me. I had no money, I couldn't speak the language, and I had very few friends. Besides working as a landscaper and a bouncer, I trained people to earn a little extra money. As time went on, I was able to open my own small karate dojo. I believe that my being able to bring the attitudes and benefits of martial arts to people helped me get through those tough times."

"It's not just physical—it's mental and spiritual. I live it twenty-four hours a day, seven days a week. I don't see anything as a challenge; my mental toughness comes from martial arts. Put anything in front of me and I will do it. That is the secret, no excuses, no stopping, no blaming. I have learned even from my losses. I review my performance, get back to the gym, double my effort, and make sure the next time I get the job done. My best advice to overcome adversity is this: when you 'hit that wall,' as we all do, it's not just about going through the wall. Look left and right—always looking for all the options to keep you moving forward towards your dream."

"If you want to aspire to be great you need to get things done. The way I get things done is by doing the things I don't like first. Then I can get to the things I do like to do. I enjoy working with to-do lists for the day, the month, and the year. There are plenty of negative people in the world. Many people—even my own family—discouraged me from fighting. It's okay to listen to other opinions, but you need to make the final decisions yourself. It's great to do things that people say can't be done!"

"Don't ever stop believing. I see people every day that can't seem to get out of their own way. Then they start working hard and training, and they become different people. They turn around their entire life because they finally decided to."

MOTI'S EMPOWERING THOUGHT: *"The memories of war and death stay with me all the time. But I have tried to take such a negative situation and turn it into a positive one. So even when I am totally exhausted, I push harder and harder for those who didn't make it."*

DO IT DAILY:

▸ ***Become a survivor.*** Reflect, regroup, and then double your efforts. These three steps will help you to shape your mind and spirit to one destined for survival and success.

▸ ***Don't ever stop believing that you can overcome.*** Get out of your own head and your own way, you can and will survive anything that stands in your way. Obstacles will arise, but you have what it takes to turn these challenges into learning lessons and meaningful experiences to be used as an asset on your journey towards success.

Nik Halik

"THRILLIONAIRE"

Nik's Journey:

CHILDHOOD ILLNESS → MILLIONAIRE BY AGE 30 → ASTRONAUT

A*'thrillionaire' is anyone willing to live a life as opposed to merely existing. Living a true life on your own terms with a personalized agenda is paramount."* This is just one of the bold views Nik Halik has on life. But he is not alone. For most highly successful people, making bold decisions and living a bold and bright life is par for the course. But it is Nik's boldness that propelled him to a level of success at a young age that few ever recognize in a lifetime.

Imagine for a moment that you are only eight years old. Now imagine, at that age, writing your biggest dreams and aspirations on a sheet of paper. Common wisdom tells us that writing down our goals is a great practice. Few of us actually do it. Even fewer follow through and achieve those goals. But bold predictions run through Nik's veins.

Nik Halik not only created his "to-do" list at eight years old, but he completed it too—well, *almost*. During our interview, Nik shared:

At eight years of age, I wrote the screenplay to my life and wrote out my top-ten goal list:

*To climb the highest mountains in the world—like Kilimanjaro
   and Everest*
To become a millionaire
To sleep in King Tut's tomb
To go into space in a rocket and walk on the moon
To run with the bulls in Spain
To own homes all over the world
To explore and travel to more than one hundred countries
To go to the bottom of the ocean and have lunch on the **Titanic**
To become a rock star

Did he do it? Yes! And he did most of it by the age of forty. Well, there is one item on that list that Nik has not yet completed: to walk on the moon. But he passionately believes he will take that walk one day. Just another one of his bold estimates he fully plans to turn into a reality.

He is the very first flight-qualified and certified civilian astronaut from Australia and is also set to become the first ever Australian and private space explorer to rocket to outer space and live on Earth's only manned outpost in orbit, the International Space Station.

Nik Halik was born in Melbourne, Australia to Greek immigrant parents, and today he is a self-made multimillionaire, adventurer, bestselling author, and global wealth strategist who runs several companies.

Nik is also the first to tell everyone:

"Individuals who seek status symbols in life have a fixation on syn-thetic wealth. People should feel good about themselves because of what they are and what they do—not because of what they have in their garages. I was born rich in potential and inherited a host of obstacles along the way."

That last statement could be true of any one of us, but in Nik's case the obstacles were substantial. That only makes his success all the more significant. He overcame his obstacles and challenges to live a life that most of us can only dream about.

Nik compares the first ten years of his life to that of the famous "boy in the bubble"—he was plagued with chronic allergies, asthma, and other health issues. The encyclopedia, he says, was his only friend. For Nik, it didn't start all that bold. Life was actually pretty gray.

"At twelve years old I stopped listening to people's B.S. I started becoming an independent thinker. And thinking that way sparked something within me—I began to feel less sick and I made a conscious decision to overcome my illness. As far back as I can remember, I always chose to listen to a drumbeat different from most people. That still works for me, and I would advise others to do the same."

"After I created my list of ten goals when I was eight years old, I really never looked back. I learned that even the smallest steps would get me closer to my goals. One of my goals was to go to outer space. When the rocket went off I was not scared—not even a little nervous! All I felt was excitement. When you look down to earth from space, you realize there are no borders, no boundaries, no religion. And there's something about that.."

When it comes to making money, Nik rejects one of the most popular notions:

"People say it takes money to make money. No, it doesn't take money to make money. It takes experience and knowledge to make money. If you lack experience and knowledge, then it does take lots of money—and you take on lots of risk. But the more knowledge and experience you have, the less money you need and the fewer risks you have to take. That's why the rich get richer."

You can't leave your fate in the hands of others. According to Nik: *"Some people will care about us and some won't, but that really shouldn't matter, because we all need to be self-reliant."*

Take responsibility for yourself. He advises: *"Put time aside daily to reflect on what needs to be done. Then create a daily achievement list. Write down the four 'must-do' things for each day. At the end of the day, write down what needs to be done tomorrow."*

It is these types of bold behaviors and practices that separate Nik from his peers. Nik knows that an extraordinary life doesn't usually happen by accident. It takes drive and consistent effort on your part. No one can do it for you, because "excellence is the result of a commitment to competence." It takes commitment to live life one step at a time. Nik urges people to "focus on each task completely, and then move on."

Maintaining your focus isn't easy. Other people want to tell you what to do. They try to tell you what's important, and they can easily discourage or distract you from your dreams. But Nik simply says:

"Don't buy people's B.S. They usually have their own agenda. Instead, get to know yourself: what is your definite purpose? Pursue a career of choice rather than settling for a 'job' of necessity. Your life's story should be written by you. It's your screenplay and nobody else's. Take responsibility for it!"

Nik Halik sees tragedy in settling for a mundane life and not deciding to live a bold one. He encourages people to live a life less ordinary, challenging everyone with this advice: *"Don't just exist—live your life! Stop putting off your dreams for 'someday.' Right now, dare to dream, live with passion, and make life an epic journey."*

Nik warns us not to let pursuing our dreams become an oppressive burden. Rather, he encourages everyone to enjoy their lives. He himself resides in Hollywood, California, but he also maintains homes in the Greek Islands as well as in Morocco and Australia.

NIK'S EMPOWERING THOUGHT: *"Dare to dream, live with passion, and make life an epic journey."*

DO IT DAILY:

- *Live a life filled with bold goals.* Stay happy and healthy, and never forget or neglect the "kid" in you. That "kid" will take you farther and allow you to dream bigger than most anything else will.

- *Author your life's story.* No one should pen your story but you. Take life by the reigns and decide, very early on, that you and you alone will dictate what happens to you.

Jacob "Stitch" Duran

ULTIMATE FIGHTING CHAMPIONSHIP (UFC) CUTMAN

Stitch's Journey:

PUERTO RICAN MIGRANT FARM WORKER → AIR FORCE → EVERYONE'S
FAVORITE CUTMAN

Cutmen are responsible for preventing and treating damage to fighters in full-contact sports. Stitch has less than one minute between rounds to fix a deep gash, a broken nose, or even an open artery. Every second counts, and his expertise has saved more than a few bouts from being stopped due to an injury. There is likely no one who knows the notion of supporting another better than he does. He not only does it for a living, he is also the best in the world at it.

In life, we all need someone in our corner. Whether in the ring or outside of it, knowing someone has got your back is imperative to truly succeeding.

He told me, *"When I work a corner and I see a fighter has nothing left, I look straight into his eyes, tell him to relax; now this is where champions are made. It's 90 percent mental and 10 percent talent. If he has prepared properly his body will respond."*

Can you really look deep into another person's soul? If it was truly possible for this to happen, I suppose there would be no one more fitting than Jacob "Stitch" Duran, everybody's favorite cutman. Stitch has become *the* go-to guy for top athletes in the worlds of boxing and Mixed Martial Arts (MMA).

An MMA fighter entering the fight cage—the Octagon—is remarkably vulnerable, fully exposed to the watching world. In those moments, a close observer can discern a lot. These warriors have spent years working on every facet of martial arts, only to put it all on the line for a few moments in the cage. As they are exposed to the talents and violence of their opponents, their family, friends, coaches, and teammates look on, but none closer that Stitch.

"When I start wrapping a fighter's hands reality sets in. It's show time—he's going into battle. A war begins in the next few minutes, and the person on the other side of the cage will try to destroy them physically and mentally, trying to take away their dreams."

As we spoke, Stitch reflected on his journey:

"I never thought I would be in this position. I started at the bottom of the barrel—growing up in a Puerto Rican migrant-farm-worker family in central California. As a twenty-two-year-old, I joined the Air Force and spent a year in Thailand where I saw my first Muay Thai match. I fell in love with the sport and started training the next day. I never turned pro myself, but I did start training other guys and eventually opened my own school in Fairfield, California. I put all the money I had into that school and spent all my time working with fighters. I became very interested in learning how to be a cutman, and with lots of reading and on-the-job training I became well known in kickboxing circles for my ability to wrap hands and fix cuts. I learned I had a real gift for working fighters' corners as a cutman. In 2001 I was approached by UFC President Dana White, who asked me to work some UFC fights. Back then the fights were really brutal, so I knew I'd have plenty

of work to do. I also saw early on that they were going to have to establish more rules to make the sport safer."

"Before each fight and between the rounds I often see fighters who may not be the most talented or the most skilled, but they have the heart to fight one more round—even when their bodies are crying out to give up. Skill is one thing, but like former heavyweight boxing champ Mike Tyson once told me, 'You have to learn and have the ability to take the pain.'"

"I'm face-to-face with these guys. They come back to the corner and I see every emotion: from fear, anxiety, and desperation to confidence and pain. Even while I'm fixing them up they look for me to tell them everything will be all right. When they see me as confident and calm, it helps them remain confident and calm."

"Same thing in life: you are not the only one on the ropes of life. Sometimes we have to challenge ourselves, or go up against the system to get the things we want. You'll see negatives and positives in life. When there's a negative you need to believe there'll be a positive right behind it."

"It's great to follow your dreams, and it's even fine to be scared. You may not know what the outcome will be, but you have to cross that finish line. You always need to keep moving forward."

"If you want to be a fighter, you need to love fighting. Money is the wrong reason. Passion and commitment only come when you really want to do something. Conditioning and discipline can separate two equally skilled fighters. So in the long run, if you don't love what you're doing, you won't have the discipline for top conditioning."

I remember as a kid hearing the announcer on *ABC's Wide World of Sports* saying, "The thrill of victory and the agony of defeat." Stitch sees that and more from up close—he has the best seat in the house. It's in his hands to fix a fighter, both mentally *and* physically, to fight one more champion-ship round.

Stitch took a somewhat thankless job, but he has become an inspiration to many as he emerged as one of the most referred-to personalities in the MMA and boxing communities. It is not just about treating a fighter's injuries. It is about elevating that fighter, and giving him strength when he truly needs it. Being recognized as the top cutman in combative sports helped Stitch land movie roles in *Play It to the Bone*, *Ocean's Eleven*, and Sylvester Stallone's *Rocky Balboa*.

Stitch sums it all up well: "I never take anything for granted. If I fail, I can always go back to picking peaches—and that's okay too!"

STITCH'S EMPOWERING THOUGHT: *"It's great to follow your dreams, and it's even fine to be scared. You may not know what the outcome will be, but you have to cross that finish line. You always need to keep moving forward."*

DO IT DAILY:

▸ *Create a formula for your personal achievement.* There's a formula for anything you want to do in life. You just need to figure out that formula and then act upon it one step at a time.

▸ *Surround yourself with a strong support system.* No one can do it alone. Even the greatest fighters need a team in their corner. The same is true in life. Find your support system and rely on them to help you reach your goals.

Juan Carlos "JC" Santana

WORLD CLASS PERFORMANCE AND FITNESS TRAINER

JC's Journey:

CUBAN IMMIGRANT → BACK TO BASICS → COLLEGE PROFESSOR

Relentlessness is one of those qualities that keeps you so enormously focused on your goals that nothing will stop you from pushing forward. It doesn't matter what shows up, it will never be enough to make you quit.

I grew up among many different athletes who shared a common mindset about strength and fitness. They were relentless across the board. It was all about how much you could bench press, squat, and dead lift. Athletes and their trainers gave very little consideration to training techniques or to understanding how the body really works on the athletic field or in the arena.

We all wanted to be the best we could be, and we were willing to put the necessary time and effort into our training. However, as the old saying goes, "You just don't know what you don't know."

When I moved to Florida, I began training at the Institute of Human Performance (IHP), founded by Juan Carlos "JC" Santana. JC is one of the world's leading authorities on training and performance and has been in the fitness industry for more than forty years. His knowledge and skills are in great demand by elite professional athletes, trainers, Olympians, police forces, and the military. JC inspires and teaches his philosophy and techniques all over the world, visiting twenty counties each year as an author, public speaker, and fitness consultant. He is relentless in his dedication to his trade.

His credentials as a college professor and his advanced understanding of biomechanics and conditioning have made JC the go-to guy for athletes from a wide range of professional organizations. He has served clients from the New England Patriots, the Boston Red Sox, the New York Yankees, the Miami Marlins, the New York Rangers, and the New York Islanders, as well as the PGA and the UFC. JC has developed training protocols that combine the stabilization, strength, balance, and endurance needed for any sporting endeavor.

JC and I reminisced about our athletic careers and agreed on one fact: *we each would have gone further than we did if we had trained like this when we were young athletes.* His high-intensity/low-impact, injury-free training methods would have extended our careers and reduced the debilitating injuries we sustained—and made us better athletes all around.

JC's functional training sounds like an easy concept, and it *is* becoming more mainstream every day. But, like all good things that quickly grow in popularity, the term "functional training" has been misinterpreted and misapplied over the last decade: everyone claims to do it—but few really know what it is.

For athletes on all levels, it pays to explore the concept of functional training and review a little history of fitness. In his book *Functional Training: Breaking the Bonds of Traditionalism*, JC explains:

"When man first evolved, life was functional—you worked hard to survive. Everything from hunting to farming required much of the body to perform many of the movements we call 'training' today."

Fitness and conditioning methods stayed fairly consistent from ancient times to the middle of the twentieth century. As training developed in the modern era of machine and bodybuilding, many of the past's effective techniques were forgotten.

In the 1960s and '70s, Universal and Nautilus pioneered resistance training with weight machines. Arnold Schwarzenegger starred in the movie *Pumping Iron* in 1977, and bodybuilding became the thing to do, but, as JC explained:

"The problem with the bodybuilding revolution was that it forgot how we moved. Traditional weight training and bodybuilding focused on contracting one muscle while ignoring the fact that all muscles work as a coordinated unit to perform a skill. Bodybuilding thus becomes the equivalent of taking all of the musicians of an orchestra and training them to be virtuosos without ever having an orchestra rehearsal; when they do try to play as an orchestra, it won't sound very good. Consequently, weight training and bodybuilding got a bad reputation with athletes needing speed, coordination, and agility. Boxers, baseball players, golfers, swimmers, tennis [players], and similar athletes wanted little to do with weight training."

For a while, the world of bodybuilding clashed with the world of function.

However, Olympian (and five-time Heavyweight Champion) Evander Holyfield proved you could combine both training approaches. After winning the Olympic gold medal in 1984 in the light heavyweight class, Evander packed on forty more pounds of muscle—with *more* speed, agility, and quickness than before. Evander accomplished this between 1985 and 1990 by hiring a mix of trainers who blended traditional bodybuilding with functional training. His impressive results showed that properly combined training methods could "grow muscle and give it hustle."

According to JC, functional training is not new; it is a return to days past—to many of the techniques used by the ancient Greeks. It is a return to the era of wooden ships and iron men.

With that warrior spirit in mind, JC explained:

"I love to discuss all things related to the will of man and where we get our strengths from. During my journey I have come to understand that strength does not come in the form we are accustomed to talking about. Even the origin of strength must be questioned! Strength does not live in the muscles we train; strength resides at the doorstep of the human will. In combat we often use the words, 'I will impose my will on my opponent.' No truer words can be spoken, for that is indeed what delineates the winners."

"I will challenge anyone to tell me they were ever a high performer without having the mindset that goes along with high performance— an indomitable will! Contrary to popular belief, the will is not forged and tested in the field of battle—that's where it is showcased. The human will is tested in 'deliberate practice'—that practice nobody likes to engage in. Endless repetitions that are focused, supervised, analyzed, critiqued, finely tuned, evaluated, and adjusted based on analysis and feedback. The cycle repeats itself for ten thousand hours or ten years! As the book **Talent Is Overrated** *by Geoff Colvin suggests, it's not talent that often sets the hall-of-famers apart—it's hard work!"*

JC moved to the edge of his seat and asked, "You want proof?"

Of course I did!

JC directed my attention to the NFL Combines (the annual weeklong showcase in which college football players perform physical and mental tests in front of NFL coaches, general managers, and scouts):

"Look at the athletes that have scored at the top of the NFL Combines. Where are they now? Most have not been successful. Now look at the NFL Hall of Fame—show me the Combines standouts. You can't find them! The Combines may measure athleticism, but they don't measure will! Jerry Rice is the poster boy for Indomitable Will Lacking Supernatural Talent. He's a true ironman of the game and the best receiver ever to lace up a pair of shoes. His talent got him into a small college and into the NFL as a sixteenth-round draft pick. However, it was Rice's will that got him through twenty seasons and a career that will never be matched."

JC offered another example of hard work paying off: twelve-time Major League Baseball All-Star Manny Ramirez. He is one of only twenty-five players ever to hit more than five hundred homeruns and earn a World Series MVP:

"We trained Manny at IHP for his batting and MVP titles, so I can speak from experience. Most people don't know how hard Manny worked. Anyone can see that he has talent, but he is by far not the best athlete on the field—not by a long shot. But when he came to IHP, he came to work. He showed up early and outworked the rest of the competition. Manny had the desire to win every time, and he put in the work that others refuse to do."

JC works with military Special Forces deployed all over the world to take out high profile targets. These are the elite of the elite, and they come in all shapes and sizes. But regardless of physique, they are all driven by the same iron will. These guys go days without sleep, food, or water; they live the unlivable. They work and fight for their lives in the most extreme elements.

"What makes these guys different is not their battlefield skills; it's the will with which they follow directions and work toward the success of each mission."

JC's message for his clients: *"**Continually reset what you are willing to endure. IHP trains the best in all fields because we understand that physical training 'resets the barometer of the human will.' It's not about the exercise, the technique, or the program—it's about integrating the training experience into the psyche of the client so at the moment of truth they can perform with inspired greatness.**"*

You would think that getting the most out of people would be easy. Just tell them, "Give me everything you've got," right? But how do you expect people to give you something they've never known, or go to a place where they've never been? By instilling relentless desire in their hearts and souls, for starters.

JC has a unique view of people's perceived limits. He refers to it as "touching the curtain." *"**People will go to the limits they know. They don't go beyond, because they see that limit as a brick wall. I suggest to my athletes that what appears to be a brick wall is actually a curtain with bricks painted on it. During training, I only ask an athlete to 'touch the curtain' repeatedly. Since they are familiar with the effort that brings them to the limit, they can repeatedly practice touching the curtain. The human spirit has always explored. If someone tells you not to open a door, what's the first thing you do when nobody is watching? That's right—you open it. So when any athlete gets comfortable touching the curtain, what happens? They naturally push on it and they post a new personal record!**"*

"You can apply this technique to any aspect of life. You know what your max is—what you've been able to achieve before. You know the feeling of giving it your all. Don't ask your body to do more; just get familiar with your best. As you practice your best, you eventually realize you have more. You push the curtain and presto! You have a new operating level—a better you!"

"What we call 'working out' is really just self-inflicted pain from physical effort. Nearly every spiritual discipline or religion has used pain from self-inflicted physical effort (fasting, suspensions, and so forth) as a method to

achieve spiritual transcendence. What is spiritual transcendence if not a form of redefining the human will?"

"Physical effort and pain can dispense the best drugs in the world—supplied by the body's own incredible pharmacy. We have this internal pharmacy that houses some of the most potent mind- and mood-altering drugs known to man. And this pharmacy opens up only when we breathe heavy from work. The heavier you breathe, the more drugs are dispensed. These chemicals explain why we feel so relaxed and in such a good mood after a good workout."

"When you combine the biomechanical aspects of training, the spiritual component of physical exertion, and the biochemical milieu of high-metabolic demands, training goes beyond anything we ever dreamed of. These elements come together to make my field the perfect combination of science and art. It's truly…spirimotional!"

Born in Cuba in 1959—the year Castro's revolution took over—JC was the son of very successful parents. His dad owned a popular restaurant, and his mom was an accountant.

"After immigrating to America, my parents had to put their egos away to survive. Dad went to work cleaning hospital floors, and Mom went from accountant to a low-level restaurant worker."

As a youngster, JC developed a love for sports and music. He has enjoyed all the trappings of being a good athlete, a college student, a touring musician, a bar owner, and a gym owner. He has become a world authority on athletic training while being a solid family man.

But his life has not been a cruise. JC has endured plenty of dark moments—from failing businesses to failing marriages. His first dark moment came in 1992. As he was trying to raise his two-year-old son, Rio, his bar went bankrupt.

As he found himself getting down to "the basics," he asked himself, "When was I the happiest?" His answer led him to enroll in Florida Atlantic University's exercise science program, and three years later he had a master's degree and was on his way to a doctorate.

JC quickly became an authority in the fitness industry. In twelve years, he has authored fifteen books and more than two hundred articles and produced some seventy DVDs. He maintains an intensive international touring schedule of twenty to twenty-five events annually.

When he opened IHP, he was a happily married man with three more children. But in 2007, the economy took a bad turn and JC was forced to hit a grueling twenty-country yearlong tour that wrecked his body and his family. That began a six-year period of total darkness for JC. He entered a deep depression that forced him into psychiatric care and heavy medication. After trying a multitude of medical treatments for depression and insomnia, JC finally went back to what had shaped him as a young athlete: self-reflection, perseverance, and hard work. Recalling this time, JC says:

"I believe I got into this deep hole because I wasn't being true to the values and principles my parents taught me. I was doing a lot more for others instead of doing for myself. I was upset at the world for what I had been through, and I became bitter toward everyone in it. I was looking at myself through the eyes of others—not through my own two eyes. Finally I realized that the power to change was in me, and all I needed was a different perspective. That was when I finally gave up all therapies and meds and got back to basics."

But as a relentless human being, his will overcame the difficult obstacles in his path.

He went on to explain what he considers to be the basics:

"The past casts a shadow on the present to ensure the future will not change. All of the problems we have are created by past experiences

that are no longer with us, but create limiting beliefs that shape our views of life and our future. Our beliefs are the program we run (i.e. our software), and limiting beliefs are like a virus."

"Now I'm in the groove again. Life isn't perfect, but therein lies its perfection. There will always be challenges, but all of these are learning opportunities. It's one's perception of what happens, and not what actually happens, that really shapes our reality. I'm not perfect, but I am in pursuit of excellence. I'm in the game!"

"If you find yourself in a dark place, try to find stillness. Get out of your mind and your thoughts. Put your full attention toward those things you want—and drive to them with full intention (i.e. focused obsession). Just keep moving forward no matter what—right foot, left foot, repeat! Even if you move backwards, you will get out of the darkness and into the light—and from there you can reassess your next move. Stay in the now and be as productive as possible. No crisis or negative emotions can live in the now. Surround yourself with the best people you can."

"Develop a purpose and a vision, and then drive your intention of that vision so hard you can feel it—all of it. Feel your intention until it makes you cry, laugh, wonder, and jump out of bed every day. That vision is your anchor when things become ugly and dark. During moments of darkness and doubt...get still, then: right foot, left foot, repeat!"

For JC, he attributes his success to his will and inability to give in. His relentlessness has always acted as a light within the darkness. That indomitable and unquestioned desire has pushed him forward and optimized the way in which he lives his life.

JC'S EMPOWERING THOUGHT: *"A day without breathlessness is a day you have not lived!"*

DO IT DAILY:

▸ ***Being relentless will overcome natural talent.*** The effort you put into perfecting your trade will always overcome natural born talent. Talent can only take you so far. A relentless mindset has no limitations.

▸ ***Touch the curtain.*** Imagination knows no boundaries. Motivation must be the order of the day. Complete dedication—along with an impeccable work ethic—reigns supreme. These qualities will help you push farther than you ever thought possible.

Herschel Walker

NFL, OLYMPIAN, MIXED MARTIAL ARTIST

Herschel's Journey:

MENTAL DISORDER → 2,500 DAILY SIT-UPS → HEISMAN TROPHY WINNER

Guts mean courage. Guts equal bravery. Guts allow you to push yourself further than most others would go. For Herschel Walker, having guts was a defining quality that led him to become one of the greatest Running Backs in college and professional history. He is remembered as a physical specimen with the heart and skills to match, all of which played a pivotal role in all that he succeeded in on and off the football field.

But maybe the greatest lesson I learned from Herschel Walker was how being humble toward others can make you friends wherever you go.

I grew up watching Number 34 play for the Georgia Bulldogs and hearing the legendary stories of the way he worked out. I felt very fortunate to spend an evening with him out to dinner after a UFC fight in Las Vegas, along with a few friends, including TapouT president Dan "Punkass" Caldwell.

Herschel, a self-described "Southern gentleman," did all he could to make me feel comfortable and welcomed. We spoke about how he trained; he explained that growing up in a poor family of seven children, he did not have access to weights. He was overweight, had speech problems, and was bullied. But Herschel was not going to be stopped by a lack of opportunities.

His guts prevailed.

In a 1991 interview with the Academy of Achievement, Herschel gave some insight into the roles God and his parents played in his life:

"My parents helped me to believe in myself. I wasn't the best-looking guy, I wasn't the best athlete in the world, but they made me feel good about myself. 'Herschel, you are somebody. Whether you are black, white, it doesn't matter. You are a person and God loves you.'"

"And then again, there was real hard work ethics. That's what we need today. Young people, adults, we need good work ethics. Because nothing is going to come to you easy. We've got too much of a competitive world for anything to come easy to you. People competing in everything. It doesn't matter what it is. Football, that's just athletics. But in the business world—doing everything—people are competing. So you got to get those very good work ethics, and I think that helped me develop my work ethics. I think God has helped me to love myself. I know who God is, and I love God."

He described his daily routine of doing twenty-five hundred sit-ups, two thousand pushups, and fifteen hundred pull-ups. He made it sound somewhat easy as he explained, "It's not what you think. I constantly change my arm positions for the exercises and often do it while watching TV." In my mind, that would not make that much of a difference, but then again I am not Herschel Walker.

"Working out like that started young for me. I was always desperate to be a great athlete; it made me feel good inside."

At the University of Georgia, he and his team won the Sugar Bowl and the NCAA Championship. Herschel earned the 1982 Heisman Trophy and was named All-American three times. But his success was just starting.

In the NFL, Herschel's twelve-year records included rushing for more than eight thousand yards and scoring sixty-one touchdowns. But Herschel loved athletics beyond the football field. He competed in the 1992 Winter Olympics in the two-man bobsled and has pursued yet another sports career in MMA. Despite achieving a fifth-degree black belt in taekwondo, Herschel told me, *"MMA was the hardest training I ever did, but I didn't enter the cage and fight for the money. It was for the love of competing and martial arts."*

Considered to be one of the greatest athletes ever to play any sport, Herschel went so far as to announce during an ESPN interview: *"I've told everyone that at fifty I might try football again just to show people that I can do that. I want to be the George Foreman of football—come back and do that one more time."*

Talk about some serious guts.

Despite his great success as an athlete, Herschel recalled in his memoir, *Breaking Free: My Life with Dissociative Identity Disorder*, that "[his] life, at times, was simply out of control." He often felt angry and self-destructive.

"To me, whenever I stepped onto the football field, the track, the bobsled run, or even playing a video game with my son, what I was participating in was a matter of life-and-death seriousness. I was that competitive. When the doctors explained to me that I had developed other personalities (alters) to help me cope with and survive the pain and alienation I experienced as a child and adolescent, I was skeptical. There may have been as many as 12 of these alters that enabled me to cope with my reality. The diagnosis was Dissociative Identity Disorder

(DID), a mental disorder previously known as multiple personality disorder."

Herschel's understanding of this disorder has helped him better understand himself:

"The truth also is that for most of my life from childhood onward, I had a form of mental illness that enabled me to simultaneously be a fierce competitor consumed by a desire to be the best and dominate in a quiet, unassuming man who let his actions do the talking."

It may be what Herschel decided to do off the field that was the greatest display of his guts. Herschel didn't have to share his personal battles with anybody, but he did—and he sees himself as an advocate for others. While some might have taken this diagnosis as a setback, Herschel used the same strength and inner human spirit to overcome the challenge.

"[I took] it on as my life's mission—not only to understand DID for my personal benefit, but also to understand it to help other people enrich their lives, lessen their level of pain, and find comfort in knowing that … [we] are not alone."

Herschel's spiritual side—like many of the individuals in this book—shines through:

"When God repairs our lives, we become the person He created us to be, with the ability to transform other lives we touch. Unless we allow God to repair us, we will never know the uniqueness of ourselves and the abilities we have to offer mankind."

HERSCHEL'S EMPOWERING THOUGHT: *"You need faith to see something nobody else can see."*

DO IT DAILY:

▸ ***Embrace who you are.*** Use your uniqueness to positively impact others. Have the guts and willingness to exit your comfort zone to make a difference in your life and the lives of others.

▸ ***Guts lead to glory.*** If you want to achieve more success than your competitors, you have to be willing to invest more into the process. Guts can lead you to glory. Be one of the few that is willing to take the chance on failing at something big rather than never even trying.

Daniel Ruettiger

THE REAL "RUDY," NOTRE DAME FOOTBALL

Rudy's Journey:

DYSLEXIC → POOR STUDENT → FEATURE FILM, RUDY

Are you one of the many who believes you will be unable to accomplish your true passion due to a perceived shortcoming? Well, meet Daniel Eugene Ruettiger, better known as "Rudy." Through Rudy's life, we will see that there is no shortcoming that can keep you from achieving what you dream.

Despite his small 5' 6", 185-pound size, Rudy wanted to play football for his favorite team, Notre Dame's Fighting Irish. Not only did Rudy want to play football, but also he aspired to be a defensive end, where the average lineman measured 6' 4" and 250 pounds.

Rudy told me, *"There are people out there that will try and knock you down and tell you things can't be done. As far as I am concerned, you should keep fighting to stay in a positive thought process; a single thought can control everything in your body."*

Rudy should know; in 1993 his epic journey inspired the hit motion picture *Rudy*.

"As a kid growing up, I had a hard time. I was the third child of fourteen in my family. I loved all sports, and I was lucky to have a baseball coach when I was only seven. He made me feel good about myself. He encouraged me."

"I came to understand that it was less about the game and more about believing in myself."

"But school was very tough for me because I was dyslexic. It held me back in almost all aspects of my life—until I joined the Navy. That turned out to be a positive turning point for me. I became self-confident and began to believe in myself. I stopped listening to people who said I couldn't do this or that."

"For me it was about continuing my goals even when I was knocked down. After the Navy, I worked in a power plant for two years, then I applied to Notre Dame. But my grades just weren't good enough. Although I was disappointed, I didn't give up on college. I applied to Holy Cross College, a small university near Notre Dame. Finally, on my fourth try, I was accepted to Notre Dame in the fall of 1974."*

"I decided to try out for the Notre Dame football team as a walk-on. My goal was to outwork everybody on the team. I made the practice squad that just works with the varsity team to prepare for real games. Going up against players outweighing me by more than one hundred pounds didn't matter because I was playing football for Notre Dame!"

"Finally, in my senior year, I got into a game. On November 8, 1975, Head Coach Dan Devine put me in as a defensive end against Georgia Tech. This was the opportunity I'd been working for from as far back as I could remember, and I wasn't about to let it pass me up."

"I was able to sack the quarterback—every defensive end's dream. And my teammates were so thrilled for me they carried me off the field in celebration. That was only the first time a Notre Dame player was carried off the field." (To this day, only two players have ever been so honored.)

Rudy's triumph is immortalized in the movie *Rudy*, and he has been honored to receive keys to cities across America and invitations to visit the White House. Each year the "Rudy Foundation," founded by Rudy and his wife Cheryl, bestows two "Rudy" Awards to recognize outstanding football players on college and high school teams. The recipients personify Rudy's "Four C's": *Courage, Character, Commitment, and Contribution.*

The Common Thread of Overcoming Adversity & Living Your Dreams is about inspiration—how each of us can get out of our own way and reach our fullest potential. So, with his permission, I offer these words of wisdom from Rudy's *Game Plans for Winning at Life*:

"It starts with a Dream. Visualize your Dream and make a commitment. Having a Dream is what makes life exciting. Never underestimate the power of a Dream. It will change your life. A Dream gives you the ability to determine your future."

"Be the person you want to be. Make the decision to take action and move closer to your Dream. Create daily success habits and surround yourself with information that will empower and inspire you. Believe in yourself and don't let anything stop you. Reinforce your Dream every day with positive information from tapes, books, and mentors."

"The greater the struggle, the greater the victory. Most people allow struggles and fear of failure to stop them. The key is to learn from your struggles and move on. Failures will make you stronger and give you the information you need to reach your Dream. Struggle will prepare you for success. Without struggle there is no success."

"Excuses will kill your Dream. What we're really talking about here is commitment. Until you make a commitment to your Dream, it's not really a Dream ... it's just another fantasy full of excuses. Fantasies don't come true because they're not real; we're not committed to them.

When we make commitments, we eliminate excuses and they become Dreams ... and Dreams are definitely real."

"Focus on your Dream and Never Quit. It is always too soon to quit. If you quit, you can't succeed. By achieving your Dream you will be an inspiration to others. You will set the example and make an enormous impact on the world. Make it happen!"

When asked about his thoughts on the film, Rudy responded:

"The movie was made to tell a story that would inspire others—to let people know that no matter what the odds are, they can overcome them, they can win. No matter what your background, your grades, your size—you can find a way. It won't come easy. The message is clear that you need to struggle; you need to prepare to earn your dream. It's all about the dream, the struggle, the victory!"

Rudy inspires all of us to be tough as nails and not accept any "shortcomings" we may feel are present in our lives. If we want to succeed, we have to be prepared to overcome any adversity and we must make a non-negotiable commitment to reach our goals.

RUDY'S EMPOWERING THOUGHT: *"Visualize your dream and make a commitment. Having a dream is what makes life exciting. Never underestimate the power of a dream. It will change your life. A dream gives you the ability to determine your future."*

DO IT DAILY:

▸ *Never quit on yourself. Never quit on your dream!* Dedication, commitment and following through are the three greatest assets to achieving your goals.

▸ ***Be tough as nails.*** If you want to succeed, you are going to have to toughen up and overcome any obstacles or setbacks along your journey.

The Common Thread

N ow it's time to apply "The Common Thread" to your life…

During the course of more than 25 years and thousands of hours interacting with, observing, and interviewing many of the highly successful people featured in this book, combined with my own life experiences and journey to becoming a success and life coach certified by The International Coach Federation (ICF), I have listened and have learned that there is indeed a "Common Thread;" in fact several common threads, that if applied to your life can greatly increase your chances of extreme success.

While crafting the conclusion for this book, it became obvious that from whatever walk of life these people came, they programmed and conditioned themselves in the practice of excellence. They have incorporated into their lives several overlapping themes that can be further broken down into six key categories that should serve as a road map to help you take charge of your own destiny:

Discovering your "WHY"
Establishing a Winning Mindset
Conquering Your Fears
Silencing the Enemy Within – "Negative Self-talk"
Pursuing Knowledge
Leveraging Your Opportunities

If you learn from these observations, and then apply these "best practices," you can dramatically improve your chances for succeeding in life and overcoming its challenges. Ultimately, this will allow you to achieve remarkable heights with the realization that you have the power to put yourself in the position to direct your own success story beyond the boundaries of even your own imagination.

Before delving into the inner workings of the highly successful people featured in this book, focus your mind on the following thoughts:

Rule number one has always been, and will forever be: Don't beat yourself, don't get in your own way, and don't come up short because of lack of effort, preparation, or self-doubt.

Achieving success isn't a "spectator sport." You must be an active participant; success is earned, not given.

Don't look to anyone else for your achievements. The moment you honestly take responsibility for all you do is the moment you begin your journey toward reaching your goals.

Your past doesn't control you. Refuse to believe that your best years are behind you.

Fight strong and hard for your happiness and success—it's worth it.

As Sylvester Stallone said in *Rocky Balboa*:

"Let me tell you something you already know. The world ain't all sunshine and rainbows. It's a very mean and nasty place and I don't care how tough you are it will beat you to your knees and keep you there permanently if you let it. You, me, or nobody is gonna hit as hard as life. But it ain't about how hard ya' hit. It's about how hard you can get hit and keep moving forward. How much you can take and keep moving forward. That's how winning is done!"

DISCOVERING YOUR WHY

Let's first set the table of what you can expect as you travel the path toward your ultimate success. We live in a very competitive world. There is no question there will be many others who have the same goals and aspirations as you. Perhaps what needs to be established more than most anything else to reach your goals is "The **WHY**."

The **WHY** is your deepest of emotions, it is personal and profound, it is beyond your motivation of what you desire. If used correctly, the **WHY** becomes a great personal asset. It is something that others cannot see, understand or even take away. Your **WHY** should dominate any and all obstacles and challenges that come between you and your goals.

The **WHY** can help you through the toughest of times—it can drive you past your fear, your pain, or just plain boredom from a tedious task. The **WHY** can make sure you stay steadfast when the going gets tough, while others wither away.

To discover your **WHY,** the first step is to be brutally honest with yourself. You must understand and tap into your most guarded emotions. This can be somewhat of a spiritual experience. To do so, take the time to relive the happiest moments of your life as well as the most difficult ones.

Reflect on when you were at your best and went beyond what you or others thought you were capable of. What were the positive feelings you experienced?

They no doubt included self-worth, confidence, and happiness, among others.

Think back to promises you made to yourself in the past that you did not keep. What were the negative feelings you experienced?

Chances are self-doubt, fear, and depression.

The emotions that come out of those experiences help create your **WHY.**

Your **WHY** should enable you to dig deep and keep you motivated and strong enough to push through until you experience those positive feelings again.

Conversely, the **WHY** should also help push away any excuses you have used in the past and remind you of the emotions you don't want to relive.

You need to have your **WHY** readily available for everyday use. Think of your **WHY** as something that is stored in a bottle. Before you roll out of bed each morning, ready to take on the world, visualize opening the bottle and using it as a powerful resource throughout the day as you face your challenges and obstacles.

Once you identify with your **WHY,** it can become part of your everyday thought pattern. Soon you will use it as an automatic tool, and your commitment to excellence will be on autopilot.

This is what successful people do. They are strong, steadfast and committed to their goals because they understand themselves, they understand their **WHY,** and most importantly, they use it to outlast and out endure the competition.

ESTABLISHING A WINNING MINDSET

Don't underestimate the impact that that your mindset has on all aspects of your life, particularly when it comes to dealing with challenges and obstacles and with pursuing your dreams. Observe yourself and others and you will see that, more often than not, the mind gives up before the physical body does. In other words, a mind under duress will likely cause you to stop moving forward before you reach your physical breaking point.

Your mind and thoughts are a strong influence on the success you will have. It can be your ally or your worst enemy, acting as a disabling handicap. It's the lens through which you see everything, including your assumptions, interpretations, self-confidence and self-esteem. Your mind and beliefs can limit you with self-imposed roads blocks and can have a direct effect on how you respond to all situations.

You may tend to have an internal battle with opposing forces. Part of your mind could say, "Go for it," while another part says, "Not today" or "Maybe tomorrow."

The super-achievers I interviewed cannot be placed into a specific demographic; however, they share a common thread—a constant demonstration of a powerful mindset that generates an inner "mental power" that extends outward and is used to deal with obstacles and setbacks. It greatly enhances the accomplishment of their goals. This mental power is consistently used in most aspects of their lives, creating a constant repeatable behavior that produces productive actions toward their desired outcome. **If you change your mindset, you can change your world.**

For those who have experienced true success, maintaining and practicing the right mindset is not a part-time job—it is actually a lifestyle. It is the understanding that there is nothing to regret—only experiences from which to learn and grow. Focusing on the past and the "what ifs" or the "what might happen" only creates self-imposed challenges throughout your journey.

Treasure hunter Mel Fisher, a former business associate and mentor whose story is told in this book, committed 16 years of his life, as well as his family's, to search for the Spanish galleon Nuestra Señora de Atocha that sunk off the Florida Keys in 1622. Despite many non-believers, Mel lived by and had the mindset of his now famous quote, "Today's the day!"

This mindset helped Mel reach his goal and find fortune and fame when he discovered in excess of 400 million dollars' worth of treasure that was lost at sea for more than 350 years. Mel had the "make it happen mindset" each and every day. Successful people consistently embrace Mel Fisher's "Today's the Day" commitment and mentality.

PUSHING THROUGH YOUR PAIN

Success requires an understanding of pain, and pain comes in many different forms. It can be physical or emotional pain, the pain of rejection, the pain of not being where you want to be in life or even the pain of being out of your comfort zone, which we as human beings often see as one of the most difficult places to be.

The manner in which your mind handles pain and the ability it has to shift the meaning of pain from something you may want to flee to something that can be used as a stepping-stone throughout your quest is key to your success. We all have our own tipping point of what makes our mindset weak. Understanding that point of no return and doing all you can to not reach that point is essential to succeeding both personally and professionally.

You will not get to the place you want to be if you do not embrace and endure the pain required to pursue your dream. To "go for the gold," a strong mindset is a must. Using your desire to accomplish your goals must overtake the pain of the necessary steps required for achievement. The anxiety of getting out of your comfort zone must be less than the anxiety of not being where you want to be.

You will most likely experience plenty of painful rejection on the road to success—a lot of "no's" for every "yes." Expect that pain, understand it, accept it and grow as an individual from it.

Often, you do not have control over your circumstances—the only thing you really have control over is your thinking and how you address and respond to situations. Many of the most successful people in the world have faced the same difficulties and obstacles that you face. They have been at great heights, and have fallen and risen again using their strong mindset as an invaluable asset.

They did not let their circumstances define them, and neither should you. My old football coach used to say, "If you get knocked down, get back up and dust yourself off." That advice holds true on the football field and on the field of life. With each painful misstep you gain wisdom and experience. It's okay if you come out of it with an emotional or physical battle scar or two. That's to be expected. But remember that you will prosper in the long run if you adopt the mindset of "dusting yourself off" and continuing to take one step after another.

Visualize a finish line out there with your name and goal on it and don't stop pressing forward until you plow through it. Behind the biggest success stories are the people who have outdone and outlasted their competitors. They leave nothing to chance or luck. They have taken the steps to solve problems that others have not; they have the "stick to it" attitude and the mindset to expect more from themselves. Their mindset does not allow for self-pity, helplessness, or a "victim mentality." They look at setbacks and mistakes as mere bumps in the road—*not* as a reflection of their true potential.

If you don't have the mindset that you are worth it, then why should others? Keep in mind that you can succeed even if nobody in the world believes in you, but you will not succeed if you do not believe in yourself.

You have the ability to be great at something. In fact, I would bet that you can think back to a moment in time when you were at your best. And I am sure you'd agree that in that moment, your mindset played a significant role in making that moment possible. You likely exhibited endless confidence and self-discipline, and did not let outside influences, pondering or self-doubt get in your way. It was that momentum of an "empowered mindset" that rocketed you towards your goals.

As you move forward, prepare your mind and get ready for the naysayers and couch critics. Beware of those who will tempt or push you toward the trap door of doubt and despair.

All too often family, friend, or foe will likely tell you why things can't be done instead of supporting and encouraging you along the way. They have their own motives and reasons for this negative behavior. Often their subconscious allows personal self-doubt and lack of effort in their own ventures to somehow justify sabotaging your efforts.

There are people out there who want to see you fail because it somehow makes them feel better about themselves and their own shortcomings. Unfortunately, that is the competitive and sometimes twisted world we live in. It is just one more thing to overcome; do not use it as an excuse or let it derail you along your journey.

DON'T LET IT HAPPEN: DON'T LET SOMEONE ELSE PUT LIMITS ON YOU!

Success does not occur by accident. Don't fall into the trap or have the mindset that somebody will come knocking at your door to give you some type of magic potion that will bring you instant success. What you can count on is your competition getting up early, staying late, and having the mindset to do the things you are not willing to do. Subscribe to the concept that success takes intense dedication and a consistently strong mindset.

Successful individuals generally have exceptional awareness and the mindset to create a game plan and strategy that motivates both them and the people around them. They are not driven to be perfect. They are driven to implement their plans. Their mental makeup helps them adapt and make necessary modifications to "the plan" in order to continue on their journey to success.

Achievers don't waste time comparing themselves to others—they have their own standards. They have the mindset to use compartmentalization to deal with one obstacle at a time. It enables them to maintain their priorities and effectively manage their day. **Their minds actively look for meaning and a better perspective of their setbacks, failures, and shortcomings. It's about finding growth behind the experience and seeing the positive outcomes that can result from what others may perceive as negative situations.** This attitude helps them take responsibility for their own actions, behavior, and circumstances.

One theme remains constant: People who have a strong mindset and use it to create a plan and outwork others achieve higher levels of real long-term success than the average person.

As Winston Churchill said: *"Some people dream of success while others get up and work for it!"*

FANNING THE FLAMES OF PASSION

I am sure you have heard that you need to have passion to succeed. That word is certainly an important one and high performers use it, but what does it really mean? Where does it come from and how can you use passion in your own life?

Geoff Colvin, author of *Talent is Overrated*, puts it this way: "Passion doesn't accompany us into the world but rather, like high level-skills themselves, develops. World class achievers are driven to improve but did not start out that way."

Throughout my conversations with highly successful people, the majority pointed out that even in a moment of defeat they saw something within themselves that could be developed and in turn increase their performance levels. That very small "thing" is what planted the seed of passion within their heart and soul to continue their efforts under any and all circumstances.

Psychologist Stephen Ceci and affiliated researchers at Cornell University developed what they called the "multiplier effect." Their findings are published in *The Psychology of Abilities, Competencies, and Expertise (Cambridge University Press)*. In essence they talk about how early, small, inborn strengths can steer somebody towards enhanced environments, helping to create a snowball effect of passion and success. As a result, small successes can build the desire and passion to practice more, which will eventually lead to increased drive and high performance.

SETTING YOUR GOALS: MILESTONES AND OBJECTIVES

You have heard it before, and the concept is correct: Establishing your goal one step at a time is the most effective way to reach the finish line. Setting goals will help you stay focused and give you something to look forward to along the way.

It all begins with the first step of being as specific as you can be with your desired outcome. To say I want to be rich or I want to get a great job is just too vague. Zoom in and put a spotlight on what you want the end result to look like. As an individual, your goal is unique and what motivates you might be different from what motivates others. That is fine so long as you have an understanding that you'll reach it only by following a specific game plan and taking the necessary steps to achieve it.

Aim high and stretch yourself to see how far you can really go; however, make it realistic, and within your reach. If you set a goal that is too high, it is likely you will talk yourself out of it before you even begin. As you reach certain goals and plateaus along your journey, be sure to reward yourself with incentives that will help keep you going, and then establish new and even higher goals.

Put a timeline on your goal. A non-specific timetable like "sometime in the future," will no doubt prevent you from taking that first step and will be ammunition for procrastination.

Create a "to-do list" of the action steps you need to take to reach your goal. If you are not sure what belongs on that list, seek out others who have "been there, done it," and have the experience and the knowledge to offer insight and input into your chosen field.

A funny thing happens when you write down your goals in a list or a letter to yourself. Suddenly, there is a plan and your belief system kicks into high gear. A good strategy many achievers implement is to keep the list at the forefront of their mind. Don't hide your list. Post it in a place you see often every day—on your bathroom mirror, your refrigerator, your car visor—any place it is consistently visible.

In 1969, at 29-years-old, Bruce Lee, world-renowned martial artist, actor and father of two, wrote himself a letter entitled "My Definite Chief Aim." In the letter, Lee declared that he would become the highest paid Oriental superstar in America and vowed that he would repay that with quality and exciting performances. He said he would achieve world fame and earn $10 million by 1980. Three years after setting these specific goals, he met and surpassed what he set out to achieve.

Was a letter to himself all it took? No, but it certainly gave Bruce a clear understanding of his goals and a road map on his way to stardom.

On your journey, be prepared for curve balls. Your plans don't always work exactly how you'd like for them to. You will need to adjust and perhaps adopt new strategies along the way.

We all would like a clear beginning and a clean direct ending, but that is just not reality. When your plans go awry, it is important to stay strong and stick to the next task at hand.

Expect setbacks. One step forward and two steps back is something that highly successful people deal with all the time. What separates them from the "average" person is that they keep moving forward towards their goals and are fixated on the final outcome.

The beginning of the process is the time for great thought concerning the necessary steps to achieving your goals. Once there is a game plan in place, it is time to turn off the thinking. All too often you can fall into a self-imposed trap of over thinking, which could lead you to unnecessary pondering and procrastination. Set your well-thought out agenda, put the thinking aside, and just move forward. Don't worry about the future or the past. Worry about each individual step in front of you.

Remember this is about you being the best you can be, and leaving nothing to chance or luck. If you are looking to separate yourself from others using more scientific-based facts and research, then it is well worth sharing with you the findings of Swedish psychologist K. Anders Ericsson, a professor at Florida State University.

He has done a great deal of work pertaining to success and is recognized as one of the world's leading researchers on expertise. His studies show that high-level success is not a birthright.

The Cambridge Handbook of Expertise and Expert Performance, written by Ericsson and his colleagues, is the first handbook where the world's foremost experts on expertise review the scientific knowledge on expert performance and how experts differ from non-experts. In the book, he explained that extraordinary chess players, business leaders, and athletes have what he calls "deliberate, well-structured practice."

I have highlighted what I believe are the key phrases and words that should be considered to reach your own personal high level of performance. My suggestion is that you read this several times to capture and take in a full understanding.

He wrote:

"[Deliberate, well-structured] practice is **focused**, programmatic, carried out **over extended periods of time**, guided by conscious performance monitoring, evaluated by **analyses of errors** and procedures **directed at eliminating error**. **Specific goals** are set at successive stages of expertise development. It involves appropriate immediate **feedback about performance**. The feedback can be obtained by objective observers—human teachers or coaches—or can be self-generated by **comparing one's own performance with examples of more-advanced expert performance**. Such objective feedback helps the learner of expertise to internalize how to identify and correct errors, to set new goals, to **focus on overcoming weakness,** and to monitor progress."

"Deliberate and well-structured practice builds on setting goals that **go beyond ones current level** of performance and thus **may lead to failures** or even lower performance. **Aspiring expert performers come to view failures as opportunities to improve."**

Using deliberate practice while working toward your goal will greatly increase your chances of success.

Embrace all the good and all the bad. It will be worth it when you have reached your journey's end.

PREPARATION AND COMPETITION

"The will to win is not as important as the will to prepare to win." – **Coach Bobby Knight**

"For every two minutes of fame, there are eight hours of hard work."
– Television News Reporter Jessica Savage

People who find happiness in competing will have the mental strength and drive to keep developing the necessary skills needed to be fully prepared. This joy of competition enables high achievers to focus on an eventual positive outcome, even when things aren't going that well. They discover a deeper understanding of growth, maturity, strength and character through competition. They face adversity and stress, but are willing to fight through it.

I had the privilege of publishing the first MMA fine art line featuring many of the top UFC fighters in the world. I was honored when I was able to work with World Champion fighter Georges St-Pierre. In his book, *The Way of the Fight*, Georges described his journey from being bullied as a kid to becoming one of the greatest champions in UFC history. He wrote about his training camp, competition, and preparing for an upcoming fight: "I want to fight guys who are better than me in all kinds of techniques. I want my training to be harder than my actual fights so I can be prepared to face my toughest opponents—so I can be ready to deal with fear."

One of the slogans used by the U.S. Navy SEALS says it perfectly: "The more you sweat in peacetime, the less you bleed in war."

Competition and preparation set the stage for physical and mental success. Keep in mind that you will have limited control over all the circumstances during your upcoming event, however, if you have "seen it and felt it" before, the day of the event will not be a surprise. This holds true whether it be an athletic event, speech, performance, or business presentation.

Putting yourself through difficult times and possible scenarios while preparing and doing things that are generally out of your comfort zone will be a positive process of self-discovery and will help you to grow as a more confident and disciplined competitor. In time, you will find yourself being more comfortable and more empowered in situations by which you were once intimidated.

High achievers understand that the success and satisfaction they get from preparing for competition enables them to stay mentally stronger just a little bit longer than their competitors, which can often be the difference between winning and losing.

A victor is created using your mind and skills, preparation, and even the sweat and tears that are seldom seen by anyone else. This applies not only for an athlete or business executive, but also for the student studying for exams or the mom striving behind the scenes to raise a family.

STAY HUMBLE

Most of the successful people I've met have a humble side. They don't feel entitled to success, and they maintain an unwavering work ethic. Using their strong minds, they face challenges, stress, and adversity with poise and the patience to work through difficult times.

They understand the importance of staying grounded. They recognize the need to be compassionate toward others and are aware that people have an underlying need to feel appreciated. They look to others for mentoring in areas where they seek development. Devoted to optimism, they realize how fragile success can truly be. Their way of thinking gives them the ability to constantly work on their coping strategies to become stronger and stronger, and willing to endure more and more hurdles even as they continually set the bar higher and higher.

Frequently, successful individuals have a connection to a higher "spiritual power," believing God has played an integral part in their lives and helped them overcome their challenges. They have a deep sense of faith and devotion, and remain grateful while giving credit to God for being with them all the time and constantly enabling them to be the best they can be.

Generally speaking, high achievers find a way to "give back" by contributing to society in a variety of ways. If you practice the art of giving, not only does it make a difference in someone else's life, but you will find that it will have a great impact on you as well.

STRENGTHEN YOUR MIND WITH PHYSICAL ACTIVITY

It might surprise you to find out that early humans traveled as much as 12 miles a day (today people walk an average of less than half a mile). Perhaps I am aging myself, but I fondly remember days gone by when I would play outside from morning till night with my friends.

I can't overemphasize the importance of physical activity and the effect it has on your success. Without question, the majority of individuals featured in this book make physical fitness a priority. The correlation between a strong mindset and physical fitness has been proven in numerous studies.

The benefits reach far beyond improving your alertness and overall health; your sense of self-worth, optimism, energy and happiness are heightened within your soul. It improves creativity, fights depression and trains you to take on demanding challenges.

I like to describe self-worth as an animal that needs to be fed; many things can feed that animal, including giving to others, accomplishments, reaching goals and a favorite of mine, physical fitness.

Juan Carlos Santana, a friend and one of the world's leading authorities on training and performance, explains the "high" reported by recreational and professional athletes. He points out that exercise can release an assortment of amazing "feel-good" chemicals from your body's own internal pharmacy. These include endorphins, dopamine, BDNF (brain-derived neurotropic factor) and serotonin, all influencing your overall happiness, sleeping habits, and satisfaction. The "pay off" of physical fitness to the mind and body does not require extreme effort—what it does require is consistency.

Even learning is greatly enriched when combined with simple specific movements. In *Smart Moves*, author, biologist and educator Carla Hannaford, PhD, has produced groundbreaking research on the essential role the body plays in learning. She says:

"Movement awakens and activates many of our mental capacities."

"In a study of more than 500 Canadian children, students who spent an hour each day in gym performed notably better on exams than less active students. Similar, men and women in their fifties and sixties, who put on a four month aerobic training program of regular brisk walking increased their performance on mental tests by ten percent."

"In another study 13,000 adults and children labeled with dyslexia in Australia, South Africa and America, a twice daily for ten minutes program of standing on a cushion and throwing a beanbag from one hand to another, or balancing on a 'wobble board,' freed all participants of dyslexia within six months."

Like so many, I say getting hooked on exercise can get you hooked on success.

It's time to put down our hand-held devices, turn off the electronics, and get out and move.

YOUR HEALTH IS YOUR RESPONSIBILITY

As a graduate with a degree in food science, I would be remiss in not suggesting and commenting on your eating habits.

I was amazed when I read Harvard professor Michael Porter's "2014 Social Progress Index," which indicated that the U.S. spends the most on health and wellness, yet we are not getting proportionate results, since we are ranked 70th in the world in overall health.

Given our culture and society, when it comes to good health practices, the odds are stacked against us.

For example, the nutritional label on a can of soda shows that there are approximately 39 grams of sugar and 140 calories in each 12 ounce serving. According to the American Heart Association, the daily sugar intake for women should be 24 grams and for men should be 36 grams, and it's even lower for children and teens.

Make it a priority to take personal responsibility for your own health and set the example for your children.

The Center for Disease Control and Prevention (CDC) estimates more than one third of American adults are obese, while nearly one third of children and adolescents are considered obese or overweight.

The World Health Organization (WHO) estimates that worldwide obesity has nearly doubled since 1980.

According to these organizations, obesity leads to heart attacks (the leading cause of death in America and the rest of the world), stroke, back pain, and diabetes.

As far as smoking is concerned—no way, no how! According to the American Lung Association, "There are approximately 600 ingredients in cigarettes. When burned, they create more than 7,000 chemicals. At least 69 of these chemicals are known to cause cancer, and many are poisonous. Here are just a few: acetone (found in nail polish remover), arsenic (used in rat poison), benzene (found in rubber cement), butane (used in lighter fluid) and formaldehyde (used for embalming)."

The availability of fast food, indoor video games, and our super-size society seems to be out of control. In schools, a constant flow of pizza, hotdogs, soda, whole milk and macaroni and cheese is readily available to our children.

Fad diets and quick fixes are not the answer. A "lifestyle" of eating "real food"—not prepackaged processed food—is just what the doctor ordered to keep your health, positive self-image, and endurance strong on your highway to success.

In order to maintain the ongoing capacity for great effort and continued strength, get your rest for the sake of your body and mind.

Look at your overall heath as a "game changer" that will make you much more prepared and vibrant for whatever comes your way.

When it comes to our health, many of us fall short and find reasons not to make it a priority. Don't embrace excuses—embrace solutions.

CONQUERING YOUR FEARS

No one can truthfully say he or she has never experienced fear in his or her life. We all have fears—fear of failure, of embarrassment, of rejection and loss, of being misunderstood or of being judged harshly. You fear the unknown, change, the process you may need to undertake, or even the outcome. You may fear physical pain. The list of fears can seem endless at times.

Ironically, your greatest obstacle or fear isn't always "the competition." Whether in sports, business or some other endeavor, your true nemesis is often your own internal fear.

It's the anticipation of pain; it's the assumption that the worst-case scenario will play out. This constant, negative flow of what "may happen" paralyzes you into inaction, or morphs into a type of "self-fulfilling prophecy" that often sabotages your own efforts, which almost always brings about the failure that you feared.

Fear can stop you dead in your tracks, it can cause you to procrastinate and focus on the "what ifs." **But how you handle your fear has a direct impact on whether or not you achieve what you desire in life.**

Many of the successful individuals with whom I spent time and interviewed offered the same answer to what I believe is a key question: Why do people have a hard time achieving their goals and reaching their full potential?

Their response was overwhelmingly consistent: "The fear of failure."

Sly Stallone has been quoted as saying, "Once in your life—for one mortal moment—you must make a grab for immortality. If not, you have not lived." If you strive for that immortality and greatness in your life, then you must deal with the variety of fears instilled in each one of us that unfortunately are often a contributing factor that can limit your potential.

Following in the footsteps of these sport legends, entertainers, and business icons who take great pride in how many times they felt and endured fear, you must learn to manage your fears, be willing to fail, to be vulnerable, and be willing to get out of your comfort zone and face harsh and uncomfortable situations.

Don't focus your attention on the difficult task at hand, but on the price you will pay for not doing the crucial things along the way to the desired outcome.

Their fear of not accomplishing what they want motivates them to stay the course. They understand it is vitally important to have fear under control to compete, to win, and to be managed throughout their journey towards success.

Overcoming fear will require you to not worry about future failures. You have to let go of past disappointments. Incredibly, most people often cling to their past failures because strangely enough they become comfortable. We all have a naturally strong resistance to change that must be conquered by our internal will to win.

Perhaps it sounds simplistic, but there is no time to remember past mistakes or potential problems. **Do not drag negative past experiences into your current situation. That will only act as an anchor that will no doubt hold you back...let it go.**

There are many benefits when you manage your fears—accomplishing your goals is just one. People who take on their fears have much more self-confidence—regardless of winning or losing. **When you face adversity, you will discover what's "inside of you." You will learn how to tap into your inner strength to not only grow, but also to thrive.**

You can embrace fear as a tool to inspire and motivate you toward success. Look into your past and recognize how the most trying times taught you the greatest lessons. Facing those challenges and those fears likely made you stronger. Hold on to those accomplishments and pull them out of your "success toolbox" when necessary. They are positive assets that should be used and reflected upon during difficult times.

In your own life, has fear held you back or caused you to procrastinate? Has fear been a factor that kept you from realizing your dream—or attempting to pursue a goal? Most likely the answer is yes.

Perhaps this thought can help: Behind fear lays opportunity, fear doesn't generally overtake us in the present moment. Rather it comes when you dwell on past negative experiences or anticipate future failure. The emotion of fear exists only in your mind. If you can work past your fears, you can then realize that whatever the outcome of the event or situation may be, it is likely much less dramatic than the outcome you originally feared. Drive yourself hard—keep practicing until your fear is under control. **Practice what you fear a hundred times, and you'll find yourself far less fearful and much more comfortable on the day of the actual event.**

If you are looking to model yourself after others who have achieved great success, try and develop their perspective: It's okay to fail, because not going after what you want clearly outweighs any fears you may experience along the way. Your fear of losing and any pain, whether physical or mental, must be overshadowed by your desire to win. Overcoming fear takes changing your perception. The internal resistance to change that we have at the very core of our being is strong, very strong, but it must be dealt with like any other challenge.

SILENCING THE ENEMY WITHIN: "NEGATIVE SELF-TALK"

Perhaps the lyrics from "Take it Easy," written by Jackson Browne & Glenn Frey of The Eagles, say it best: ***"Don't let the sound of your own wheels drive you crazy."***

Your inner monologues, self-talk, and self-defeating internal chatter can and will dramatically affect your outer performance. But you'll find that your internal voice is difficult and sometimes—almost impossible—to control. When it condemns and criticizes, it can create self-doubt, fear, anxiety, procrastination and hesitation. Without question, it can be a powerfully destructive influence on your goals and dreams. It can be your fiercest critic—a self-imposed weapon used against you.

This internal dialogue is powered by our human brain that weighs only about three pounds, but what an influence those three pounds have.

The National Science Foundation estimates that the average person has over 50,000 thoughts per day:

*"The vast majority of them are pure nonsense. **We often dwell in the past or the future, obsessing about mistakes we might have made, battling guilt, planning ahead or worrying.** We are constantly drifting into fantasy, fiction, and negativity."*

"Consequently, an absolute minuscule number of our thoughts are actually focused on what is truly important and real: the present moment. The moment is all that is, ever was and will be. Everything else is elusive and illusory, particularly as our subjective awareness and feelings are concerned."

Unproductive self-talk can lead you to believe that you have no options. The process of your own self-defeat, depression and hopelessness will be in place, and soon you'll believe that you are destined for failure.

Upbeat, positive and productive self-talk creates an atmosphere of options and, as cliché as it sounds, when there are options, there is hope.

The truth is many successful people with limited financial resources, no so-called connections, or even a poor education have succeeded by employing a constant flow of positive self-talk.

Your inner conversation should play a more productive role in shifting your thoughts away from self-doubt and cause you to become more confident, optimistic, happier and successful.

What can be realized with a productive thought pattern is that optimism becomes a choice. Adversity and uncertainty will come and go—that's life. But the better you can handle uncertainty with a more optimistic thought pattern, the better your quality of life, and the less likely you'll get on that emotional roller-coaster. Develop a thought pattern that says, **"Problems make me smarter, more resilient, innovative and stronger, and help take me to the next level."**

An additional benefit of filling each day with positive, productive and optimistic thoughts are that they will dramatically influence your happiness.

Truly happy and successful people know how to immerse themselves in optimism and move away from negative thinking. They know how to have fun—how to be their own advocate and best friend.

"Human [happiness] is produced not so much by great pieces of good fortune that seldom happen, as by little advantages that occur every day." – Benjamin Franklin, **The Autobiography**

In other words, this Founding Father's message is that happiness is not obtained by winning the lottery or finding the pot of gold at the end of the rainbow, but rather, by finding joy in the little positive things that happen each day that all too often are taken for granted, ignored, or overlooked.

What else can be done to relieve negative self-talk? **Let go of resentments, jealousy and regrets. Forgive yourself and others, lugging the past on your shoulders will only weigh you down and impede your progress.**

Recognize the fact that there is so much more to you than your own perceived weaknesses—whether it's your past setbacks, your financial limitations, your physical appearance, or anything else that troubles you.

Keep in mind that self-doubt and low self-esteem are dream killers. You are not defined by your past unless you allow it to define you. Do not build your identity around past regrets or perceived shortcomings.

Stop with the internal hate speeches directed at yourself. Imagine your response if you heard your worst enemy saying to you the critical things you have said to yourself. You would want to grab that person by the throat and say, "How dare you speak to me like that?" Yet, we do it to ourselves way too often.

If you allow it to do so, your "inner critic" will control your life. If you've allowed your self-defeating inner thoughts to hijack your dreams, it's time to stop and declare a moratorium on this self-imposed destructive behavior.

PURSUING KNOWLEDGE

"If a man empties his purse into his head no one can take it away from him. An investment in knowledge always pays the best interest."
– Benjamin Franklin

Like a carpenter with his toolbox of hammers, screwdrivers, and more, you need to equip yourself with your own tool belt of wide-ranging skills in order to accomplish what you desire. If a skill is important to your long-term success, then take the time and energy to master it!

One of the things famed treasure hunter Mel Fisher taught me was that before a ship can leave port, there must be a manifest of its inventory. Before you set sail on your "sea of life" journey, you also must create a personal manifest of skills, techniques, and knowledge.

Knowledge truly is power.

Nothing will build your confidence more than adding new skills and incorporating them into your daily activities. Information and know-how will pay dividends throughout your life and can play a critical part in significantly closing the gap against any individual that may have far more resources than you.

Consider the growing $11-billion-per-year self-improvement industry. You can find an incredible array of products and services—from motivational speakers and personal-growth seminars to instructional DVDs, books and personal-coaching services. You'll find opportunities to learn about networking, spiritual growth, diet and exercise, personal affirmation and much more.

Now look at your own industry and the environment in which you want to compete. Are there opportunities to gain knowledge? Without question: yes. Does learning new skills and competencies take a lot of money? The answer is no.

Nearly every industry looks big at first glance, but under closer study, you'll find each one is likely smaller than you thought, with experts willing to give free advice. Walls and barriers to knowledge are a thing of the past.

Perhaps the strongest example is the World Wide Web. In the days of old, it took lots of resources and money in order to obtain a decent education. Not that long ago discrimination denied much of our society access to education. The exciting part is that today, if you feel you are missing a skill set or desire a new skill, you can get out there and acquire it like no other time in history.

Is there a learning curve? Absolutely, accept it as part of the process. Just about anything you want to become better at is available for free on the internet—articles, videos, scientific research, planning templates, best practices, newsletters, internships, even motivational support. You will find that people love to share and help others, and it's all at your fingertips.

Once you discover the vast assortment of resources available to you, you will find they can have an enormously positive impact on your life. They can help you transform your world and bring you closer to what you desire and who you desire to be. You will gain a newfound confidence in your field.

Commitment, dedication and belief in yourself, combined with old-fashioned effort and diligence, is still the right formula to gain the knowledge required to truly make a significant impact on your life.

Go out of your way and develop a habit to learn something new every day; this will better equip you to come up with sound strategies and creative solutions to problems, goals, and challenges you face.

Keep in mind nobody was born with, or has a complete repository of, knowledge. All knowledge has to be learned and then developed.

Do not hesitate to look to others for help. Every individual interviewed for this book demonstrated their willingness to learn from others. Ironically, the people who already possess the most knowledge continue to hunger for more. Their appetites for knowledge are insatiable, and they are committed to becoming experts in their respective fields. In turn, they grow to become lifelong learners with the commitment to never lose out because someone else has more knowledge or smarts than they do.

LEVERAGING YOUR OPPORTUNITIES

"Opportunity is missed by most people because it is dressed in overalls and looks like work." – Thomas Edison

Let's get it out in the open: The notion of a "level playing-field" is a myth. Not everyone has the same opportunities. Nor should you expect the world to be tailored to your exact needs.

There are countless factors and experiences that began as early as your childhood that affect and influence your development, success and opportunities.

Your upbringing, parenting and family structure, nurturing, the environment in which you were raised, your education and exposure to early reading, your peers, and your role-models—both positive and negative—are just some of the influences that likely had a profound impact on you.

Despite your past, present or future circumstances, a fire in your belly must exist in order to cut through any and all obstacles and challenges.

The truth is that there are many individuals who were brought up with very similar backgrounds and resources, yet some hold on to the past as an excuse to use when things don't go their way, while others use their past as a motivator to go far beyond what they saw and experienced to get more productive results.

Success features people from all different walks of life who have learned to recognize and take advantage of their options.

Each day arrives with a variety of opportunities, both big and small. It can take a keen eye to identify all of them, but trust me—they are there. With the right attitude, you will see opportunities where others do not.

Building success is about seeing the barely noticeable little doors, opened just a crack, as a pathway to your golden ticket. Don't make a mistake and believe that success somehow happens overnight. Countless stories about "overnight successes" actually reveal people who have followed a series of the smallest steps—the first step leading only to the next step, then the next step and the next step, until they achieved their dreams.

My martial arts instructor, Sensei Anthony Arango put it very simply during my 10-year pursuit of earning my back black, "A black belt is a white belt that never gave up."

That theme stuck with me and should stick with you. Engage challenges as opportunities. Expect to be uncomfortable and learn to bounce back from disappointments. **Problems and challenges are the price we pay for progress—they come with the territory.** If handled correctly we learn, and in turn an opportunity is born.

It's not only the richest, smartest, best athletes, nor the most gifted musicians, entrepreneurs or entertainers that make it to the top. Those who have risen to greatness are those who have learned to be strong during the difficult times. They have developed and harnessed their true potential by not allowing a perceived lack of opportunities to hold them back.

People like Jackie Robinson, Bruce Lee, Wayne Gretzky, Michael Jordan, Albert Einstein, Sigmund Freud, Elvis Presley, John F. Kennedy, Henry Ford, Steve Jobs, Mark Twain and Abraham Lincoln were not destined for greatness. They chose to take each opportunity and use it to the fullest to become the legends they are.

Nurture that quiet storm of rage inside your soul. Stay hungry and determined to remain personally accountable for your own success. Look for help when you need it; accept help when it's offered. But in the end, it's up to you to make the most of each opportunity. The potential has always been there. Whether you have recognized it or not, it has always been inside of you.

The highly successful individuals in this book have been described as tenacious, gritty, passionate, committed, dedicated, and strong. Their personality traits include determination, competiveness, boldness, and courage.

It is now time for you to welcome and invite those words into your life. To take a stand for yourself, to get off the sidelines and take massive action by using the insights and wisdom shared in *The Common Thread of Overcoming Adversity and Living your Dreams,* and begin the process of reaching your greatest potential.

Stay strong, be a warrior, and keep moving forward!

CPSIA information can be obtained at www.ICGtesting.com
Printed in the USA
BVOW08s1228010915

416050BV00004B/139/P